Contemporary British Fascism

Also by Nigel Copsey

ANTI-FASCISM IN BRITAIN

Contemporary British Fascism

The British National Party and the Quest for Legitimacy

Nigel Copsey
Senior Lecturer in History, University of Teesside, UK

First published 2004 by
PALGRAVE MACMILLAN
Houndmills, Basingstoke, Hampshire RG21 6XS and
175 Fifth Avenue, New York, N. Y. 10010
Companies and representatives throughout the world

PALGRAVE MACMILLAN is the global academic imprint of the Palgrave Macmillan division of St. Martin's Press, LLC and of Palgrave Macmillan Ltd. Macmillan® is a registered trademark in the United States, United Kingdom and other countries. Palgrave is a registered trademark in the European Union and other countries.

ISBN 1–4039–0214–3

This book is printed on paper suitable for recycling and made from fully managed and sustained forest sources.

A catalogue record for this book is available from the British Library.

Library of Congress Cataloging-in-Publication Data
Copsey, Nigel, 1967–
    Contemporary British Fascism: the British National Party and the quest for legitimacy/ Nigel Copsey.
        p. cm.
    Includes bibliographical references and index.
    ISBN 1–4039–0214–3 (cloth)
        1. British National Party (1982–) 2. Political parties–Great Britain.
3. Fascism–Great Britain. I. Title.
JN1129.B75C67 2004
324.241'093–dc22   2003067785

10   9   8   7   6   5   4   3   2   1
13 12 11 10 09 08 07 06 05 04

Printed and bound in Great Britain by
Antony Rowe Ltd, Chippenham and Eastbourne

To the memory of William Francis Copsey

Contents

Acknowledgements

In the first place, my thanks go to those people whose assistance proved especially valuable when it came to collecting research materials for this book. They are Martin Durham, Monty Kolsky at the Board of Deputies of British Jews, Mike Hartman from the Tyne and Wear Anti-Fascist Association, Graham Macklin, Paul Meszaros from Bradford Trades Council, and Christine Woodland, Archivist at the University of Warwick's Modern Records Centre. My thanks also go to Michael Newland for answering my queries. David Renton commented on parts of the manuscript and I am grateful to him for his suggestions and advice. The University of Teesside's History Research Group helped support this project and I am indebted to colleagues for supplying teaching cover. For permission to re-use material from a prior publication, I acknowledge the Political Studies Association and Blackwell Publishers. As always, I owe a special thanks to my family for their encouragement and forbearance.

NIGEL COPSEY

Introduction

For many years, tainted by the horrors of the Second World War, Europe's right-extremists were political pariahs who occupied the dark, outer reaches of political existence. Since the 1980s, however, Europe has been revisited by the spectre of the extreme right. Over the last two decades millions of votes have been gathered by right-extremists on the continent, above all in France, Italy, Belgium and Austria. Yet Britain always seemed out of step, that is until the turn of the new millennium when the localised emergence of the British National Party (BNP) opened up the possibility that Britain's right-extremists were set to fall into line with many of their continental counterparts and break through into the national arena of mainstream politics. This prospect, all but unthinkable barely a year or so ago, demands a clear, accessible and thorough study of Britain's leading far-right party – the British National Party.

Our subject might have appeared unexpectedly but it is not a 'new' political party. Originally formed in 1982, its history stretches back over 20 years. Not until the 2001 general election, however, with the exception of a local council by-election victory in Tower Hamlets in 1993, did the party attract much in the way of wider recognition. In the wake of the worst race riots that Britain had experienced for some 15 years, the BNP hit the headlines with an impressive poll in Oldham. What followed on, first in the north-west of England and then else-where, was a sequence of local election victories. One after another, as a series of local council seats fell to the BNP, the name of the party, and its leader Nick Griffin, entered the political limelight. Yet for those of us with a long-standing interest in the field, the character most synonymous with the party is not Nick Griffin, but John Tyndall. Chairman of the BNP from 1982 until 1999, when he was forced to surrender the leadership to Griffin, expelled from the party in 2003 and later readmitted, Tyndall governed the British National Party like a personal fiefdom. Noted more for his staying power than for his tactical sense, it was not until Nick Griffin took over and set about transforming the party's strategy that the BNP experienced a dramatic upturn in its electoral fortunes.

Two principal figures therefore dominate our picture: John Tyndall and Nick Griffin. It is to the former that we direct our attention at the outset. A leading figure on Britain's far right – Chairman of the National Front (NF) for most of the 1970s – John Tyndall was crucial to the formation of the British National Party in 1982. It is only through retracing his political career that we are able to identify the source of the British National Party and understand its creation. Our first chapter therefore turns the clock back to the 1950s and takes us from Tyndall's political baptism in the League of Empire Loyalists through neo-Nazi organisations like the National Socialist Movement and the Greater Britain Movement, into the National Front before finally arriving in the early 1980s at the British National Party.

If the longevity of the British National Party is a surprise, then the provenance of the party's name may also be an eye-opener. In the course of Britain's fascist tradition, organisations calling themselves the 'British National Party' have surfaced here and there with regular frequency. A former member of Mosley's prewar British Union of Fascists established the first British National Party in August 1942. However, following an anti-fascist campaign by the Communist Party, this disbanded shortly afterwards.[1] Another version of the BNP was launched in February 1960. No relation to the former, it included Tyndall as a leading activist. This BNP lasted until the end of 1966 when it was amalgamated into the National Front. It also counted John Bean, current editor of *Identity*, the magazine of the present-day BNP, as its national organiser.[2] In the 1970s, meanwhile, Eddy Morrison, a former NF stalwart established a British National Party in Leeds. But this venture was short-lived too. Morrison was later to become a youth organiser for Tyndall's British National Party.[3]

That the latest version of the British National Party has had a far longer existence than any of its predecessors is clear. Yet this could not have been predicted in the 1980s. As we show in our second chapter, there was little resonance for right-wing extremism in Britain during this period. The far right had practically vanished from Britain's political landscape. Despite everything though, the British National Party laboured on. But there was more to it than that. The 1980s saw a 'struggle for the soul of British nationalism', as Tyndall refers to it, a period in which the BNP and the rival National Front battled it out for control of the right-extremist fringe. Winning this 'struggle' was central to the party's political objectives and yet it has failed to catch the attention of academic researchers.

Into the 1990s and there was the promise of a new dawn. A local election victory for the British National Party in Tower Hamlets in 1993 led observers to first question whether the far right in Britain was threatening to follow the continental model.[4] We analyse the reasons behind this 'success' in our third chapter. Yet this was the party's one-and-only win under Tyndall – its moment of destiny failed to arrive – and so we also address its subsequent failure. Not surprisingly, jubilation in the party's ranks soon turned to demoralisation. In the once fertile area of Tower Hamlets support for the party collapsed. By the close of the 1990s, as we shall see, Nick Griffin was able to successfully unseat John Tyndall whereupon the British National Party underwent an intensive course of cosmetic surgery.

Before evaluating Griffin's attempt to re-package the party we depart from chronology for a moment. Our fourth chapter takes a more thematic approach and probes the ideology of Tyndall's British National Party. Here we are careful to delineate 'right-wing extremism' and 'fascism', two of our key terms of reference. That Tyndall's BNP should be seen as fascist is important not least because, as we shall see, even if image and tactics have changed under Griffin there has been little modification to the party's core ideology. Chapter 4 therefore offers more than a dry taxonomic exercise: it provides the background context to the fifth chapter where we subject Griffin's ambitious 'modernisation' programme to closer scrutiny. Through reference to Griffin's own blueprint, we seek to examine the 'modern' face of today's British National Party.

Moving on and the focus of the penultimate chapter is the recent upturn in the party's electoral fortunes. By taking us through the sequence of British National Party local electoral breakthroughs, in Oldham, Burnley and elsewhere, the sixth chapter constructs a clear picture of recent BNP activity in these areas and explains why this upsurge has happened. Griffin sees these local electoral gains as the springboard to a national breakthrough and so in our study we will reflect, however tentatively, on the possibility of such a breakthrough occurring in the near future. In the final chapter we survey Western Europe's extreme right. Here we locate the relative position of our subject in its broader context. At this point we engage with the international field of the extreme right and this leads us to regard the electoral rise of the BNP in terms of common causes and wider trends.

As we shall see, no single factor accounts for the electoral rise of extreme-right parties. But be that as it may, the most crucial part of our argument is that the construction of legitimacy is a necessary dynamic in extreme–right electoral breakthrough. In the realms of political theory, the concept of legitimacy is, of course, most often associated with systemic authority, obedience and consent.[5] However, it clearly has wider application, and for the purposes of our study we take it to mean that many in society regard the party, whether in the local or national arena, as socially acceptable. The point about this type of legitimacy is that it can be both engendered from within and accorded from without. It is our contention that even if far-right themes are legitimated by the mainstream, right-extremists will still struggle to make any electoral impression if they decide not to moderate and adapt to the norms of the system. And since the British National Party has long been regarded as a political pariah, its quest for legitimacy must be seen as central to its electoral fortunes.

This is the first detailed study of the British National Party. As such, the scope of this volume will go beyond anything that has been published to date. Existing work in the historical field of British fascism is profuse but coverage of the BNP is, by comparison, thin.[6] Admittedly, the party has been written about in occasional chapter contributions to edited collections and in a small number of journal articles, but a detailed monograph that covers the history of the party has long awaited its author.[7] Given both the topicality and significance of the subject there is a need to fill this lacuna with a well-researched and readable monograph, now more than ever. Yet it is in the nature of contemporary studies that until the future course of events reveals itself, the full story of this latest incarnation of the British National Party cannot be written. Nonetheless, given the interest that British fascism continues to invite from historians, our subject is sure to be revisited by the academic community sooner rather than later.

1

'Back to Front': John Tyndall and the Origins of the British National Party

In the mid-1950s, after two years of national service, John Hutchyns Tyndall was ready to answer the call of politics. Yet there was little shaping his early radicalism at that time other than hard-nosed patriotism, an impassioned devotion to the cause of the British Empire and growing hostility to the permissiveness of liberal society where the 'smell everywhere was one of decadence'.[1] Even so, these beliefs were sufficiently potent to induce Tyndall towards the right-extremist political fringe. But what Tyndall was to discover there was of somewhat limited appeal. The most prominent figure on Britain's far right in the 1950s remained Oswald Mosley (1896–1980), but he was now a political veteran who had lost much of his legendary messianic zeal. The postwar political resurrection of Mosley and his Union Movement had already been thwarted by 1950 and what is more, as Tyndall recalls, he was 'immediately put off' by the Union Movement's policy of union with Europe.[2]

The only other realistic alternative to Oswald Mosley was the ultra-patriotic League of Empire Loyalists (LEL). This group, as Tyndall later acknowledged, was not ideal. Though the Empire Loyalists did infrequently contest elections, it was more a conservative-imperialistic pressure group than a serious political party. Its major contribution to political life was through the mischief it made disrupting Tory Party conferences, heckling opposition speakers and throwing bags of flour (and even entrails) at dignitaries. As George Thayer found out in his 1960s study of the British political fringe, the Empire Loyalists had become a natural home for the less sophisticated right-wing Tory reactionary horrified by the demise of the British Empire.[3] But despite a reputation for Colonel Blimps and schoolboy political 'pranksterism', the leader of the Empire Loyalists did have an extremist provenance: Arthur

Kenneth Chesterton (1899–1973), a cousin once removed of the writer G.K. Chesterton, had been a leading spokesman for the prewar British Union of Fascists (BUF) and had founded the Empire Loyalists in 1954. Moreover, though Chesterton had become disillusioned with fascism, had cut himself off from Mosley in 1938 and had never returned to his fold, Chesterton was still wedded to a dogged belief in conspiratorial anti-Semitism.[4] Sure enough, in the 1950s Chesterton became a 'natural magnet' – to borrow Richard Thurlow's words – for those neo-fascist extremists who were against Mosley.[5] And so it was to Chesterton's fringe group of Empire Loyalists that Tyndall would be first drawn.

Born in July 1934, Tyndall was therefore in his early twenties when he became active with the League of Empire Loyalists, but much of the detail of his political philosophy was yet to be defined.[6] He did not have the advantage of a liberal university education; at his suburban grammar school in Kent his achievements had been on the sports field rather than in the classroom and he had left school with modest qualifications. As a child, it had been his mother who had chiefly influenced his political education. She had possessed what Tyndall loosely refers to as 'a kind of basic British patriotism'; his father, in contrast, had been committed to internationalist principles in spite of having been raised in Ireland in a strong Unionist family.[7] As for John Tyndall's upbringing, this had been both emotionally stable and materially secure. There is certainly no indication that any of Tyndall's political beliefs can be attributed to a psychologically disturbed or materially deprived childhood – a point that he is careful to make.[8]

From League of Empire Loyalist to National Socialist

Tyndall recounted the first steps in his passage to the far right of British politics in a speech he delivered to North American right-wing extremists in 1979: 'One day in about 1956 I was sitting at home watching television and I saw a news item about a demonstration by a group calling itself the League of Empire Loyalists'. And so he continued: '… as an imperialist I thought I would find out more about this group'.[9] Following his instincts Tyndall dropped in on the League's basement office in Westminster, and from that moment on his long political career was set in motion.

As John Tyndall made his entrance to the League of Empire Loyalists' office, a selection of A.K. Chesterton's publications was brought to his notice, the sum and substance of which immediately impressed itself on Tyndall's incipient political consciousness. What Chesterton's writings revealed to Tyndall was that the decline of the British Empire could be attributed to an iniquitous Jewish conspiracy. As he read through the pages of Chesterton's journal *Candour*, the door was opened to a new political understanding. '*Candour* brought me face-to-face for the first time with what is sometimes called the "Conspiracy Theory"',[10] recalls Tyndall:

> Bit by bit, it started to come home to me, in the form of incontrovertible evidence, that there was present in Britain and around the world a definite Jewish network wielding immense influence and power... The truth was inescapable.[11]

When confronted by the full gravity of this Jewish 'menace', Tyndall decided on leaving behind all thoughts of a normal career at some point during 1957–58. From this time forth, he would fully commit himself to a life of political struggle.[12]

He was not alone. Attracted by A.K. Chesterton's adaptation of classic conspiracy theory to modern times, a new generation of young extremists also gravitated towards the ranks of the League of Empire Loyalists. In days to come these figures would make up Tyndall's closest associates and, most significantly, this cluster would shape the future course of right-wing extremism in Britain. One key figure was John Bean, an industrial chemist by profession who in 1956 became the London secretary of the Empire Loyalists. Tyndall first encountered Bean in February 1957 after stepping into the breach and volunteering to help support the Empire Loyalists' candidate at a by-election in North Lewisham. Electoral hopes went unrealised, however, and the LEL candidate lost her deposit.[13] In consequence, and more or less coming to a decision in unison, both Tyndall and Bean were now of the opinion that there was little mileage left in the League's political strategy: there could be no way forward in making appeals to weak-willed middle-class Tories who when it came down to it were quite prepared to sacrifice the Empire.

What both Tyndall and Bean aspired to was something more radical and hard-edged. They proposed a new political party that would combine 'nationalism' with a 'popular socialism', a serious organisation that was clued-in to the ordinary concerns of the working class, appealing particularly to those concerned by the effects of black immigration – an issue that was to burst onto the political scene in the wake of racial disturbances in Notting Hill and Nottingham in 1958. And so, both Tyndall and Bean walked out on the Empire Loyalists and in April 1958, along with a handful of south and east London members of the LEL, formed the National Labour Party (NLP) based in Thornton Heath, Croydon.[14]

Another former LEL activist who later joined company with Tyndall (and Bean) was Colin Jordan, a Cambridge graduate in history and a secondary-school teacher by profession. During his time at Cambridge and for some years thereafter, Jordan had gravitated towards Arnold Leese (1877–1956), the leader of the prewar Imperial Fascist League (IFL). Although the IFL had been numerically insignificant, indeed a tiny rival to the BUF, of all the prewar fascist organisations in Britain it seemed to copy the racial ideology of German National Socialism to the letter. During the early 1950s Jordan had founded the Birmingham Nationalist Club, yet it was within the Empire Loyalists that he had made his presence felt. By 1956 Jordan was its Midlands organiser and a member of its National Committee. But cast in the same mould as Tyndall and Bean, Jordan grew disillusioned with the 'moderate' stance of the Empire Loyalists and so founded his own dissident group known as the White Defence League (WDL) in 1957 – a racial nationalist pressure group with an express wish to 'Keep Britain White'.

Though first established in the Midlands, the White Defence League's base of operations soon switched to 'Arnold Leese House' at 74 Princedale Road, Notting Hill once Leese's widow had made Jordan his political heir in 1958. Both the White Defence League and the National Labour Party were now navigating a parallel course. This was a fact made obvious to both groups during the summer of 1958 when by most accounts the NLP and the WDL played a central role in stirring up racial tensions in Notting Hill.[15] Before long they would co-operate with one another, and in 1960 the National Labour Party and the White Defence League finally merged to form the 1960s incarnation of the British National Party. In point of fact, this was really a 'Bean–Jordan' merger as Tyndall had briefly resigned from the NLP only to later reemerge in the BNP taking sides with Jordan.[16]

The third key individual, also a political debutante with the Empire Loyalists and later on a close lieutenant of Tyndall, was Martin Webster. A former grammar-school pupil, Webster had joined the ranks of the Empire Loyalists in his teens shortly after the departure of Tyndall and Bean. But after three years of League activity, he too experienced a loss of faith. Webster was another, like Tyndall before him, to find fault with the Empire Loyalists' 'light-weight' political strategy. For Webster, the problem was that they 'were not bound together by the discipline of an ideology and were not driven on by the will to win'.[17] But it was also rumoured from elsewhere that Webster possessed little enthusiasm for the League's unorthodox methods. Passing judgment on Webster's contribution to the LEL, one former activist remarked: 'He was never very much use to us and always seemed rather frightened.'[18] By the early 1960s Webster was ready to change tack and was soon drawn into Tyndall's orbit. With Webster's eyes opened to the 'juvenile' nature of the League's political activities on hearing a John Tyndall speech in Trafalgar Square in 1962,[19] a political association between the two was soon constituted. Significantly, this lasted close to 20 years and reached its zenith in the 1970s when as Chairman and National Activities Organiser respectively, Tyndall and Webster dominated the National Front and when, for at least one author, they took on the character of 'political Siamese twins'.[20]

At the start of the 1960s, however, the young Tyndall was still serving his political apprenticeship. For a short time, having turned his back on Chesterton, Tyndall found a new mentor in the Hitler-obsessed figure of Colin Jordan who had stepped into Leese's shoes (or more appropriately his jackboots) as Britain's führer. By this stage Jordan had become something of a high flyer on the British far right. He had not only been appointed leader of the newly formed British National Party, but his cachet also extended to the international arena where Jordan had established a series of contacts with overseas neo-Nazis by means of shadowy organisations such as the Northern League.[21] Nonetheless, even before his introduction to Jordan, it was clear that Tyndall had already imbibed pro-Nazi ideas.

Tyndall recalls reading *Mein Kampf* sometime in the 1950s[22] and, whilst in the National Labour Party, had penned an article for the NLP journal that had been suffused with Nordic racism. Gripped by a fear that Jews were conspiring to destroy 'Aryan' culture, Tyndall warned his readers that:

> By his systematic attack on all European culture the Jew is polluting and destroying the European soul... If the European soul is to be recovered in our country and throughout Europe, it can only be by the elimination of this cankerous microbe in our midst.[23]

But if Jordan was not the immediate source of Tyndall's emerging pro-Nazism, it is not so easy to see Chesterton as its author either. Chesterton had berated Hitler's aggressive imperialism in 1939, had been commissioned into the British Army during the Second World War and had been sickened by the horrors of the Nazi

genocide. Though Chesterton was obviously anti-Semitic, his antipathy towards Jews was grounded in conspiracy theory and not biological racism.[24]

Once ensconced within the newly founded British National Party,
Tyndall became a close confidante of Jordan whose hard-line ad-
miration for German National Socialism he increasingly shared.
Emboldened by Jordan's leadership, Tyndall was encouraged by his
'führer' to form a body of elite activists within the BNP known as
'Spearhead'. This body, which in all probability never exceeded more
than 60 activists, took postwar mimicry of National Socialism to new
heights as it clothed itself in jackboots, grey shirts, armbands, belts and
carried out regular sessions in ideological and paramilitary training.[25]
Rather improbably, Tyndall has since claimed that this was a self-
defence force brought into being as a consequence of the violent
tactics of anti-fascist opponents – Tyndall had recently been arrested as
a result of a scuffle with an anti-fascist.[26] This, however, does not
explain why the Spearhead squad found it necessary to engage in
military manoeuvres such as simulating a series of attacks on an old
tower in the Surrey countryside, nor does it explain the handling of
explosives.[27]

Spearhead 'caused a great deal of dissension in the BNP' as Tyndall
later conceded.[28] For some time, Bean, the party's deputy leader, and
his principal ally, Andrew Fountaine, a wealthy Norfolk landowner
and former Tory, had grown increasingly anxious about overt Hitler
worship and the downgrading of indigenous racial nationalism. Under
Jordan's encouragement, the BNP had recently undertaken campaigns
in support of Nazi war criminals Rudolf Hess and Adolf Eichmann –
campaigns that were hardly likely to purchase much in the way of
public sympathy. By early 1962, with a view to bringing about wider
public support for the BNP, which it has to be said never had more
than a few hundred members, both Bean and Fountaine had decided
that the move towards overt neo-Nazism had to stop. The Spearhead
experiment was the final straw: Jordan, Tyndall and the Spearhead
officers had to go. Following a meeting of the BNP's national council –
deliberately convened so as to make certain of Jordan's non-
attendance – Jordan's faction was given its expulsion notice. Even so,
Tyndall did not yield; his support for Jordan remained resolute. As a
result, Spearhead was not disbanded and within a matter of weeks
Jordan had regrouped his 20 or so followers as the National Socialist
Movement (NSM), launched on 20 April 1962, the anniversary of
Hitler's birthday.

Emerging from the British führer's shadow: from the National Socialist Movement to the National Front

Even though he was still Jordan's subordinate, Tyndall was a far-right leader in the making and by the early 1960s he was carving out a niche for himself in British fascism's hall of fame. Along with his organisa-tion of Spearhead, Tyndall had now turned productive in propaganda work and the publication of his pamphlet *The Authoritarian State* under the NSM banner in April 1962 quickly established his credentials in this domain. From start to finish, *The Authoritarian State* inveighed against democracy, which for Tyndall, quoting from the *Protocols of the Elders of Zion*, was a 'modern farce' perfidiously conjured up by Jews as their 'ladder to power'. The Jew is 'diabolically clever', warned Tyndall. On the one hand he uses democracy to appeal 'to the vanity of his gentile victims by persuading them that it is THEIR crowning achieve-ment, and not his', and yet at the same time the Jew 'even goes to the point of attacking Communism in order to advance it'.[29] The genre of *The Authoritarian State* was classically conspiratorial and provides yet further confirmation of the accuracy of David Edgar's inspired comment that 'conspiracy theory runs through contemporary British fascist ideology like Blackpool runs through rock'.[30] Hence: 'Liberalism or Bolshevism, whichever the people follow – there is only one master – Judah, the all powerful!'[31] Tyndall's solution to this 'Jew-inspired' democratic fraud was an authoritarian form of government whereby absolute power would be invested in the prime minister or 'Leader'.[32]

As Tyndall made clear, his pamphlet did 'not dwell upon every department of national policy';[33] it was over to Colin Jordan's pam-phlet, *Britain Reborn* to fill in the remaining gaps: the introduction of measures to protect and improve 'Aryan, predominantly Nordic blood', 'folk socialism', the rejection of both capitalism and communism, the 'encouragement and expansion of our native Aryan cultures... and the eradication and exclusion of all detrimental alien influences', 'a whole-some national community based on blood and soil', the creation of a compulsory National Socialist Youth Movement, and so on. To bring all of this about, the NSM would not organise itself as a political party but as a 'movement of regeneration', a 'task-force' that would recruit and prepare its cadres for the impending crisis when democracy finally breaks down and it is to the NSM that the people turn for salvation.[34]

Predictably the NSM attracted few converts to its ranks. Martin Webster was one of a small number – estimates of membership in August 1962 were in the 30–50 range.[35] All the same, its activities and particularly those of Spearhead caught the attention of both the media – excited by the prospect of sensationalist copy – and Special Branch. In July 1962 Tyndall was arrested for using insulting words likely to occasion a breach of the peace following a National Socialist Movement rally at Trafalgar Square – he had recklessly referred to Jews as a 'poisonous maggot feeding on a body in an advanced state of decay'[36] – but worse followed. The following month, Spearhead activity at a four-day NSM camp in the Cotswolds triggered a police raid on the NSM's London headquarters, and at their subsequent Old Bailey trial Tyndall was found guilty of forming a paramilitary organisation under Section Two of the 1936 Public Order Act. Along with two other activists, both Tyndall and Jordan were sentenced to prison (nine months for Jordan, six months for Tyndall). Thankfully other NSM initiatives also hit the buffers, such as Tyndall's attempt to secure substantial funds for the NSM's 'anti-Zionist' campaign from a London embassy official of the United Arab Republic.[37]

In years to come the whole NSM episode would return to haunt Tyndall and exact a heavy price on his political ambitions. During the 1970s, in order to hammer home the neo-Nazi background of the National Front leadership, anti-fascists availed themselves of old photographs of Tyndall proudly dressed in Spearhead paraphernalia and reproduced them in a series of leaflets, in television documentaries and in the press.[38] Not surprisingly, when reflecting on his time with the NSM, Tyndall now maintains that his involvement with the National Socialist Movement was a 'profound mistake'.[39] The most disturbing aspect of this entire episode is Tyndall's insistence that his conscience is clear. Tyndall's 'defence' was that he was 28 years old at the time, he 'still had a lot to learn' and, besides, 'when one sees one's nation and people in danger there is less dishonour in acting and acting wrongly than in not acting at all'.[40]

In the spring of 1964 Tyndall's collaboration with Jordan ended. The break came at the moment Tyndall, backed by Martin Webster, tried and failed to force Jordan's resignation as leader of the NSM. With no going back, Tyndall then made the obligatory move and founded his own political organisation – the Greater Britain Movement (GBM). One known factor in Tyndall's break with Jordan was a deep personal feud arising from Jordan's marriage to Françoise Dior, heiress of the French perfume House and a militant neo-Nazi. Aside from their political affiliation, both Tyndall and Jordan shared a weakness for Dior who subsequently broke her engagement with Tyndall in order to marry Jordan.[41] Somewhat predictably, Tyndall later denied that this love wrangle played any part in his rift with Jordan and no matter what, their past history has now been forgotten: 'Years later CJ and I met again, shook hands and buried any antagonisms that had arisen during this period of conflict'.[42] As a matter of fact, Tyndall invited Jordan to join the National Front in 1972.[43] Though somewhat evasive about the whys and the wherefores, Tyndall would like the split with Jordan in 1964 to be understood in terms of differences arising solely over political and organisational matters.[44]

What the contemporary documents reveal is that Tyndall and his colleagues had taken umbrage at Jordan's woeful neglect of leadership duties and the recklessness of Jordan's domestic life. His marriage to Dior had quickly deteriorated, attracting negative publicity in the popular press that had 'reduced the cause of National Socialism to the status of tragic-comedy in the eyes of the public'. Another gripe was that Jordan had supposedly deviated from pure National Socialism by privately expressing 'contempt for certain tenets fundamental to the Hitler faith'.[45] Tyndall maintained that this ideological betrayal would not happen under his leadership and promised his fellow national socialists that:

Aside from this change of title, let it be understood that there is no question whatsoever of any change of ideology. The Greater Britain Movement will uphold, and preach, pure National Socialism. [46]

Indeed, though Tyndall's Greater Britain Movement now sought to project an image that was identifiable with British patriotism, he kept true to his word. When the official programme of the GBM was published, it privileged the creation of a British national-socialist state where: 'Only those of British or kindred Aryan blood should be members of the nation' and where 'The removal of the Jews from Britain must be a cardinal aim of the new order'.[47]

Looking back, however, Tyndall claims that his Greater Britain Movement was a 'stop-gap measure'[48] – a transitional base from where a spirit of unity could be promoted on the extreme right, chiefly through his new magazine, also named *Spearhead*. There is some truth in Tyndall's contention as he began to initiate approaches to other far-right organisations in 1965. Yet it was surely the harsh reality of being just one splinter group in the midst of many others that made Tyndall's new way of thinking a political necessity. Indeed, such was the GBM's insignificance, Tyndall would resort to desperate measures to win publicity such as Webster's assault on the Kenyan head of state,

Jomo Kenyatta, in 1964 and a 'rigged' shooting incident at the GBM's Norwood headquarters in 1965 which Tyndall allegedly used to incriminate anti-fascists.[49]

At that point, no less than five different organisations competed for hegemony on Britain's right-extremist political fringe: Tyndall's GBM, Jordan's National Socialist Movement, Bean and Fountaine's British National Party, Chesterton's Empire Loyalists and Mosley's Union Movement. What is more, each of these separate organisations had failed to exploit racial populism to its full advantage and none of them had any following worthy of note. The Empire Loyalists had reduced in size from its late 1950s highpoint of several thousand to around one hundred.[50] Meanwhile, the Board of Deputies of British Jews estimated that the Union Movement had less than 200 active members, the British National Party had a paper-membership of some 500 but its active strength was much lower and the combined strength of the GBM and NSM was not likely to exceed 100.[51]

Yet for all its ineffectiveness Tyndall remained sanguine about the future prospects for Britain's extreme right. Following the Labour Party's victory at the February 1966 general election and with the Conservative Party apparently in demise, he mused in *Spearhead* that by making an appeal to disaffected patriotic Tories, Britain's far right now had an historic opportunity for political success. If it was to take advantage of this situation, it was therefore incumbent on him and his colleagues to overcome their divisive mentality and unite their numerous fragments. And so, Tyndall wrote:

> For no matter how powerful the arguments for division may be, they fade and collapse when confronted with the decisive fact that continued division is going to mean continued weakness, and continued weakness is going to mean continued failure.[52]

All the same, unity was not an easy furrow for Tyndall to plough. An obvious sticking point was his penchant for national socialism, and to have the ear of 'moderates' such as Chesterton and Bean, Tyndall would have to satisfy them that he was no longer a staunch national socialist or that, at the very least, he could keep his iron hand in a velvet glove.

With this in mind, *Spearhead* abandoned its open neo-Nazism from early 1966 onwards.[53] Tyndall also published a new pamphlet in 1966 – *Six Principles of British Nationalism*. A unity programme for Britain's extreme right, it was predicated on the formation of a new organisation capable of winning a critical mass of electoral support. What caught the eye about this document was its democratic spin. It was shorn of all references to Jewish 'conspiracies' and to national socialism. All through this document Tyndall gave the impression of a seasoned political campaigner that by distancing himself from his neo-Nazi past had now come to terms with contemporary political realities. Significantly, Chesterton received it favourably.[54] Eager to merge his dwindling numbers of Empire Loyalists into a new formation, Chesterton opened discussions with Tyndall. What Tyndall proposed to Chesterton during the summer of 1966 was a merger between his Greater Britain Movement, the British National Party and the Empire Loyalists in an amalgamated body known as the 'National Front' – the name taken from a short-lived group led by Andrew Fountaine in the early 1950s.

As it turned out, Chesterton and Bean (with whom Tyndall had also negotiated) ran with his proposal but cut Tyndall off from further discussions fearing that his previous neo-Nazi indiscretions might well put unity at risk. If, as Chesterton remarked, 'The true motive is to ensure that the National Front is taken seriously as an acceptable challenge to the political parties',[55] then there could be no place for Tyndall and his GBM. The BNP's journal *Combat* declared that since anti-Semitism and pro-Nazism would certainly not be part of NF policy, Tyndall's Greater Britain Movement would be excluded from the NF.[56] Therefore, when the Front was officially launched at the start of 1967, it was without Tyndall and his Greater Britain Movement. But Chesterton and Bean were being disingenuous. Tyndall's isolation was never intended to be permanent and he was soon rewarded for his efforts. For all Chesterton's assurances that the NF would not become a home for the 'man who thinks this is a war that can be won by mouthing slogans about 'dirty Jews and filthy niggers',[57] in the spring of 1967 Tyndall had come to a private understanding with Chesterton.[58] It was agreed that Tyndall and the Greater Britain Movement would be allowed to join the National Front later that year 'on probation'. Bean has since come clean about the importance of Tyndall's contribution to the formation of the National Front: 'Tyndall's work in bringing about the founding of the National Front was significant. Understandably, he was annoyed that this was not acknowledged at the time, because of his past.'[59]

Leading from the Front

In explaining John Tyndall's rise to prominence in the National Front – he first became Chairman in 1972 – commentators have made use of two main approaches. According to Michael Billig's understanding, the Front emerged from a coalition of extreme-right groups that comprised both those who saw themselves as heirs to non-democratic fascist traditions and those who wanted to work within democratic structures.[60] Billig maintains that the coterie preserving the non-democratic tradition, that is to say Tyndall and his associates obtained the controlling positions in the Front. Their plan was to bring a two-sided strategy into play whereby the 'respectable' language of racial populism would be used to draw in large numbers of people. From the ranks of these new recruits, the most committed would be allowed to enter an inner ideological core where they could be proselytised to national-socialist ideas and traditions. For Billig, here was the real purpose of the (Tyndallite) coterie – 'to transmit ideas and traditions across time; its principal function is to guard the past for the sake of the future'.[61]

There is much that rings true about this interpretation, not least the persistence of radical anti-democratic ideology at the Front's core. Nonetheless, a more convincing approach, simply because it fits the historical record of the party's development more accurately, is the argument forwarded by Richard Thurlow. What Thurlow reveals is that whatever their original intention, though ex-GBM members 'did play an important role in the NF in the 1970s, the evidence suggests they were a coterie of mutually suspicious individuals whose actions owed more to anarchy than conspiracy'.[62] Thus, during the early years of the Front, Tyndall remained a loyal supporter of Chesterton, even supporting him when a group of militant rebels on the NF Directorate, including former GBM members, revolted against Chesterton's leadership in 1970. But this is not to deny that Tyndall lost sight of the Front's leadership. For the moment he would bide his time by constructing a base within the fledgling party as editor of *Spearhead*, his own private property but which subsequently became the NF's *de facto* monthly.

By all accounts thoroughly worn-out by the various intrigues against him, Chesterton announced his resignation at the end of 1970.[63] By 1972 Tyndall felt strong enough to make his move. He was now the NF's Vice-Chairman and could count on the loyal support of Martin Webster, who had recently ingratiated himself with Chesterton and in 1969 had been made the Front's National Activities Organiser. At last, during the summer of 1972 Tyndall's opportunity came when Chesterton's successor, the Powellite John O'Brien, a Shropshire fruit farmer and former stalwart of the Shrewsbury Conservative Association, along with eight of his supporters on the NF Directorate resigned and left the Front following revelations that through the

Northern League, both Tyndall and Webster had kept close connections with German neo-Nazis.

Following their exit Tyndall was simply requested by the NF's rump Directorate to assume control. As it was, Tyndall took over the reigns just at the right time. As Chairman of the National Front, he now presided over its period of most spectacular growth triggered by the Heath government's admission of the Ugandan Asian refugees. Feeling betrayed at the Conservative government's leniency over this issue, the racist constituency flocked to the National Front. Membership of the Front doubled between October 1972 and July 1973 and possibly jumped as high as 17,500.[64] It was during this period that Martin Webster polled 16.2 per cent of the vote in West Bromwich, the highest poll for a NF candidate in a parliamentary election. But the success was short-lived and criticism of Tyndall and Webster soon began to manifest itself.

A set of disappointing results at the 1974 general elections gave confidence to the growing opposition to Tyndall and Webster from two groups of opponents within the NF. A curious coalition came together in order to depose Tyndall and Webster and a protracted dogfight ensued. On one side of the pincer was a group of so-called 'moderate populists' who were led by John Kingsley Read and Roy Painter, both defectors from the Conservative Party. They were less ideologically driven than the incumbent leaders and saw Tyndall and Webster's past as an electoral liability. As for the other group, it based itself around the NF's newspaper *Britain First* and was led by young radicals Dave McCalden and Richard Lawson. This group of so-called 'Strasserites' – named after the prewar Strasser faction of the German National Socialist Workers' Party[65] – wanted the Front to adopt a more 'left-wing' ideological orientation but they were also opposed to Tyndall's authoritarian leadership. Outmanoeuvred from both sides, Tyndall was replaced as the NF's Chairman in October 1974 by John Kingsley Read.

Though demoted to Vice-Chairman, Tyndall was not prepared to give up the ghost, and throughout 1975 he tirelessly worked on the grassroots and on those hardliners who had supported him in the past. Even so it still took a court battle for Tyndall to regain control. In November 1975 Tyndall had been expelled from the Front by a NF disciplinary tribunal; the following month, Mr Justice Goulding of the High Court overturned that decision. As a result the 'populists' and the 'Strasserites' split from the NF and founded a breakaway National Party in January 1976. To begin with the signs were good for the 2,000 to

3,000 dissenters that cut loose. At local elections in May 1976 the National Party won two seats on Blackburn council. Since the NF had never won any seats at either council or parliamentary level, in straightforward electoral terms the National Party actually proved more successful. But destabilised by internal ideological contradictions, the National Party collapsed in the late 1970s.

Tyndall was therefore back at the helm as chairman in 1976 when the NF experienced a further period of growth triggered by popular resentment at a new wave of Afro-Asian arrivals – this time from Malawi. It was not the actual numbers of immigrants that sparked off the Front's revival: in this case 130 as opposed to the 27,000 Ugandan Asians that had arrived four years earlier, it was the hysterical manner in which it was reported in the popular press.[66] What's more, the upward momentum looked set to continue and when the NF polled 120,000 votes at the Greater London Council elections in 1977, the popular impression was that the NF was now on course to become Britain's third largest political party. Buoyed up by raw expectancy, the Front quickly pledged to contest over 300 seats at the 1979 general election. Under Tyndall's leadership, the Front looked set to make its historic electoral breakthrough.

But expectations were poles apart from reality. Not only had the Front overestimated the scale of its potential support, contradictions were also abound in the Tyndallite NF that fatally undermined its electoral credibility. The root of the problem was its failure to adapt itself to the political environment. If the Front were to succeed in the electoral arena then it would have to repudiate its hard-line ideological principles. Yet in order to counteract the 'deviationist' National Party, Tyndall had returned to a more robust ideological position in the mid-1970s supported by Martin Webster and Richard Verrall,[67] a newcomer to Tyndall's inner circle who was appointed editor of *Spearhead* in 1976. Thus, in articles such as 'The Jewish Question: Out in the Open or Under the Carpet?' Tyndall revisited the conspiratorial anti-Semitism that he had first imbibed from Chesterton in the 1950s where: 'no race on earth has done more to undermine the idea of the nation state than the Jews'.[68] Meanwhile, Verrall took Tyndall's belief in the inequality of human 'races' and tried to legitimise it with appeals to the biological sciences. In one notorious article – 'The Reality of Race' – Verrall incorporated 'scientific' drawings of three skulls in order to demonstrate that on the evolutionary scale, the cranial capacity of 'Negroes' was in-between that of Orang-Utans and Europeans.[69] None of this, of course, made it possible for the Front to portray itself as a respectable political party with any plausibility. Moreover, as the Front increasingly found out from 1977 onwards, the pressure to disclaim its extreme ideological views became all the more acute once the media and oppositional groups such as the Anti-Nazi League began to increasingly expose the NF as a 'front for Nazis'.[70]

The logic of adaptation obliged Tyndall to stand down and remove his ideological coterie from its position of power. When Tyndall and Webster's past indiscretions were combined with the content of articles in *Spearhead*, the NF found it impossible to throw off the stigma of neo-Nazism. Yet Tyndall remained predictably steadfast. There was no point in 'dressing up patriotism in clothes that cannot offend', Tyndall argued.[71] But inevitably, his dogmatism did nothing to forestall the Front's electoral collapse or prevent its rapid turnover of members. In fact, whenever the Front's membership increased, the party resembled a bath with its taps running fast and the plug out. Possibly some 12,000 joined and left in the 1970s[72], though, rather improbably, others have put this figure as high as 60,000–70,000.[73] Many defections occurred as a consequence of new members being exposed to thinly disguised fascist ideology at the party's core. Such was the rate of desertions that paid-up membership of the Front had fallen to approximately 5,000 by 1979.[74]

If Tyndall had presided over the periods of the Front's greatest growth, in 1972–74 and during 1976–77, he was now presiding over the Front's electoral decline. With its remaining political legitimacy melting away at the end of the 1970s, the Front was about to return to the political ghetto. Needless to say other factors played a part in its demise, such as the rightwards shift in the Tory Party under its new leader Margaret Thatcher, but these were essentially factors beyond Tyndall's control.[75] What Tyndall did have a say in was the party's public image, but even after its May 1979 general election debacle in which the NF polled a derisory 1.3 per cent of the vote, he still refused to give way on the need to adapt and attain respectability. For Tyndall, respectability meant the National Front losing its distinctive identity, of 'diluting its policies out of all recognition to their original substance', it meant betraying the original founders of the movement and it meant 'naïve chasing of moonbeams'.[76] In the Tyndallite NF, if the tradition of racial nationalism was to be kept alive there could be no room for such a compromise, as Tyndall would assert in June 1979:

> I do not believe that the survival of the white man will be found through the crest of political respectability because I believe that

respectability today means one thing, it means your preparedness to be a lackey of the establishment... I don't want respectability if that is what respectability means, preparedness to surrender my own race, to hell with respectability if that is what it is.[77]

Schism at the 'gay' National Front and the birth of the British National Party

In November 1979, following his failure to unseat Tyndall from the party leadership, Andrew Fountaine – who had recently formed a breakaway National Front Constitutional Movement – described the relationship between John Tyndall and Martin Webster as a 'symbiosis, a word that describes the parasitic relationship that exists between two organisms that are mutually dependent'.[78] Such was the resilience of this symbiosis – a political collaboration that had lasted nearly 20 years – Fountaine could be forgiven for not anticipating that the Tyndall–Webster partnership would come to an end in a matter of months. In a dramatic turn of events, Tyndall moved against his former confidante as recriminations in the aftermath of the 1979 general election burst out into the open. In order to free himself from all blame for the NF's major setback, all that Tyndall required was a pretext. Tyndall's mentality is such that, as Ray Hill, an informant for the anti-fascist magazine *Searchlight*, makes clear:

If anything went wrong, when the party suffered setbacks or failed to accomplish some task it has set itself, you may be quite sure that nowhere in the catalogue of blame would the name of John Tyndall feature. The 'führer principle' to which he was so devoted had been elevated into something resembling papal infallibility.[79]

Notwithstanding differences of opinion that were emerging between Tyndall and Webster over Front strategy (Tyndall was hostile to Webster's procurement of skinheads), the pretext that Tyndall found to use against Webster was the latter's homosexuality. An 'incensed' Tyndall claimed that he was shocked to discover a 'homosexual network' amongst the leading officers of the National Front.[80] But in truth, Tyndall's claim that he was unaware of Webster's sexual preference is barely credible. The reality was that Webster's homosexuality was widely known amongst Britain's contemporary fascists – 'as bent as a nine bob note' as one activist informed John Bean around the time of the NF's formation.[81] And as Hill puts it, 'If Tyndall had not been aware of it until shortly before the split, he must have been the only nazi in the western hemisphere who had not.'[82]

Nonetheless, Tyndall crafted an alternative explanation for the Front's electoral demise in which he argued that it was not the Front's extreme policies that had alienated 'patriotically-minded British people', nor was it the violence that typically occurred whenever the Front marched, 'No, there is some other factor that has caused the NF to fail to exploit its full potential in terms of national support.'[83] What had invited the public's contempt in 1979 and demoralised the party's membership was, according to Tyndall, a series of scandalous Sunday press reports that had uncovered a web of homosexuality within the Front. Tyndall insisted that at first he had doubted the reliability of these press reports – after all, the Front was noted for its homophobic attitudes – but a letter had come into his possession in October 1979 that had convinced him that Webster was abusing his position in the party by making homosexual advances to young NF members.[84] Webster had seemingly written a letter to a Young National Front activist in the West Midlands inviting him for a weekend stay in London. Moreover, in a further letter that was sent to Tyndall from a party activist in the West Midlands, it was claimed that Webster had been caught caressing and kissing the son of an activist following a local National Front social evening.[85] The upshot of this party scandal, Tyndall contended, was that the NF was in crisis: 'vast numbers of members' were dropping out and, above all, 'In the West Midlands – once a major area of NF strength – the party has virtually collapsed as a result of it.'[86] One Tyndall loyalist from Cheshire even maintained that 65 per cent of the membership had failed to renew 'solely because of the homosexual Webster'.[87]

In a bid to turn the tables on Webster, Tyndall raised the issue of homosexuality as a matter of extreme urgency at a meeting of the NF Directorate on 5 October 1979. It was here that Tyndall called on Webster to resign from his post as National Activities Organiser for having committed an act 'prejudicial to the security of the Party'. But the NF's Directorate frustrated Tyndall's plan. Suggestive of Tyndall's diminishing status, Webster won a vote of confidence from the Directorate – Richard Verrall included – and subsequently apologised for his past conduct.[88] Having found his path blocked, Tyndall then attempted to instigate changes to the NF's constitution in order to have greater authority placed at the command of the Chairman – more power in his own hands needless to say. Tyndall first tried tabling a resolution to this effect at the NF's AGM on 27 October 1979, but having been thwarted yet again, Tyndall then tried to browbeat the NF Directorate with an ultimatum in January 1980: either summon an EGM or accept his resignation. Suspecting that Tyndall was after dictatorial powers, the Directorate vetoed Tyndall's demand. With only Richard Edmonds,[89] a staunch Tyndallite prepared to offer his support, Tyndall resigned at the NF Directorate meeting held on 19 January 1980.[90]

In an open refusal to bow down to the authority of the NF's Directorate, Tyndall then established a parallel organisation, the New National Front (NNF) – the immediate precursor to the British National Party – in June 1980. 'I have one wish in this operation and one wish alone', insisted Tyndall, 'to cleanse the National Front of the foul stench of perversion which has politically crippled it'.[91] So, unlike the other factions that had splintered from the NF following its 1979 general election disaster, that is to say the National Front Constitutional Movement[92] and the British Democratic Party,[93] the New National Front was dedicated to the eventual reunification of the National Front. Tyndall looked forward to the day when the New National Front's strength would surpass that of the old National Front – this would leave the Directorate with no other option but to negotiate a reunification on his terms. The original intention behind the New National Front was therefore quite straightforward: Tyndall saw it as nothing more than a pressure group for wresting control from the NF Directorate in order for him to reform the existing party. As a result, the NNF remained committed to the political ideals of the original NF whilst at the same time offered an alternative leadership to disaffected Front members.

When the New National Front was launched, it claimed to have acquired the support of possibly around one-third of old NF members.[94] Among Tyndall's immediate entourage were his father-in-law and benefactor, the Brighton businessman Charles Parker,[95] along with Dave Bruce[96] and Richard Edmonds.[97] By March 1981, the NNF boasted that support between the old National Front and the New National Front was now 'extremely evenly divided'.[98] Yet on further reflection, this claim was exaggerated. Certainly Tyndall's NNF absorbed many disillusioned NF members, but as Ray Hill has suggested the NNF only had around 1,200 members in 1981.[99] As for the NF, its membership was likely to have been in the order of 2,000.[100] Almost immediately, the rivalry between the old NF and Tyndall's NNF descended into a rather farcical and pathetic 'numbers game' with each group trying to outdo the other in terms of making exaggerated claims as to relative numbers on demonstrations, those attending respective AGM's and so forth.[101]

In the midst of all this petty rivalry, at least in public, Tyndall continued to stand his ground. The National Front would be a united party once again when nearly all NF branches had been captured.[102] In its newspaper, *New Frontier*, the NNF remained committed to winning this 'internal struggle' and called on members of the old National Front to register their repudiation of Webster and thereby facilitate unification through one of two courses of action: declare to the NF Directorate that unless Webster is removed, they will refuse to undertake any more activity or contribute any more money; alternatively, they could simply 'crossover' to the New National Front.[103] Privately, however, a different picture was emerging. What Ray Hill has revealed is that already, by the summer of 1981, Tyndall had been forced to accept that the only way to defeat Webster and the NF leadership would be to reunite Britain's far right under the ambit of a reorganised party.[104] This was becoming increasingly self-evident because, in the first place, the NNF's early momentum had started to falter – it had stopped 'catching up' with the Front. Secondly, the ideology of the old NF was being reworked under the influence of new party chairman, Andrew Brons,[105] and as such the old NF was betraying its original (Tyndallite) principles. Brons had argued that the NF had become unsure of its 'fundamental philosophical assumptions' following its internal upheaval, and so a 'clear-cut ideological identity' was urgently required.[106] But for Tyndall, under the Brons, Webster and Verrall triumvirate, the clamour for ideological renewal was deviating the Front towards 'infantile and puerile leftism'.[107]

Though it was hard to swallow, the fact that Tyndall could no longer recapture the National Front also meant that his claim to the Front's brand name would now have to be sacrificed. If he was to secure a political future, the only alternative was to constitute an entirely new political party. Ironically, however, the first step towards the formation of what later became known as the British National Party was actually taken by an anti-fascist, the *Searchlight* spy, Ray Hill. It was Hill, at that time a former leading activist in the British Movement – an organisation founded by Colin Jordan in 1968 as the successor to his National Socialist Movement – who first contacted Tyndall with a view to reunifying the various fragments on Britain's extreme right in January 1981. The plot that Hill hatched was to bring together a new party with the intention of ultimately unravelling it and thereby further debilitating the far right by causing yet more schism. According to Hill, his duplicitous plan was to encourage the BNP to grow and 'split it down the middle by provoking a life and death leadership struggle between myself and Tyndall, and then begin the cycle of internal war all over again'.[108] In the event, however, Hill's covert scheme never came off. Convinced that the BNP had run aground, Hill decided against contesting Tyndall's leadership. He went 'public' instead and revealed his true colours in 1984.

But this plan was still within the bounds of possibility in 1981; all the more so when, following Hill's approach to Tyndall, a furtive meeting took place in London in May 1981. Here, Hill sounded out Tyndall and, as far as we know, Tyndall never suspected that Hill's motives were anything other than genuine. At Hill's base in Leicester, it was then decided to launch a new political party under Tyndall's leadership that would draw its members from the New National Front as well as from the British Movement and the British Democratic Party, organisations in which Hill had previously established loyal followings. Approaches would also be made to other fragments such as the National Front Constitutional Movement. What was required, however, was an appropriate vehicle to bring this unity about and so a 'Committee for Nationalist Unity' (CNU) would be set up. Well-known far-right activists would front this whilst Tyndall would remain behind the scenes providing the CNU with financial support and facilities.[109]

Some months later, in January 1982, the CNU was formally launched bearing names from all the respective extreme-right organisations – it even included two representatives from the National Front. The CNU subsequently issued a circular to 200 leading right-extremists and invited those who registered a positive reply to a conference that took place in London at British Rail's Charing Cross Hotel on 27 March 1982. Unsurprisingly, the NF leadership dismissed this initiative out of hand; Webster declared that Tyndall was up to his usual tricks, once again trying to 'poach' NF members.[110]

In spite of the NF's call for its members to boycott the CNU, a tiny NF faction did attend this unity conference. All together, around 50 extreme-right activists were there, including 22 delegates from the New National Front. The end result was an agreement whereby a new political party would be established calling itself the British National Party – though some, including Tyndall, favoured the name 'National Party'. In essence the party would be constituted from the New National Front but it would also embrace defectors from the British Movement, the British Democratic Party, the Nationalist Party (hitherto known as the NF Constitutional Movement) and the National Front. Its leader would be John Tyndall.[111] Some two weeks later, on 7 April 1982, the party was formally launched at a press conference in a hotel in London's Victoria. On the platform alongside John Tyndall were Ray Hill, the elderly figures of Charles Parker and Capt. Kenneth McKilliam (chair of the CNU conference and founder of the NF's ex-servicemen's organisation) and John Peacock, a pro-unity campaigner from the British Democratic Party. With an air of incorrigible optimism, Tyndall declared that the BNP would be like the 'SDP of the far right' – people would flock to it as a substantially stronger and more viable formation than either the National Front or the British Movement.[112]

To all intents and purposes, the founding of the British National Party saw John Tyndall retrace his footsteps and go 'back to Front'. Thus, in 1982 Tyndall merely picked up from where he had left off two years earlier. As an extension of the New National Front – an organisation that had identical political objectives to those detailed in the NF's Statement of Policy (1977) – the BNP was more or less a rerun of the 1970s National Front. Hence, when the principles and policies of the BNP were first published in 1982, we find ourselves on familiar Tyndallite ground: national unity and national sovereignty, withdrawal from the EEC, rebuilding the British Commonwealth into a strong association of white ethnic communities, economic nationalism, racial integrity, compulsory repatriation, restoration of law and order, an independent national defence, and so on.[113] As Tyndall later confirmed, the National Front's 'political objectives as they stood, needed no alteration'.[114] But, as was the case with the 1970s National Front, these political principles undoubtedly masked a more radical ideological core, as we shall see.

Nonetheless, the BNP was not a carbon copy of the 1970s National Front. A major distinction lay in the BNP's constitutional basis. Throughout the 1970s, in order to back up the party's claim that it was committed to democratic principles, the National Front built the principle of 'democratic' collective leadership into its constitutional framework. Yet this had been a recurrent source of irritation to Tyndall. In October 1974, elections to the Directorate by a ballot of all the party's members had allowed Tyndall's opponents to temporarily dispossess him of control over the Front. More recently, the Constitution had, Tyndall argued, become nothing more than 'a pawn in the hands of the Directorate, to be bent and manipulated at the Directorate's will'.[115] For Tyndall, it was not the Chairman but the dominant faction on the Directorate, in this case Webster and his 'Gay Lobby', that now controlled the Front. Accordingly, when the BNP was established,

Tyndall was determined that a new constitution should be adopted in which full executive powers would be vested in the Chairman thereby authorising the party leader to act decisively in all internal matters.[116] Moreover, since any candidate for election to the party leadership must have served at least five years of full membership, Tyndall believed that should the party enter a period of rapid growth, he had immunised himself against any potential challenge from 'populist newcomers' of the Kingsley Read/Painter ilk. As it turned out, however, Tyndall was eventually deposed in 1999 not by a 'populist newcomer' but by a seasoned campaigner of the far right, Nick Griffin, onetime leader of the 1980s National Front.

What this chapter has shown, then, is that John Tyndall, a founder and first leader of the British National Party, possessed an unbroken line of far-right activity that stretched back to the 1950s. As he openly accepts, the basis of his political beliefs had been 'laid early in my life, probably by the time I was 22 or 23 years old'.[117] Without doubt, the seminal influence on his political thinking was A.K. Chesterton. In January 1971, when reflecting on Chesterton's resignation from the Front, Tyndall felt compelled to acknowledge that 'I can say without hesitation that what understanding I may have been able to acquire of political affairs today I owe much more to A.K. than to any other single person.'[118] What Tyndall absorbed from Chesterton's writings was a visceral and unshakeable belief in Jewish conspiracy theory. But there was always a wider picture to Tyndall's ideological development. By the early 1960s he was openly advocating neo-Nazism and, although he puts this down to 'youthful exuberance', there is much evidence to suggest that Tyndall remained wedded to national-socialist ideology during the 1970s even if semi-hidden behind a mask of 'British patriotism'.

As for his political methods, these were, as Tyndall says, 'being formed gradually in the hard school of experience, trial and error'.[119] Despite a flirtation with other means, Tyndall had become convinced by the mid-1960s that the only route to power was through the ballot box. Yet his experiences with the National Front – an organisation that he had played a significant part in founding – had left a bitter aftertaste. Hence, by the early 1980s Tyndall was on guard against several enemies within the gates: 'liberal' constitutions, ill-disciplined mores and not least those 'moderate' racial populists who, in their quest for political respectability, were ready to forgo what Tyndall proudly regarded as his revolutionary political mission. For Tyndall, adaptation to the political environment had its limits and loss of original ideological identity could never be countenanced. As Tyndall reminds us:

> The whole purpose of those who founded the National Front in 1967 and took part in its early battles to gain recognition was that it should become a revolutionary challenge to that system, not a pale copy of it.[120]

What applied to the 'founding pioneers' of the National Front equally applied to those who launched the British National Party in 1982, some fifteen years later. Of course, the one notable exception in all of this was Ray Hill – a 'founding father' of the British National Party for whom Tyndall later rewrote history. As far as BNP operations were concerned, Tyndall implausibly declared: 'we never let him get too close to ours'.[121]

2
The Struggle for the Soul of British Nationalism

For Britain's extreme right, the election of Margaret Thatcher in 1979 brought with it the first cold winds of a long and miserable winter. Unable to compete with the Conservative Party for ideological space and debilitated by its own disunity, the electoral performance of the extreme right during the 1980s went from bad to worse. At the general election in June 1983, the vote for right-extremist parties across the country averaged out at below 1 per cent in the seats contested.[1] In June 1987, as Thatcher celebrated election to her third term, both the British National Party and the National Front had all but vanished from Britain's electoral landscape. Only the most dedicated of academic observers could ferret out the two or three far-right candidates that did stand.[2] This was undoubtedly a time of electoral decline and sterility for Britain's right-extremist fringe, but it should not be dismissed as a period in which Britain's far right merely limped on with little or no purpose. On the contrary, with the BNP and the NF now vying for the 'soul of British nationalism', the far right became a hotly disputed territory fractured by internecine struggle and ideological quarrel. As Tyndall understood it, if the BNP were to recover the political strength of the 1970s NF, winning this struggle would become imperative and by 'all means necessary' if need be.[3] But it was not until the end of 1989 before this struggle had finally played out. Where Tyndall had survived, others such as archrival Martin Webster had fallen. Now Tyndall had the upper hand, and at long last as the British National Party entered the 1990s it had succeeded in displacing the National Front as Britain's leading far-right party.

Establishing itself: the BNP in its early years

As well as incorporating the whole of the New National Front, when the BNP had been instituted in 1982, it had been given a further boost by support from various other far-right fragments – the British Democratic Party, the British Movement, the Nationalist Party and defectors from the National Front for whom the Front's progressive radicalisation went against the grain. Nonetheless, even though the National Front's membership had fallen to an unprecedented low, the BNP still fell some way short in comparison.[4] Consequently, if the BNP were 'likely to emerge as the most powerful movement in the nationalist camp in the next few months' as Tyndall optimistically predicted in *Spearhead* in April 1982, it was essential that the party did not merely exist on paper.[5] What impressed itself on Tyndall was the need for the BNP to establish its name, institute a firm organisational structure, build up a regional network of branches, place itself on a sound financial footing, turn out regular publications and fulfil a major activities programme. With all of this in mind, over the course of the next year, Tyndall's BNP set itself on a path of 'continuous and steady' development.[6]

In the months that followed, as the NF leadership woefully struggled to manage its declining numbers, the impetus passed to Tyndall and in terms of building the party significant steps forward were taken. In the first place, numerous NF branches defected and as the BNP established itself as the leading extreme-right party in a series of provincial towns and cities such as Liverpool, Manchester, Leeds, Hull, Gateshead, Glasgow, Plymouth and Bristol, branch organisation around the country gathered momentum.[7] However, London remained largely infertile territory where the National Front reigned supreme amongst the capital's far-right flock. For a moment, this situation could have been turned on its head had Tyndall not, following advice from Ray Hill and Tyndall's benefactor, Charles Parker, committed a serious error by snubbing overtures from Joe Pearce, Young National Front leader.[8] In Ray Hill's opinion, had Pearce delivered the ranks of the Young National Front to the BNP – the Young National Front was at its strongest in London – the NF would have been put out of action. Consequently, in order to keep the far right in fragments, *Searchlight* spy Ray Hill brought it home to Parker and Tyndall that Pearce was untrustworthy. Having turned Pearce down, this political opportunity passed Tyndall by.[9]

Nonetheless, the party's organisational development did not desist. A stream of publications appeared, its financial position was secured – start-up costs were minimised as the BNP was run from Tyndall's 'Seacroft' home in Hove, East Sussex – and the first edition of the British National Party's constitution was published in November 1982.

As we have seen, Tyndall, frustrated by the National Front's Directorate structure, inspired it and in place of a Directorate structure, full executive powers were vested in the party leader. A disciplinary code was also built in which intended to 'thwart at birth any subversive or disruptive actions or tendencies in the party by conferring powers of summary dismissal on the party's leadership'.[10] That these developments were intended to fashion the BNP into a disciplined and unified outfit under Tyndall's authoritarian control, a party with staying power is clear. But none of this could take away from the fact that as far as the ordinary public was concerned, it was the National Front that remained the household name. The NF still held the lead as it possessed the 'brand label' even if as Tyndall remarked, 'the winning product had gone'.[11]

For the BNP not to be a wasted effort, it had to make itself known to the British public. At first its work in this direction rehearsed the publicity-seeking antics of the League of Empire Loyalists. In June 1982 some BNP members led by Ray Hill attempted to bring the party to wider attention by interrupting a BBC radio transmission of 'Any Questions' in Peterborough. When the panel was asked who they thought was the best person to lead the country, Hill jumped on his seat and shouted 'John Tyndall, leader of the British National Party'.[12] But as for other possibilities, marches and rallies apart, the BNP was more than a year old before a major publicity opportunity presented itself. By standing over 50 candidates at the June 1983 general election, the BNP could qualify for five minutes broadcasting time on TV and radio thereby making its presence known to millions – 'this election will make the BNP known in every household' as one local BNP bulletin boldly forecast in March 1983.[13] By setting up a special election fund in order to finance the deposits of a number of 'ghost candidates' and by calling on its branches to raise the £150 deposit for each seat via collections, voluntary members' levies, jumble-sales, raffles and soliciting of special contributions from 'better-off-than-average' members,[14] the BNP was able to put up candidates in 53 constituencies.[15] Rather than winning votes – in only five constituencies were election addresses delivered to every household – the central purpose of the British National Party's 1983 election campaign was to win publicity and recruit new members. For some time prior to the election, party membership had levelled off at 2,500.[16]

Even if only 14,000 people voted BNP[17] and its highest vote was a derisory 1.3 per cent in Walsall South, over 13 million people almost certainly saw its party-political broadcast. This featured Tyndall, flanked by Union Jacks, regurgitating well-worn themes: the failure of the 'old parties', opposition to mass immigration, withdrawal from the Common Market, and so on. Yet his party's commitment to compulsory repatriation went undisclosed – a sop to political respectability, perhaps.[18] But in the founding *Principles and Policies of the British National Party* (1982), which remained true to 1970s NF policy, repatriation was cast in stone:

> Immigration into Britain by non-Europeans...should be terminated forthwith, and we should organise a massive programme of repatriation and resettlement overseas of those peoples of non-European origin already resident in this country.

Buried within the detail of *Vote for Britain*, the party's 1983 election manifesto, the presence of Tyndall's inveterate racial-biological determinism could be discerned too. Underpinning this repatriation policy was Tyndall's refusal to accept the idea of 'racial equality', a 'myth' that in Tyndall's eyes had been deliberately spread by Westminster politicians:

> It is time this crackpot idea was abandoned once and for all, and that we recognised that among the races of the world there are **inherently different** aptitudes for development which environmental, economic or political changes will never alter – a fact that has been borne out by the very different levels of achievement between white and coloured races in Britain, both in the schoolroom and in subsequent employment.[19]

But in the broadcasting shop window, what Tyndall put on view was slightly more refined and, with these election broadcasts proving sufficiently attractive to invite 3,000 enquiries to the party, the BNP won 'hundreds' of new recruits.[20]

Yet by the same token, the National Front also benefited. In over 50 constituencies the NF stood candidates and, like the BNP, adopted an election strategy geared more to winning publicity, attracting enquiries and winning new members than to winning votes. Since the turn of the decade the NF had expressed the view that it could not possibly come to power under conditions of political, social and economic stability and, in consequence, elections were to be primarily fought to gain publicity and to recruit new members – votes were a 'secondary consideration'.[21] A sensible position perhaps given that the NF only averaged

1.1 per cent of the vote at the 1983 general election. Nonetheless, the Front did receive more than 2,000 enquiries as a result of its election campaign and 242 new members had joined by the end of July 1983.[22] Yet looked at from another angle, conversion rates were low – typically 10 to 15 from every 100 enquiries. The problem the NF encountered was that branch organisers were usually responsible for chasing up enquiries and, where branch organisation was weak, follow-up rates fell short. One way through this problem, the BNP thought, was to invite those members of the public that had enquired about the party following its election broadcasts to a series of indoor meetings. However, these meetings only seemed to occur in those provincial cities where branch organisation was already at its strongest.[23] Progress was thereby checked, and while the BNP had certainly established itself on the far-right fringe by 1983 and had more or less caught up with the National Front in terms of membership size, its struggle for dominance over Britain's extreme right was far from won. Moreover, in terms of its wider political recognition, the BNP may have briefly established its name during the 1983 general election but as for its wider impact, this remained negligible.

The holy grail of 'Nationalist Unity': the British National Party and the challenge of the National Front, 1983–87

Before the 1983 general election, the British National Party had approached the National Front with a proposal for merger on condition that Martin Webster and his 'Gay faction' stepped aside.[24] Unsurprisingly, given the acrimonious dispute between Tyndall and Webster, at the National Front's 1983 AGM, a motion rejecting 'Nationalist Unity' had been proposed by Webster.[25] But as the Front's National Activities Organiser, Webster's tenure was nearing its end. In December 1983, a band of young radicals led by Joe Pearce and future BNP leader, Nick Griffin, conspired to oust him and Webster found himself expelled from the Front in early 1984. The occasion for all of this was not Webster's refusal to countenance reconciliation with Tyndall, but Webster's bid to inhibit ideological radicalism and factionalism within the Front itself.

While tensions came to a head in 1983, the beginnings of the Front's radicalisation can be traced back to 1980. As the NF's radicals understood it, the impetus for ideological change came from them, that is to say, from a group of young and inexperienced activists who had served their political apprenticeships in the Young National Front – such as

Nick Griffin[26] who, in 1979, had led the Young National Front's Student Organisation whilst also serving as the assistant editor of *Tornado*, a local NF newssheet in Ipswich. Other key radicals included Derek Holland,[27] Graham Williamson[28] and Patrick Harrington.[29] In reality, however, the first move towards radicalisation came from the Front's 'adult' leadership and, in particular, new Chairman Andrew Brons who sought to prioritise the Front's ideological development in the wake of the 1979 general election debacle.[30] The absence of a 'clear-cut ideological identity' had been raised as a serious problem at the NF's Directorate Conference in early February 1980, and the following month it was Brons who reminded the rest of the Directorate that they had decided to invite party members to submit a 5,000-word paper on how the NF should develop its ideology.[31] Moreover, it was Brons who first introduced the radical ideological concept of Distributism[32] to the National Front.[33]

But even if radicalisation chimed with the concerns of the NF Directorate, Webster always endeavoured to keep the younger generation of party radicals in check. At the outset, the seedbed of the Front's radicalisation was *Nationalism Today*, a magazine founded in 1980 that was independent of the NF at first but which was later adopted as its official publication.[34] Within the pages of *Nationalism Today*, a stream of articles appeared that took the NF down a radical anti-capitalist and anti-communist course. During the second half of 1983, however, the activities of party members associated with a new magazine – *Rising* (1982–85) – aroused most concern, especially from Webster who feared the development of 'a party within a party'. Co-edited by Derek Holland, *Rising* was a semi-clandestine publication. It styled itself as a magazine of 'the vanguard leadership of the Revolutionary Nationalist Movement', a magazine that 'may go beyond' what could be considered acceptable 'in patriotic circles'.[35] One member of the NF Directorate, having received an unsolicited copy of this magazine, dismissed it as a 'Jewish dirty trick operation' – so taken aback by its content.[36]

Certainly *Rising*'s contents came across as a curious creed, especially for those accustomed to run-of-the-mill authoritarian racial populism. For inspiration, *Rising* drew from 'Third Position'[37] revolutionary nationalism, disseminating the esoteric ideas of fascist philosophers Evola[38] and Codreanu[39] in particular. Throughout, it concentrated its attack on the spiritual 'abyss' of urban materialism and the liberal-capitalist system, calling instead for the creation of a New Man – a 'political soldier' – selflessly committed to nationalist rural and spiritual revolution. But while domestic right-extremists fronted the *Rising* project, its principal ideological driver was in fact a group of far-right Italian political refugees belonging to the Armed Revolutionary Nuclei (NAR), who had sought refuge in London following the 1980 Bologna station bombing. This London-based NAR group, led by Roberto Fiore,[40] had been introduced to Holland and Griffin through Michael Walker, former central London organiser of the NF. Griffin's association with Fiore even ran to a business partnership too – a 'London guide' business known as 'Heritage Tours'.[41] Evidently, 'behind the scenes' the radical wing of the Front was becoming closely meshed with Italian neo-fascism, and there can be little doubt that Griffin, Pearce and Holland, working in conjunction with the Italian exiles, were planning to take over the Front.

Even so, despite an urgent internal inquiry into *Rising* – it had uncovered a series of covert ideological training sessions attended by Griffin and some of the Italian exiles – the Front's Directorate took no action. Indeed, whether or not this was so in private, certainly as far as the Directorate minutes record, Webster seems to have been initially satisfied that Griffin's involvement with *Rising* was not motivated by 'malice'. Griffin's defence was that since the NF's Education and Training Department's seminar activity had lapsed, he had been attracted to *Rising* by default and henceforth would give 99 per cent of his effort to promoting the NF.[42] Yet Griffin was clearly playing for time, and such was the desire of the radical faction to gain control over the Front that Webster found himself the victim of a party coup shortly afterwards as both Pearce and Griffin threatened their resignation in joint protest at Webster's failure to deal with falling party morale.[43]

Watching events from a distance, Tyndall congratulated himself. He saw Webster's removal as a total vindication of the position he had adopted in 1980. Moreover, with Webster finally out of the way, Tyndall again offered up the possibility of reconciliation: 'I can only say again that our door is open'.[44] Yet if truth be told, what 'reconciliation' meant for Tyndall was victory over the Front and unity on his terms, in other words, a new 1970s NF-style coalition but with Tyndall in full control. However, though Webster's expulsion had removed one important obstacle to this political goal, as regards the Front's ongoing radicalisation, Tyndall had to bridge an ever-widening gap. His response was to try to disabuse the Front's supporters of the notion that ideological radicalisation held the key to future political success. The 'more ideological baggage the movement carries, the more there is to disagree, argue and fight over' Tyndall argued and therefore, 'A few very basic principles rooted in the primacy of **Race** and **Nationality** are sufficient; more than these are superfluous.'[45] And once again Tyndall repeated his mantra that the failure of the 1970s Front was not the failure of ideology but the failure of collective leadership.

Rather predictably, however, little common ground could be found with the new generation of Front leaders who decried the 1970s NF for having been little more than a 'broad church' pressure group, held loosely together by popular racism. For its radical activists, the 1970s Front had been an ill-fated 'rag-bag' of a party comprised of 'black-hating Tories' who, after the 1979 general election, soon returned to their 'natural home', 'social inadequates, bar room politicians, hooligans looking for an excuse for violence – and, of course, a body of genuine, if unsophisticated nationalists'.[46] With such odd bedfellows, what had brought schism to the Front after the 1979 general election, they insisted, was its lack of ideological coherence and identity. Any return to a broad, ill-defined programme was therefore out of the question. And so it followed that during the winter of 1984, writing in *New Nation*, the NF's journal, the Front made it clear that it jealously guarded its new ideological direction and whilst issues of 'Race' and 'Nation' were of 'immediate importance', it was not prepared to sacrifice its radical opposition to capitalism.

As the 'parent movement', the National Front insisted that unity could only occur if other 'nationalists' join or rejoin the National Front and only if they accept the radical ideological position of the NF in its entirety.[47] Sure enough Tyndall's approach came to nothing. The following year, at a meeting in North London called by the BNP to promote 'Nationalist Unity', chaos ensued as NF members shouted abuse and insults at the platform. From now on, as far as Tyndall was concerned, further contact with the NF should be ruled out 'unless the initiative to establish that contact came, for a change, from the other side'.[48]

When such a proposal finally came forward, it was during the spring of 1987 and the work of Andrew Brons, onetime GBM activist who had remained faithful to the NF even after the expulsion of both Tyndall and Webster. But Brons had resigned as NF Chairman in 1984 and had now come out in opposition to Griffin's 'young guard'. In fact, by this time, the National Front had split into two warring factions after an episode of fratricidal conflict had torn the Front apart in 1986. Ostensibly, this schism occurred as the 'political soldier' faction led by Griffin, Holland, Harrington and Williamson disengaged the Front from an electoral strategy altogether. Other than recruiting an elite corps of hardcore political activists, the strategy of these 'political soldiers' lacked clarity, however. Nonetheless, at least one contemporary academic observer thought it had become a 'proto-terrorist' organisation.[49] Those NF members who dissented from this course of action – the majority in fact – formed themselves into a dissident National Front Support Group (NFSG) otherwise known as the 'Flag Group', which kept the Front committed to the more orthodox electoral path.

From within the Support Group, Andrew Brons took it upon himself to open a dialogue with Tyndall through the BNP's Northern England Chairman, Stanley Clayton-Garnett,[50] a leading critic of the extreme right's inability to overcome its 'factional psychosis'. Revealingly, Clayton-Garnett had earlier called for unification in 1985 based on the 'indisputable and sacrosanct' principle of a 'Nationalist party with a radical Socialist dimension' (namely, a national-socialist party).[51] According to Clayton-Garnett, these fundamental ideological precepts were 'the rock upon which a united party must be built'.[52] Such an ideological position did not deter Brons who presumably felt that his own working-class Strasserism could be fitted into this design.

Since Brons had quietly sought collaboration with the BNP in Yorkshire for some time, his approach to Tyndall did not come entirely out of the blue. Yet the impression we get from *Searchlight*'s Gerry Gable is that Brons' initiative may have been part of a grander conspiracy orchestrated by the veteran 'Nazi godfather' Colin Jordan, a close friend and neighbour to Brons. According to Gable, Jordan had emerged from self-imposed exile in 1986 in order to pen an article for the League of St George's[53] journal that set out a blueprint for the future of Britain's far right whereby right-extremists were encouraged to strictly separate their efforts into either legal and illegal activity. In this way, by bringing the NF and BNP together, the public face of the far right could be maintained whilst the 'political soldiers' went underground.[54] In line with this reading, the NF's 1986 split could be considered a purely cosmetic exercise orchestrated by Jordan. But whilst this conspiracy theory carried a whiff of plausibility, the animosity between the NFSG and the NF's 'political soldiers' was far from illusory as their published exchanges clearly testify.[55] The reality is that NF's 1986 split did not occur as a consequence of Jordan's master plan. For Patrick Harrington, this grand conspiracy theory was 'just rubbish its [sic] as simple as that';[56] the basis for it was growing intra-party conflict over the ideological and strategic direction that the Front was taking. Under the influence of the 'political soldiers', the NF had reneged on its long-standing commitment to Ulster, banned all mention of scientific racism from *Nationalism Today* and wasted time engaged in 'adolescent paramilitary fantasies'.[57]

In May 1987, Tyndall met with Brons in Leeds. This was the first meeting of the two in seven years. On the discussion table were the terms of a Nationalist Alliance between the BNP and the National Front Support Group, not dissimilar in nature to the mainstream SDP–Liberal Alliance: an electoral pact where both agreed not to compete with one another in elections; a free flow of publications; the pooling of resources for joint activities; and the institution of exploratory talks aimed at minimising and eventually eliminating ideological, policy and constitutional differences. A Liaison Committee with Clayton-Garnett as its Chair would oversee all this.[58] Following this meeting, Brons recommended the Nationalist Alliance to the NFSG's steering committee and a first meeting of the Liaison Committee took place in July 1987.

But things were not right. The NFSG's steering committee backtracked, and to Tyndall's frustration the deal was undone. On 9 August 1987, an audience in Leeds expecting to hear that the alliance had been sealed, instead heard Brons declare that the NFSG's steering committee had 'democratically reversed the previous decision and the partnership was off'.[59] The NFSG claimed that certain BNP personnel had informed them that Tyndall would never agree to merger between the two parties unless his leadership went unchallenged and that the BNP's constitution and its basic policies prevailed. However, as Tyndall pointed out, his intentions were far from secret: 'So my position is – yes, if there is to be a union of forces, I lead it – until such time as a man more competent than I appears.'[60] Elsewhere, Clayton-Garnett, Tyndall's proxy, blamed the 'iconoclastic mentalities of certain segments of opinion extraneous to the BNP' and drew particular attention to 'considerable differences' in political philosophy between the BNP and the NFSG. In other words, the sticking point had been the NFSG's working-class radicalism.[61] Browned-off by continued division of the far-right camp, Clayton-Garnett left the BNP shortly afterwards. Declaring himself 'non-aligned', he wrote in *Spearhead* in August 1988 that he was now working for the 'creation of a united nationalist movement which embraced the total area of acceptable nationalist opinion'.[62] In truth, Clayton-Garnett was prime-mover in a covert bid to hijack the BNP in Yorkshire and establish a National Socialist League in Leeds.[63]

Perhaps the most likely explanation for why the Nationalist Alliance miscarried, however, was that Martin Wingfield, editor of the NFSG's

Flag newspaper, which had ruled out any possibility of merger in its editorial, had sabotaged it for no other reason than he still nursed a personal grudge against Tyndall and Charles Parker. Though later reinstated, Wingfield had been expelled from the Front in 1980 whilst Tyndall was its chairman, following disciplinary action inaugurated by Charles Parker, Tyndall's father-in-law and the NF's Brighton branch organiser. Originating from the time when Wingfield had contested Parker for regional control over the NF's Sussex area, there had been a history of bad blood between Parker and Wingfield. Frustrated by Parker's lack-lustre leadership, Wingfield had made trouble for himself by organising a group of disaffected Front members for whom he had independently published *Sussex Front* without permission of the local branch.[64] For this breach of discipline, and for other 'troublesome conduct' – the suggestion is that Wingfield was guilty of financial irregularity – he was forced out of the NF.[65] Despite an interval of many years, extending the hand of friendship to Tyndall was not part of Wingfield's plans.

With the ground cut from under Tyndall's feet, it looked as if it was a case of 'back to square one' for the BNP. Over half a decade had passed since its formation and Tyndall seemed no nearer to winning the struggle for supremacy on Britain's far right. The National Front had not been thrown into the shade and, as we have seen, all attempts at securing the BNP's hegemony through the 'unity trail' proved futile. 'SHED NO TEARS for the rapid demise of the Nationalist Alliance', declared one contributor to *Spearhead* in a bid to strike an upbeat note.[66] But pessimism and defeatism were the order of the day. Yet Tyndall's efforts at 'reconciliation' had not been entirely wasted. Taking advantage of its 'open door', most of the NF's Tower Hamlets branch broke away and joined forces with the BNP. Of course, at the time, the true significance of this would be lost on Tyndall, but as it turned out it was this branch that made a decisive contribution to the party's first electoral victory – in September 1993 in Millwall, within the London borough of Tower Hamlets.

On or off? The BNP and the electoral trail

If supremacy on the far right via the 'unity trail' had been exhausted, lest we should forget that as a party intent on winning power at the ballot box, the British National Party had committed itself to the electoral trail as well. But other than having the far-flung point of political power as its final destination, this trail was haphazardly mapped out.

Indeed, over a five-year period (1984–89), elections were only sporadic-ally contested by Tyndall's BNP and, what's more, its forays into the electoral arena became ever more irregular and intermittent. Many commentators have drawn attention to the fact that the BNP steered clear of the 1987 general election, and in those elections that it did contest results were extremely modest, typically in the 1–3 per cent range though punctuated by occasional 'highs' – the 11.7 per cent of the vote that a BNP candidate polled in a local council by-election in Sunderland in 1984[67] and occasional 'lows' – the 15 votes that a BNP candidate polled in a by-election in Plymouth that same year.[68]

For the most part, this fitful electoral strategy was the consequence of Tyndall's decision, taken after the 1983 general election, to concen-trate the resources of his party on long-term organisational develop-ment 'rather than continually butt its head against the brick wall of the electoral system' where 'it had no hope of making any significant dent'.[69] Without doubt, Britain's far right was stonewalled by a polit-ical climate in the 1980s where, in journalist Angus Roxburgh's memorable phrase, the Conservative Party 'stretched the concept of the 'mainstream right' to its limit'.[70] Nonetheless, the itch to fight elec-tions remained persistent, especially amongst local party activists for whom, in the absence of more meaningful electoral engagement, branch activity lacked fire and imagination – the regular drill of door-to-door leafleting and routine paper sales hardly infused them with vitality. Occasionally, therefore, so that the enthusiasm of party activists would not be deadened, Tyndall gave his reluctant consent to electoral forays.

Yet in truth there was a mingling of attitudes in Tyndall's mind. Now and then he saw positive benefits from such electoral activity, as during 1985 when policy was modified to encourage the contesting of elections in order to secure council premises for meetings from which Tyndall hoped to attract local and national publicity.[71] By 1985 the BNP had largely returned to public obscurity and since these meetings would typically attract some committed anti-fascist opposition, publicity was frequently generated, as in Bradford in April 1985 when Clayton-Garnett polled 4.1 per cent of the vote fol-lowing a council by-election campaign in which the BNP's election meeting had ended in serious disorder.[72] The following year, how-ever, barely any importance was attached to electoral activity – only one BNP candidate stood at the 1986 London borough council elec-tions. The reason why is not hard to find: John Tyndall along with John Morse, editor of the BNP newspaper, *British Nationalist*, had received one-year prison sentences for incitement to racial hatred.[73] Though they only served four months, the BNP's programme of activity largely ground to a halt during 1986 despite the labours of Richard Edmonds and Bromley branch organiser, Alf Waite, who stood in whilst Tyndall and Morse were detained at Her Majesty's pleasure.

On his release from prison, Tyndall returned to the helm. However, stormy waters lay ahead as he soon found himself having to navigate the forthcoming general election. It was Tyndall's belief that if the BNP contested the 1987 general election, it was essential for the party to make a 'credible showing'. The influx of new members after the 1983 general election would have been greater had many not been dissuaded by the paltry votes that the BNP candidates obtained, Tyndall thought.[74] But the party was clearly up against it. In the first place, as we have seen, disunity prevailed on Britain's far right. For the moment, the idea of the 'grand' Nationalist Alliance was still being mooted, and therefore the BNP would have to go it alone and contest the general election from its own limited resources. Secondly, since 1983 the party had not appreciably gained in strength, it had not benefited from any sizeable financial windfall and, due to Tyndall's imprisonment, had undergone a damaging period of internal disruption. Thirdly, with the raising of electoral deposits from £150 to £500, the BNP would have to commit itself to spending at least £25,000 in order to contest 50 seats. With around £10,000 in its coffers, plus some £3,000 raised following a special election fund appeal launched in April 1987, the party's scarce financial resources would only allow it to contest 20 to 25 seats at most, clearly not enough for it to secure any broadcasting time.

When it came down it, however, Tyndall was unconvinced that the BNP could make a credible showing in these 20 to 25 seats, even with a plentiful supply of campaign literature. One problem was lack of party strength at the grassroots, as one local bulletin moaned: 'Head Office has informed us that there are some areas of the Country where the local B.N.P. is not in a fit state to fight a parish election, let alone a General Election.'[75] More than that, the popular appeal of the Conservative Party with its blend of free-market liberalism and social authoritarianism, had kept the extreme right in the political backwaters since 1979. The BNP's derisory showing at the Greenwich parliamentary by-election in London in February 1987 – it polled 0.3 per cent of the vote – suggested that the possibility of the BNP obtaining a credible vote in this political climate was remote. With Tyndall loath to put the BNP's financial security at risk, on the late afternoon of 11 May – the day the election was called – an internal party bulletin was hastily despatched informing all branches and groups of his decision not to field any candidates at the general election the following month. Taking into consideration the monies saved from not fighting the election, Tyndall sweetened the pill by promising his supporters that a party headquarters premises would be acquired in the near future.

Even so, Tyndall's last-minute decree was met with dismay at the grassroots. For a party seeking mass popular support, this ruling clearly dampened the spirits and, even if the overwhelming majority of members observed Tyndall's directive, all did not pass without incident. Two prominent local BNP officers, Alf Waite in Bromley[76] and Michael Easter from the BNP's West Kent branch, broke ranks and declared their intention to stand as BNP candidates. In so doing – Waite stood in Ravensbourne and Easter in Tonbridge – the leadership was defied and a serious challenge to Tyndall's authority became a distinct possibility. However, with Tyndall determined to retain party unity and discipline, he moved quickly and terminated their party memberships. To all party members in the Kent and Bromley areas, Tyndall sent out a special bulletin voicing his determination to put a stop to internal indiscipline. In a further letter, addressed to BNP members in Bromley, Tyndall claimed that Waite's actions had resulted from deterioration in their working relationship following Tyndall's return from prison. Waite was said to be under much personal strain and was suffering from ill-health.[77] Yet despite his best efforts to bring these dissident activists on side, there was now an open breach with local activists in south-east London and parts of Kent; large-scale defections to the National Front Support (Flag) Group subsequently took place.[78]

Yet Tyndall was to emerge from this stormy episode with his authority still intact, in all probability because he was proved right – the two unofficial BNP candidates polled less than 1 per cent of the vote. Nonetheless, there could be no avoiding the sense of dejection at local branch level: 'We ask of you who share our disappointment to grit your teeth and carry on with promoting the principles of the British National Party', was the rallying cry of the West London branch.[79] However, elections were now second-order priority. Over the course of the next year or so, Tyndall's immediate objective was to strengthen his ailing party. In consequence, it was 1990 before the British National Party rekindled its electoral aspirations.

The 1980s draw to a close: the BNP at the end of the road?

With the Nationalist Alliance having come to naught and having played no part in the 1987 general election, party morale had hit rock bottom by 1988. Unsurprisingly, some members had lost heart. By now, according to *Searchlight*'s figures, membership of the British National Party had fallen to barely 1,000 though Tyndall claimed, perhaps disingenuously, that over the course of the past two to three years membership had been 'just about maintained' where rates of new enrolments had almost kept pace with drop-out rates.[80] But without doubt the party was sunk in gloom, and as 1988 opened, Tyndall's address to the troops railed against the prevailing sense of defeatism within the party. What gave Tyndall particular cause for complaint was the attitude of local leaders for whom criticising the national leader-ship for the party's inactivity had become an easy means of escape. Exonerating himself for the party's current plight, Tyndall declared that success or failure depended '95 per cent' on local effort put in by party activists. Moreover, winning support did not hinge on moderat-ing the party's image or 'ideological cosmetics'; the way forward was through branch activity and the sheer perseverance of local party activists.[81]

What Tyndall had in mind for 1988 was the completion of five prin-cipal tasks, all of which were geared towards strengthening the party. Contesting elections was a deliberate omission, 'first things first', Tyndall said.[82] To start with, he sought a 50 per cent increase in party membership. On this point, Tyndall specifically linked high rates of recruitment to the widest possible distribution of party literature. Hence paper-sales had to rise by 50 per cent and leaflet/sticker distribu-tion by at least 100 per cent. Second, he promised to deliver a party headquarters building where a party official would be available on the end of a telephone at any time during the working week – for the moment there was no central office with a telephone number that could be made available to the public. Third, Tyndall pledged to win the struggle for the 'soul of British nationalism' by turning the BNP into the strongest faction on the far right and thereby unify 'the members of the other factions (at least those of them worth having) under us by the gravitational pull of our superior strength'.[83] A further promise was to instigate a training programme for party activists, and to end with he announced his intention to publish a book – *The Eleventh Hour* – scribed, not unlike Hitler's *Mein Kampf*, whilst in prison. From this publication Tyndall aspired to attract a wave of new recruits of sufficiently high calibre to form the BNP's layer of 'middle management'.[84] That, at any rate, was the plan. By May 1988, however, in light of reports of a series of defections to the rival NF Flag Group, *Searchlight* was asking whether Tyndall's BNP had in fact reached 'the end of the road'.[85]

In the midst of all this adversity, the failings of the BNP were thrown into sharp relief by the unprecedented success of Jean-Marie Le Pen, leader of the *Front National*, in the first round of the French presidential elections in April 1988 – Le Pen polled 14.4 per cent of the vote, some 4.4 million votes. This gave Tyndall much food for thought. In relation to its French counterpart, the extreme right in Britain was poles apart; the contrast in political fortunes was vast. From Tyndall's vantage point, looking across the Channel from his home close to the white cliffs of Dover, the decisive factor accounting for the electoral rise of Jean-Marie Le Pen had been the 'credibility' factor. According to Tyndall, at some point between 1981 and 1988 (he could not identify when), Le Pen had broken through a barrier of electoral 'credibility' with French voters 'before which they were regarded as not having a chance and after which they were seen as having something of a chance'.[86] In Britain, meanwhile, the BNP languished because voters saw it as weak and irrelevant. Of all things, it was therefore 'credibility' that had accounted for Le Pen's spectacular change in electoral fortunes. For Tyndall, the lesson from France was that the BNP had to attain credibility and thus, 'we should be looking for ways to overcome our present image of **weakness** and **smallness**'.[87] Whether by design or not, it was obvious that Tyndall had overlooked one important factor in all of this: the rise of the *Front National* had been occasioned by the construction of political legitimacy, brought about in part through a process of self-induced internal moderation.[88]

Yet moderating the party's image and ideology was never a vital concern for Tyndall. But it would be wrong to assume that he attached no importance to it all. As Roger Eatwell has previously noted, during the 1980s Tyndall endeavoured to keep the skinhead element and football hooligans at arm's length;[89] this fraternity gravitated more towards the ranks of the National Front. Nonetheless, as far his French lessons were concerned, Tyndall had much to learn. Within his immediate entourage he kept faith with hard-line racists, individuals with criminal records for violence. Tyndall's deputy, Richard Edmonds for instance, who had convictions for smashing the Nelson Mandela statue on London's South Bank and who, over the course of the previous three years, had allegedly been a key player in the distribution of over 100,000 copies of *Holocaust News* – a newssheet that declared the Holocaust a myth. This publication, which carried the imprint of the BNP's own 'Centre for Historical Review', was described as 'a wonderful statement of the truth' by Edmonds in the course of one TV interview.[90] During 1988, 30,000 copies alone were mailed out to MPs, lawyers, schools and to Jewish communities across Britain.[91] Another close associate of both Tyndall and Edmonds was Tony Lecomber,[92] formerly the BNP's youth officer, who was convicted in 1986 for handling explosives.[93] During 1989, Lecomber had contributed a series of articles to *Spearhead* on genetics and culture, including one which in true Hitleresque fashion had called for a programme of compulsory sterilisation of the mentally sub-normal, of the physically handicapped and of certain criminal and anti-social cases.[94] Indeed, where the BNP's ideology was concerned, Tyndall could see no need for compromise: 'We should not be looking for ways of applying ideological cosmetic surgery to ourselves in order to make our features more appealing to our public', Tyndall declared.[95] When one local organiser had challenged his party leader over this issue in 1987, Tyndall's response was to hold the local organiser responsible for the BNP standing still in that particular locality. The local organiser subsequently resigned.[96] Here we can detect Tyndall's rule of thumb yet again – a change of political clothing was not the answer.

Despite everything, however, Tyndall managed to keep the BNP afloat, due in part to the dedication of local party activists particularly within the Yorkshire region where Eddy Morrison, a former youth organiser for the BNP, reinvigorated the grassroots.[97] Morrison, a veteran of a host of far-right organisations – the National Front included – had set up his own British National Party in Leeds during the 1970s.[98] In September 1988 he returned to Tyndall's fold after earlier being frozen out for pouring scorn on Charles Parker's Masonic connections. With Morrison determined to instil new life into the Yorkshire region, *Searchlight*'s prediction that Tyndall's BNP was doomed, proved premature.[99] Nonetheless, save for publication of his book, Tyndall had clearly fallen a long way short as far as his principal aims for 1988 were concerned. Indeed, as 1989 arrived, party membership had not moved beyond the 800-1,000 range,[100] nor had the BNP eclipsed the National Front.

Over the course of next 12 months, however, the clouds of gloom gradually lifted, and the British National Party finally established itself as Britain's premier far-right organisation. What revived the BNP during 1989 was a combination of factors of which the collapse of the rival National Front was singularly the most important. During the late 1980s, the ideological posturing of Nick Griffin's 'political soldiers' – the 'official' NF – had become ever more radical and esoteric, so much so that the ideology it espoused came across as entirely alien to mainstream right-extremists. From the pantheon of far-right ideology, the 'political soldiers' threw out biological racism for a start.[101] With the 'political soldiers' now supporting the cause of black separatists such as Louis Farrakhan and Marcus Garvey, there was no place for crude anti-black racism in the NF. 'Black Is Beautiful', the *National Front News* declared in August 1987 (somewhat at variance with *Bulldog*'s crude racist headlines in the early 1980s when 'We don't want wogs. We don't want snobs. We want jobs!' had been the norm).[102] For those brought up on a daily diet of anti-black racism, all of this was rank heresy, and so the 'political soldier' faction set about destroying its credibility of its own accord. Incredulously, the 'official' NF even extended a hand of friendship to the Jewish community and unreservedly condemned anti-Semitism,[103] though this was belied by its support for black Muslim anti-Semites and Islamic Third World and anti-Zionist causes, such as Iran's national revolution and Gaddafi's regime in Libya.[104] It perhaps should be mentioned, too, that this was not just empty talk. During 1988, Griffin, Holland and Harrington visited Tripoli as official guests of the Libyan regime; they went in search of lucrative funds, but returned only with bulk copies of Gaddafi's 'Green Book'.[105]

The ideology of what became known as the 'Loony Front' was clearly a non-starter – it is difficult to see how these iconoclastic beliefs could have ever raked in enthusiasts from within extreme-right circles let alone from within society at large. Yet the seeds of the official NF's collapse also lay in the way in which it restructured itself. In seeking to create an elite corps of 'political soldiers', membership became a privilege; not only did membership dues increase to £120 per year in 1986, but it also took members about three years before they could become cadres of the National Front. Unsurprisingly, the 'official' NF quickly incurred membership losses. According to *Searchlight*'s estimates, membership had fallen to some 600–800 by January 1989.[106] A further blow for the 'political soldiers' came during 1989 when their ideological mentor, Roberto Fiore, was exposed as a probable MI6 informant.[107] The final straw, however, was the decision taken by Patrick Harrington to contact the *Jewish Chronicle* with a view to opening a dialogue with the Jewish community. Nick Griffin and Derek Holland soon departed along with 50–60 others to form the International Third Position. By

January 1990, the point at which Harrington disbanded the 'official' National Front, the 'political soldiers' had dwindled to probably no more than 15 activists.[108]

Meanwhile, the National Front Flag Group – the 'unofficial' NF – which had an estimated membership of 3,000 at the start of 1989,[109] also experienced a significant haemorrhaging of support. In a document that the BNP claims to have obtained, it was revealed that during the course of 1989 the NF Flag Group had contracted down to just 10 active units.[110] Its major fiefdom was the West Midlands where at the start of 1989, 75 per cent of the Flag Group's newspaper print run of 2,000 was distributed.[111] But according to the BNP, a Flag Group rally held in Birmingham in June 1989 had attracted only 100 marchers; the local press was less generous and put the figure at just 50 NF supporters.[112] The reason for the Flag Group's demise was almost certainly ineffectual leadership. As a matter of principle, with the 'political soldiers' eschewing electoral politics, the Flag Group had staked all its credibility on electioneering. However, not only was this a time when the electoral soil was especially difficult to till, the Flag Group's electoral strategy was more often than not chaotically pursued with little regard given to either financial outlay or to the location of constituencies.

Rather than carefully targeting seats, the Flag Group made a point of contesting parliamentary by-elections whenever the opportunity arose. Predictably, therefore, its succession of electoral forays was an unmitigated disaster. In December 1988 it contested a parliamentary by-election at Epping Forest and polled 0.8 per cent of the vote. This was followed in June 1989 by a parliamentary by-election in London's Vauxhall when the Flag polled a sorry 83 votes. On the same day, in elections to the European Parliament, the Flag's Martin Wingfield polled just 0.82 per cent of the vote in Birmingham East. Since December 1988, the Flag Group had wasted close to £8,000 on futile electoral contests – all that it obtained in return was humiliation.[113] The ultimate embarrassment came in March 1990 when the Flag Group contested the Mid-Staffordshire by-election, polling a mere 0.5 per cent of the vote and defeated by the late Screaming Lord Sutch of the Monster Raving Loony Party.[114]

As both factions of the National Front faded from view, Tyndall's BNP finally came to the fore. At last, because monies were not wasted on election deposits and also generously part-financed by Richard Edmonds, Tyndall delivered on his promise and a party headquarters building was secured in early 1989. Premises were found at 154 Upper

Wickham Lane, Welling in Kent.[115] Welling was chosen because it was thought to be in a 'safe' Conservative district, an area known for 'white flight' and potential reservoirs of racist support.[116] And significantly, by functioning as a central point for information and distribution, the BNP turned its new premises to good account. Before long, circulation of *British Nationalist* and *Spearhead* had begun to outstrip the publications of its rivals. Moreover, in place of electioneering, a controversial programme of national activities during 1989 that was intended to maximise publicity and create the impression of party strength was pursued instead. In particular, Tyndall hoped to capitalise on anti-Muslim sentiment arising from the death threat issued in February 1989 by Ayatollah Khomeini against Salman Rushdie – author of *The Satanic Verses*. Thus, in a rerun of the 1970s NF policy of 'kicking its way' into the headlines, the British National Party made plans for a series of provocative and high-profile demonstrations in multi-racial 'hot spots' scheduled for the summer of 1989.

In the event, its gaze fixed itself on the West Yorkshire town of Dewsbury. This was not only an area where the BNP could muster up enough activists to make a serious incursion, but Dewsbury had also made a name for itself as a racially segregated town. In September 1987, 26 Dewsbury parents had refused to send their children to a local school because 80 per cent of the pupils were Asian.[117] It was potentially fertile terrain. So BNP activists from Yorkshire, supplemented by Tony Lecomber, tirelessly worked the ground and announced plans to stage a rally in the town on 24 June 1989. The previous Saturday, Asian youths and police had clashed in nearby Bradford and this march was clearly intended to fan the flames of racial tension – the BNP had spread rumours that a copy of the Koran would be burned at its rally. Hundreds of local people, eager to vent their hostility towards the local Asian community, joined forces with the BNP contingent. The deliberate release of a smoke bomb in front of the counter-demonstrators sparked serious disorder and some 80 or so Asian youths were arrested.[118]

This episode alone 'succeeded in its aim of putting the BNP on the map', another *Searchlight* spy, Tim Hepple claims.[119] For sure, with the National Front in organisational disarray, Dewsbury won the BNP recognition amongst its extreme-right constituency. In bidding to out-rival the NF, it was a potent weapon for anti-NF propagandists like Tony Lecomber who, during extensive travels across the country in the seven months prior to Dewsbury, had derided the weaknesses of both factions of the National Front. Writing in *British Nationalist* after

Dewsbury and other 'successful' outings, such as a rally in Darlington, Tyndall made the grandiose claim that the 'name of our party, for long languishing in obscurity, is now on thousands of lips'.[120] But had the pace of new recruits really 'started to quicken', as Tyndall maintained? Perhaps, although even if recruitment was on the increase, the party's upward curve was modest. For a start, the BNP failed to push home its advantage in Dewsbury where fear of possible charges of incitement or conspiracy to riot had led Eddy Morrison to lie low for a month. Hence, as Hepple remembers, 'All the energy and good work went down the tubes.'[121] As *Searchlight*'s figures suggest, party membership was still only 1,000 in January 1990.[122] Therefore, even if Tyndall had won the 'struggle for the soul of the British nationalism', and in so doing had finally outmanoeuvred the National Front, the BNP's position *vis-à-vis* the political mainstream had not altered in the slightest. As it entered the 1990s, Tyndall's British National Party still remained cut off from the centre of British political life.

As we have seen, there was certainly a wretched cold wind blowing across Britain's far right during the 1980s. What weighed heavily against any right-extremist revival was the fact that Thatcher retained a hard-line on the issues of 'race' and immigration as well as law and order. Consequently, Britain's right-extremists struggled for political space. As one commentator put it, 'Certainly, while Mrs Thatcher was the leader of the Conservatives, they could not hope to compete successfully with her for the ideological far-right vote.'[123] Moreover, during the 1970s the NF had often benefited from protest votes particularly where Liberal candidates did not stand, while during the 1980s, as one BNP activist complained, 'a large part of the electorate was infatuated with the media-manufactured 'alternative' to Labour and the Conservatives, namely the Liberal–SDP Alliance'.[124] Alongside all this, it should be pointed out that economic factors were incidental – in periods of both economic recession (the early 1980s) and economic boom (the late 1980s) the far right failed to flourish. If economic factors had little bearing on the far right's fortunes, in stark contrast Britain's right-extremists were certainly debilitated by their own disunity. Factional warfare and ideological schism undermined political credibility. The ideological experimentation of Britain's far right during the 1980s – the Third Positionism of the 'political soldiers' and the Strasserism of the Flag Group – clearly did nothing to broaden its appeal. And even if the BNP remained more 'old school' and kept its policy modelled on the 1970s NF, the continued cultural association of the extreme right with the stigma of Nazism and Fascism was a major obstacle. Throughout, Tyndall's BNP remained a political pariah and yet he still clung to the notion that credibility rather than respectability held the key to electoral breakthrough.

Nonetheless, as a new decade began, the British National Party faced the future with renewed confidence. Even before Thatcher's unexpected fall from power in November 1990, it had already detected a change in public mood. Looming on the horizon were a series of issues that could 'play into its hands', such as a rise in Islamic fundamentalism, the Gulf crisis, the possible arrival of the Hong Kong Chinese and moves to closer European union.[125] Therefore, have no doubts, one local BNP activist declared in September 1990: 'Instead of having a roaring gale blowing in our faces as we try to press forward, we now have a slight breeze at our backs.'[126] And as events over the next few years were to prove, he was not wrong.

3

A False Dawn in Tower Hamlets: The British National Party in the 1990s

In September 1993, as the British National Party won its first council seat in Tower Hamlets, the optimism with which the BNP had greeted the 1990s looked surprisingly prescient. Heralded by a triumphant John Tyndall as a political earthquake, 'the tremors of which are likely to reverberate for many months, even years',[1] this electoral victory was the first election success for the extreme right since the heady days of the 1970s when a National Front offshoot – the National Party – had won two seats on Blackburn council. All but a political non-entity during the 1980s, Tyndall's BNP now seized upon this result. It might have only been the election of just one representative to one local borough council, but for Tyndall it was 'the most tremendous step forward the party has ever made'.[2] However, soon enough, the BNP found its electoral progress cut short. At its peak, in 1994, the average vote for BNP candidates in its fiefdom of Tower Hamlets had been 8.9 per cent; four years later, its average share of the poll across this district had fallen to just 4.53 per cent.[3] If the first part of the decade had showed all the signs of promise, the remainder of the 1990s belied expectations. Without doubt, September 1993 proved a false dawn and what lay in store for Tyndall from the mid-1990s onwards were the closing moments of his reign – a period that saw diminishing electoral rewards, continued disappointment and, in the end, his ejection from office as party leader.

Of the final stages of Tyndall's term in office, we will return to later. To begin with, our concerns start with the party's electoral advance in Tower Hamlets and the factors that gave rise to its first-ever election victory. This is a question that Angus Roxburgh recently claimed has 'baffled' academics.[4] Yet several authors, myself included, have previously addressed this issue and there is little sense in which we are at a complete loss in our accounts.[5] In light of Roxburgh's remarks, however, it does seem appropriate to cast another critical eye over this local arena and, besides, since publication of my original essay, work by Roger Eatwell on the BNP's Tower Hamlets electoral breakthrough has brought forward new theoretical insights that demand closer reflection.[6] Yet there is also a further important question which has so far escaped the attention of academics, and this is our second concern: why did the BNP subsequently decline as a political force in Tower Hamlets and elsewhere after 1994? That the BNP suffered a slow but sure decline from this moment onwards is clear, and yet it has attracted only passing comment. The fact that some of its members sought thrills elsewhere, in amongst the diehard neo-Nazi ranks of Combat 18 (C18), has been noted as one factor. But little is known of those activists that remained within the party. On the occasion of the BNP's 1999 leadership contest, just 30 per cent of the total membership voted for the incumbent leader.[7] No doubt many of Tyndall's once faithful followers were becoming increasingly dissatisfied and impatient with his style of leadership, but what lay at the root of this disaffection?

Making gains at the ballot box

The borough of Tower Hamlets, established in 1965 from a union of the metropolitan boroughs of Bethnal Green, Poplar and Stepney, is located within the inner East End of London, an area which, in the history of right-extremist political agitation in Britain, occupies a special place. As a locality, it can lay claim to a rich tradition of extremist activity that stretches back at least to the late nineteenth and early twentieth centuries when the East End was at the forefront of political agitation against Jewish 'aliens' – the British Brothers' League having been founded in Stepney in 1901.[8] With its local tradition of anti-Semitism, the East End gained notoriety in later decades as a stronghold for Oswald Mosley's British Union of Fascists (BUF). Indeed, where Mosley's Blackshirts obtained their most noteworthy electoral scores, they did so in East End districts at the London County Council elections in 1937 – the BUF polled 23 per cent of the vote in North East Bethnal Green, 19 per cent in Stepney and 14 per cent in Shoreditch.[9] Moreover, immediately after 1945, the activity of postwar Mosleyites in the British League of Ex-Servicemen and then the Union Movement was further sustained by this local anti-Semitic culture and fiefdoms of support were established around Bethnal Green, Shoreditch and neighbouring Dalston junction.[10]

At the end of the 1950s it was the turn of the National Labour Party to encroach on East London whilst, later, the 1960s incarnation of the British National Party held a regular newspaper pitch in Bethnal Green.[11] But by this time, both with the exodus of the East End's established Jewish community and the arrival of immigrants from the New Commonwealth, in particular from Bangladesh, antipathy towards incoming Asians now superseded anti-Semitic agitation. The term 'Paki-bashing', first coined at the end of the 1960s, is believed to have originated in the Collingwood Estate in Bethnal Green.[12] During the 1970s the East End became one of the National Front's major heartlands, and towards the end of the 1970s its last bastion of strength: in local elections in 1978 the NF obtained 23 per cent of the vote in St Peter's Ward in Bethnal Green.[13] Thus, according to Chris Husbands, what makes the East End 'unique amongst almost all working-class communities in Britain' is its 'history of white working-class insularity and of hostility to outsiders'.[14]

Yet the significance of such local cultures of intolerance can be overstated. During the 1980s, even if the East End had been fertile terrain for the far right, this did not stop its decline in the area. The NF could only muster 4.3 per cent of the vote in a by-election in the St Peter's Ward of Bethnal Green in 1984.[15] And as late as 1988, the British National Party's candidate in the Lansbury ward of Tower Hamlets polled a mere 1.9 per cent of the vote.[16] Moreover, examples from elsewhere cast doubt on the extent to which such long-standing local traditions are necessary factors in extreme-right electoral breakthroughs. For instance, just prior to the September 1993 election of the BNP's candidate in Tower Hamlets, another BNP candidate stood in Burnley, an area like East London with a relatively large Asian population. Here, the party captured some 10,000 votes in 2002. But there is little sense of a strong extreme–right tradition in this particular locality: in August 1993 the BNP candidate in Burnley polled a pitiful 9 votes.[17]

That being so, let us return to Tower Hamlets where, in 1990, the BNP's upturn started with a series of local elections. In May 1990, the BNP candidate and former NF activist, Steve Smith, polled 290 votes in the Holy Trinity ward of Tower Hamlets (Globe Town). This represented some 9.71 per cent of the total vote, while the local BNP thought it corresponded to around 13.5 per cent of the white vote.[18] Two months later, in a local by-election in the Park Ward of Tower Hamlets (Bow), Smith captured 8.4 per cent of the vote (or, according to the BNP, 10 per cent of the white vote). Then, following the death of Brenda Collins, the Liberal leader of Tower Hamlets council, a further opportunity for the BNP to put its new-found electoral credibility to the test came with a by-election in August 1990 in the St Peter's Ward of Bethnal Green. In this former Front stronghold, the BNP candidate, Ken Walsh, polled 12.1 per cent of the vote, which was said to have represented 'at least' 16 per cent of the white vote. This result was by far the best gained by any far-right party in East London since 1978.[19]

Consequently, at the 1992 general election the BNP concentrated its efforts on the two East End constituencies of Bethnal Green and Stepney, and Bow and Poplar. It was here that the BNP recorded their best scores with Richard Edmonds obtaining 3.6 per cent of the vote in Bethnal Green and Stepney and John Tyndall garnering 3 per cent of the vote in Bow and Poplar. While these results may seem unexceptional, the BNP did win the support of between 5 and 6 per cent of white voters and, in certain neighbourhoods, it claimed to have polled over 10 per cent of the vote.[20] Of particular note was the Millwall ward in the Bow and Poplar constituency, from where local party activists believed that a significant 'slice' of its vote at the 1992 general election had come from despite a lack of local activity.[21]

Notwithstanding the odd derisory performance – the 82 votes that a BNP candidate won in a by-election in Spitalfields in August 1992 – it is clear that during this period the BNP was becoming a potent political force in Tower Hamlets. This was confirmed in October 1992 when its candidate Barry Osborne polled 20 per cent of the vote in a local by-election in Millwall (657 votes) where, following encouraging general election results, local BNP activists had invested most of their energies. This was a ward that had received little attention from the party in the past since it was geographically isolated in the southern part of the borough, on the Isle of Dogs peninsula. Bethnal Green had been the traditional hunting ground, but after Osborne's promising performance, and with a view to the 1994 local elections, the focus was now on Millwall.

As the area was being primed, the BNP's opportunity came early. The resignation of a Labour councillor triggered a by-election in the very same Millwall ward as the '20 per cent campaign' of October 1992. In the event, on 16 September 1993 some 1,480 people voted for the BNP candidate, Derek Beackon. At local elections in May 1990, Beackon had polled just 93 votes in the Redcoat ward of Stepney.[22] On that occasion he had attracted a mere 3.71 per cent of the vote, this time his share of the vote increased almost thirty-fold to 34 per cent, around one-third from a 42 per cent turnout. By a narrow margin of just seven votes,

Derek Beackon was elected local councillor, serving on the Isle of Dogs Neighbourhood Committee. For John Tyndall, all this represented the BNP's 'moment in history'[23] – the first time that any of its candidates had been elected to public office. In his mind, this was the dawn of a new era. A deluge of membership enquiries soon followed. Tony Lecomber claimed that 800 new members were recruited immediately after Millwall.[24] That Tyndall later denied ever 'hyping up' this victory was somewhat disingenuous.[25] There can be little doubt that Tyndall thought that the BNP was now on its way from the 'back streets' of Millwall into the British political mainstream.

For sure, the BNP's election victory became the immediate focus of national attention. But as the condemnatory nature of the mainstream response shows, the door to the political mainstream was immediately shut. Leading politicians, the Archbishop of Canterbury, London's police chief and the press all roundly condemned the BNP as a 'thoroughly nasty' party promoting racist politics that took it beyond the pale.[26] Moreover, in some sections of the national press the BNP stood accused of being a fascist party, as in the *Daily Telegraph* which conjured up memories of the British Union of Fascists in the East End during the 1930s and additionally remarked that, 'One would have thought the East End's subsequent experience of fascism – in the form of Hitler's Blitz – would have cured it for ever of the affliction.'[27] Similar words echoed from the *Daily Mail*: 'when 1,400 souls trotted out to vote for the British National Party many started from homes built over craters made by Hitler's bombs'.[28] Meanwhile, the *Daily Mirror* also thwarted the mainstreaming of the BNP; it featured a photograph of Beackon giving a Nazi salute, accompanied by the headline: 'SIEG HEIL... and now he's a British councillor.'[29]

Over the longer term, however, commentators started to put forth reasons for the BNP's election victory. Significantly, all the major lines of interpretation saw the experience of Millwall as essentially atypical; in the words of British Home Secretary, Michael Howard, it was 'an isolated event caused by a combination of particular local circumstances'.[30] One factor was the manipulation of 'race' as a political issue by the local Liberal Democrats who were widely known throughout the East End as London's 'secret racist party'. By entering the arena of covert race politics in Tower Hamlets – the only multi-ethnic borough in London under Liberal Democrat control in the early 1990s – the local Liberal Democrats had made racism politically respectable and thereby paved the way for the BNP's electoral victory.[31] Elsewhere, commentators focused on the insularity of Millwall's white voters, 'a peculiar breed: insular, proud of their docklands heritage and identity as a community, and notoriously suspicious of "outsiders"'.[32] Thus, voting for the racist BNP represented a particularly 'belligerent' defence of community.[33] With Tower Hamlets ranked eighth amongst the most materially deprived boroughs in the country, others pointed to the Isle of Dogs as an inner-city ghetto, an enclave of 'urban despair'.[34] As local residents stared 'from the windows of high-rise blocks as rich City types commute past them to the gleaming towers of Canary Wharf', their sense of relative socio-economic deprivation had supposedly been radicalised by the 1980s 'Yuppie' redevelopment of the Docklands.[35]

However, as recent events have clearly shown, in Burnley, Blackburn, Halifax, Stoke and so on, the belief that this 'freak' election result could only happen in such an 'atypical' place now seems rather naïve. As the director of the Runnymede Trust[36] wrote to the *Independent* in September 1993, 'For the Isle of Dogs is not an island, entire of itself.'[37] In other words, the racism of the Isle of Dogs was nothing out of the ordinary but merely part of a wider popular racism that permeates British society. Hence, for David Cesarani, BNP voters in Millwall were 'racists, but no more so than the millions of Tory voters who responded to Mrs Thatcher's sly promise to resist the 'swamping' of Britain by people of another culture'.[38] Even so, it would still be wrong to deny that local circumstances did not play an important part in the BNP's electoral emergence. On this issue, as I have argued elsewhere,[39] we must bring to the fore the processes by which the BNP obtained its local legitimacy. Whilst nationally, as we have seen, the party remained a political pariah, in Tower Hamlets a different picture emerges. Most significantly, the BNP sunk local roots and, in so doing, became a 'respectable' political actor in the local arena. In this way, the BNP played a decisive part in its own rise to local prominence.

'Rights for whites': the BNP and the quest for local legitimacy

Where during the 1980s the BNP had purposely refrained from heavy engagement in local electoral arenas, at the beginning of the 1990s the Tower Hamlets branch stole the initiative and set itself on a course of local electioneering. The origin of this strategy did not lie with John Tyndall, who rarely left his Sussex redoubt, but with Eddy Butler the Tower Hamlets branch organiser, described by Richard Edmonds as 'the commander' on account of his intimate knowledge of the territory.[40] The key to Butler's strategy was local community politics, addressing neighbourhood concerns through a populist campaigning style that went under the heading 'Rights for Whites'. This slogan, as Derek Beackon remembers, was not original – it had been around in the 1970s.[41] If truth be told, Martin Webster had used it a decade or so earlier to organise a series of demonstrations against the Notting Hill Carnival.[42] In Tower Hamlets, however, as one BNP activist pointed out, 'the use it was put to was altogether different. It was used to get among the downtrodden white population, in a similar manner to the Black Civil Rights movement in America in the 1950s and 1960s'.[43] Its aim was simple: to neutralise the Nazi 'smear' through local contact and thereby establish the BNP as a legitimate defender of local white residents.

In 1990, what set the ball rolling was an attack on a white school-boy, John Stoner, at Morpeth School in Bethnal Green by a group of Asian children. The upshot was a protest march to Bethnal Green police station on 24 February 1990 by 300 white residents, organised by George Happe, John Stoner's foster grandfather. Happe denied that the family was racist and publicly disowned the BNP, yet some 50 BNP activists joined this march and a series of racist slogans were chanted from start to finish. But this was no 1970s NF-style demonstration. Instead of confrontational disorder, Liz Fekete has described 'a carn-ival-style atmosphere', where 'white residents leaned from windows to greet them, waving Union Jacks and occasionally bursting into rendi-tions of "Rule Britannia" and "maybe it's because I'm a Londoner"'.[44] After that, as one local BNP organiser recalls, 'another local white was attacked in a potentially fatal incident. We therefore decided to hold our own activity to give angry and frustrated whites an opportunity to express their grievances in a legitimate political way'.[45]

The Tower Hamlets 'Rights for Whites' campaign was thus brought to life. As the opening gambit, just two months prior to the May local government elections, a 'Rights for Whites' demonstration was announced for 11 March 1990. A fortnight of intensive door-to-door leafleting followed, in which the BNP deliberately presented the 'Rights for Whites' campaign as a community-based initiative. Accordingly, its 'Rights for Whites' leaflet had a rough and ready 'home-made' feel to it. Since householders tend to receive (and ignore) high volumes of quality advertising material through their letterbox, it was thought that leaflets produced in this way would be more distinctive. Therefore, in simple black felt-tip and type, supporters of the 'Rights for Whites' campaign were asked to write to a post-office box in East London. It was not immediately obvious that the campaign was sponsored by the

BNP, but the post-office box belonged to a local BNP activist (and former NF member) David Ettridge. In the event, around 400 people turned out; the most pleasing aspect to this march, local BNP activist Steve Smith recalls, was that 'a large percentage of the procession were ordinary members of the public without any previous connection to the party'.[46] At this moment, the BNP made itself known as the architect of the 'Rights for Whites' campaign, and in so doing handed out further leaflets, distributed stickers and purportedly sold 'hundreds of copies' of *British Nationalist* to local residents.[47]

It should now be obvious that a vital ingredient in the construction of the BNP's legitimacy in Tower Hamlets was the way it attached itself to local protest and then embedded itself within the white community through its 'Rights for Whites' campaign. By doing so, local BNP members caught the mood of the moment and were able to speak

> to literally thousands of local people, selling papers and creating the image that they wanted to create of the BNP, as opposed to the negative media stereotype, or the equally negative traditional nationalist image.[48]

The BNP's message was 'reasonable' and 'unextreme', 'public-spirited' even: we will defend the rights of white residents in the areas which affect their everyday lives, as Eddy Butler implored, 'We must stop talking just about what we like to talk about and start talking about the things that local people are crying out to hear.'[49] For that reason, the BNP had picketed Tower Hamlets Town Hall against the closure of a local nursery in the run-up to the Park ward by-election in July 1990. On this occasion, local mothers had welcomed the BNP, it was no longer seen as 'outside' their community and they had chanted its slogan 'Rights for Whites'.[50]

Regrettably, academic commentators have generally overlooked the fact that similar 'Rights for Whites' tactics were quickly extended beyond their original test bed. But during 1991, in the absence of further electoral contests in the East End, such tactics were used in support of local electoral campaigns elsewhere. In May 1991, at local elections in Rochdale, the BNP used the same ploy as in Tower Hamlets – the stabbing of a white youth, allegedly by Asians – to argue that whites were the real victims of 'racist' tensions.[51] Meanwhile, in the capital, the focus of BNP activity shifted south of the river Thames. In Bermondsey, at local elections in 1990, the BNP candidate Steve Tyler, a former Tory and Monday Club member, had polled 7.36 per cent of the vote in the Rotherhithe ward.[52] In August 1991, Tyler, now standing in the Brunswick ward, chose to engage 'Rights for Whites' tactics. In this instance, the BNP targeted a local housing officer for allegedly being more concerned with evicting 'white residents for being "racist" than evicting the drugged up and drunken squatters that infect our estate'.[53]

But concrete election results proved disappointing. In Rochdale the BNP candidate Ken Henderson polled a derisory 158 votes or 3.98 per cent of the vote; Tyler a mere 132 votes.[54] In truth, with regard to the creation of legitimacy, the party was negligent in both cases. Those who turned out on party activity in support of these campaigns frequently succumbed to open and aggressive displays of neo-Nazism. Following a pre-election rally in Rochdale, Tyndall had issued a special directive to party officers on 1 May 1991 demanding that they got 'their act together' and 'straighten out those who are letting us down in public or otherwise get rid of them'.[55] Yet to borrow a cliché, old habits die hard. And, at a BNP counter-demonstration in Bermondsey in August 1991, the party had brought a violent reputation on itself after a number of BNP activists had ambushed a black protest march against racist attacks.[56] But because the popular press did not really pick up on it, any damage to the BNP's reputation was probably restricted to the Bermondsey area. It was the weekend of the Notting Hill Carnival and the cynical suggestion from the BNP is that the media 'wanted to avoid a major black riot in retaliation'.[57]

By way of contrast, in October 1992, when the BNP contested the Millwall ward for the first time, local activists in Tower Hamlets had become convinced that the BNP could gain tactical advantage if violent disorder was avoided. In the past, such violence had played into the hands of anti-fascists as it typically placed the extreme right outside mainstream democratic norms and thereby denuded it of political respectability. Notwithstanding occasional lapses, such as in February 1992 when Eddy Butler had supposedly led a 30-strong BNP contingent on a violent raid against anti-fascists,[58] absolving itself from violence became a key part of BNP electoral practice. The party, through a series of seminars and organisers' meetings – 'From Street Gang to Political Party' – had begun to promote this line more widely from the beginning of 1992.[59] Moreover, as a defector from the BNP has recently disclosed, the leadership also encouraged some 300 party activists to infiltrate the Conservative Party in order to sow division at Tory grassroots and thereby trigger a switch of membership to a less 'extremist' BNP.[60] Thus, in the run-up to the October 1992 by-election, public meetings were eschewed (because of the violence that they would typically invite) in favour of solid door-to-door canvassing and community politics. Significantly, according to local BNP organiser Steve Smith, this 'brought us into contact with the electorate and helped build a rapport, which over the next year would reap enormous political dividends'.[61]

Not surprisingly, with the BNP's candidate Barry Osborne having polled 20 per cent of the vote in October 1992 – the BNP's best election performance to date – the same tactics were repeated when it came to the second Millwall campaign in September 1993. Each night of the campaign, a team of 20–30 BNP activists took to the streets canvassing and leafleting the Isle of Dogs.[62] As Derek Beackon, the BNP's winning candidate remembers, his campaign involved 'putting out three to four different leaflets for the whole Island and canvassing the entirety of it'.[63] Looking back, Beackon says:

> I think the main and most important lesson we learned during Barry's campaign was not to have a public election meeting, that is, winding up the reds and giving them the opportunity to cause trouble and blame us and make us look like thugs in the eyes of the electorate.[64]

Yet in all truth, violence was never too far away. Some three miles from Millwall, on the evening of Saturday 11 September, a group of some 30–40 BNP members ran amok in Brick Lane, smashing windows and attacking Bangladeshi restaurants.[65] But within Millwall itself, alert to the dangers of negative association with violence and extremism, the party sought to develop its appeal as the custodian of the local white community. In its campaign literature, the BNP urged all white voters to 'get together as a community and give a massive protest vote', to 'elect Derek Beackon and have someone to speak up for us Whites'.[66] By offering to empower the white community, to restore its 'lost birthright', this talk undoubtedly struck a respondent chord with local white residents: 'I'm not in full agreement with all the BNP stands for but "Rights for Whites", yes', was how one BNP voter justified her choice of vote.[67]

Thus, from its beginnings in 1990, 'Rights for Whites' defined the BNP's political identity in Tower Hamlets. As its trademark, it even extended as far as the polling papers – Beackon gave his affiliation as 'Rights for Whites – British National Party'. But what's more, as we have seen, its 'Rights for Whites' campaign used legitimate methods of political campaigning, was carried out on the doorsteps and became rooted within the local community. In consequence, the BNP main-streamed itself in Tower Hamlets despite the best efforts of the local *Docklands Recorder* to convince its readers on the eve of the election not to be fooled by the BNP since its manifesto was 'based on hatred, no different in ideology to that of Mosley or Hitler'.[68] Other opponents, such as the Anti-Nazi League (ANL), also failed to cut the BNP off from the local white community. Typical of the genre, the ANL's 'hard-hitting' leaflet exposed the BNP's true nature by featuring Beackon giving a Nazi salute and declared that the BNP 'are the British NAZI Party'.[69] Yet all the indications are that the BNP's doorstep politics can-celled out these 'smears'. As one BNP voter (and lifelong Isle of Dogs resident) put it, 'I fought against Hitler, but these are not fascists as we knew it then. They're nationalists who stand for the rights of English people in this country.'[70] But this is not all. The local respectability that the BNP obtained also drew additional strength from another source: the covert racism of the ruling Liberal Democrats.

London's 'secret racists': a helping hand from elsewhere

At the national and regional level, the Liberal Democrats had been aware of the problem of its local councillors pandering to racism in Tower Hamlets since 1990. However, no action had been taken.[71] Since the Liberal Democrat approach to electioneering was 'bottom-up' whereby election literature was produced at the level of the election, local activists had much autonomy in terms of deciding the content of their election material. In Tower Hamlets, the local Liberal Democrats were described by the BNP as being more akin to a Residents Association, a party that had 'transformed themselves from being com-posed of a small group of early yuppie outsiders, to being the party of the local frustrated housewife'.[72] In the course of all this, local Liberals had turned to (racial) populism as an election-winning technique. This was the racism of political expediency.

When the Liberal–SDP Alliance had taken control of the council in 1986, the majority of its voters had been white. The Labour Party, on the other hand, had been taken over by the 'new London Left' and came to rely heavily on the local Asian vote. To keep the faith of its white electorate, the incoming Liberal administration introduced a series of controversial policies that were covertly racist. Housing policy was the domain in which this took place but this was no coincidence. For a start, the most distinctive feature about the housing stock in

Tower Hamlets was that it was predominantly public-sector owned. In fact, more housing in Tower Hamlets came under the council's responsibility than it did under any other council in the country.[73] Not surprisingly, housing allocations policy was a fiercely contested issue, but into the bargain it was also an issue charged with racial tension. Under the previous Labour administration, local tenants associations had already complained of preferential treatment for Bangladeshis.[74]

It was against this background that, in 1987, the ruling Liberals introduced a 'Sons and Daughters' housing scheme. This was intended to allow sons and daughters of local residents to be rehoused within Tower Hamlets close to their parents. However, it disproportionately favoured white applicants by using residency points based on length of parental residence in the borough. The largest ethnic minority population – the Bangladeshi – was of recent arrival, and many families had still to be reunited. Not surprisingly, one study showed that only 8 per cent of applicants under the 'Sons and Daughters' scheme were Asian but Bangladeshis amounted to 69 per cent of the borough's homeless people in July 1988.[75] Hence, for some time prior to the BNP's local intervention, the Liberals were perceived as the local party that defended white interests. Moreover, the local Liberal Democrats endeavoured to maintain this impression during the May 1990 local elections when their election literature played on the 'Sons and Daughters' theme and generated the impression that the Liberal Democrats were in favour of giving 'local', that is to say white, residents preferential treatment in housing allocations. At the same time, the Liberal Democrats circulated a bogus Labour leaflet in which it was declared that the Labour Party had pledged to 'scrap these policies and see that Bangladeshis are treated fairly'.[76]

Fortuitously for Tower Hamlets BNP, the fact that 'race' continued to dominate the local political agenda over the course of the next few years was grist to its mill. Without doubt, the local Liberal Democrats were instrumental in setting this agenda and thereby provided the BNP with political space. Most crucially, this was legitimate mainstream space. It was created for the BNP and not merely a space that by ignoring the 'race' issue the mainstream had left 'open' for the BNP to enter: in November 1991, the *East London Advertiser* reported that a Liberal Democrat councillor was travelling to Bangladesh to tell them that Tower Hamlets had 'no room left for immigrants'.[77] At the 1992 general election, he then distributed a leaflet in which he claimed that he had been victimised for boasting that he had 'fought and spoken up for local youngsters (and had been called "racist" as a result)'.[78] During the same election campaign, one Liberal Democrat councillor refused to lower the Union Jack from council offices in Globe Town. This councillor (who had been present on the Stoner protest march) was praised by the *East London Advertiser*, which printed a full page Union Jack for readers to cut out and display despite the fact that the Union Jack had become a well-known symbol of the BNP.[79] The Liberal Democrats also distributed three incriminating leaflets at the 1992 Millwall by-election (when Osborne had polled 20 per cent). One suggested that Liberal Democrats favoured the resident white community; another attacked Labour's positive discrimination policy; and a further leaflet claimed that the local Labour Party had said 'NO to Island Homes for Island People'.[80]

What the BNP therefore obtained in Tower Hamlets, as Roger Eatwell has usefully described it, was a form of 'syncretic legitimation'.[81] In other words, since the BNP additionally benefited from the legitimation of its racist politics by the local political mainstream, the BNP's local legitimacy was not entirely of its making. In the main, the guilty party was the Liberal Democrats and they were hardened offenders, and coded racism was again in evidence in leaflets distributed in September 1993.[82] But the Labour Party was also a part cause in the BNP's electoral victory. On the defensive, local Labour Party activists had firstly implied that they supported a housing policy that favoured white residents. Secondly, by providing false canvass returns in September 1993, which raised the possibility that the BNP could win the Millwall ward by-election, a local Labour Party agent, Stephen Molyneaux, had raised the BNP's electoral credibility. As Nicholas Holtam and Sue Mayo have recognised in their account, 'This shock was intended to win back Labour voters. Instead it gave credibility to the BNP, and the concentrated attention of the media ensured a self-fulfilling prophecy.'[83]

Yet the BNP still had to 'corner' the racist vote. Cas Mudde has argued that a key problem the far right has faced in Britain has been its failure to 'own' the 'race' issue. Thus, for Mudde, 'In Britain, the Conservative Party traditionally owns 'extreme right' issues like law and order, immigration and (opposition to) the European Union.'[84] But in Tower Hamlets, things were different. The mainstream party that took ownership of the 'race' issue was the Liberal Democrats and significantly, from 1990 onwards, ownership of this issue began to transfer from the Liberal Democrats to the British National Party. What accounted for this was the potency of the charge the BNP levelled against the Liberal Democrats: that for all their 'racism', once in power they betrayed whites and always favoured Bangladeshis. This was Barry Osborne's line in his election literature in October 1992: 'The Liberals' Sons and Daughters scheme is just a con – Bangladeshis are still put first in housing in Liberal Neighbourhoods like Bethnal Green and Poplar.'[85] And Derek Beackon merely repeated Osborne word for word in his election literature in September 1993.[86] Evidently, the point was hammered home, especially when, as a result of a borough-wide housing lettings policy, 28 per cent of properties on the new Mast House Terrace estate in the Isle of Dogs went to Bangladeshis.[87] When, following Beackon's election victory, it commented: 'The Liberals repeated last year's shabby trick of playing the "race card", by trying to pretend that they were against immigration. The trick failed, as local whites had heard it all before, and this time were not taken in', the BNP hit the nail on the head.[88]

From his analytical sweep of a number of far-right electoral break-throughs – the BNP in Millwall included – Roger Eatwell has proposed an explanatory model that accounts for increases in right-extremist voting. This model, which he refers to as 'efficacy–legitimacy–trust' is three-dimensional in its approach.[89] According to Eatwell, extreme-right electoral breakthroughs require a conjunctural combination of the following three factors: the first is 'rising personal efficacy', that is to say, a sense in which people feel they can influence policy by voting for an extreme-right party. In this respect, a party's credibility is obviously important. The second factor is 'rising political legitimacy', as Eatwell says, 'whilst some voters are attracted to parties precisely because they seem beyond the pale, this is not true in the main for the most successful ethnocentric parties like the FN'.[90] Finally, there must be 'declining system trust', that is, a decline in socio-economic and/or socio-political system trust. In Tower Hamlets, Eatwell's three-dimensional approach seems compelling. For a start, the BNP's credibility did rise as it reaped the rewards from the Labour Party's canvass returns. Moreover, not only did the BNP acquire local legitimacy, but there was also a decline in local system trust, especially with regard to housing policy.

On closer reflection, however, Eatwell's model is not without its problems. Clearly far-right parties need to pass a certain credibility threshold, but if that threshold was passed after the BNP won 20 per cent of the vote in October 1992, why had 657 people already voted for it? Following his election in September 1993, Beackon had come across as a poor-quality and inarticulate councillor. He was often un-familiar with the council agenda and was apparently confused by council bureaucracy. Consequently, one might assume that BNP voters would lose confidence in their candidate – a decline in personal efficacy – yet at local elections in May 1994, Beackon actually polled 561 extra votes. If there was declining system trust, why, in a survey of 524 voters in Millwall, did BNP supporters declare that they would favour Labour as their second preference? One would expect that given their declining trust in the mainstream parties, if no BNP candidate was available, BNP supporters would be those most likely not to vote.[91] This point about declining system trust certainly requires some further qualification – a MORI poll undertaken in 1990 revealed that Tower Hamlets had an above average approval rating for an Inner London authority. In Globe Town, where the BNP polled 9.71 per cent of the vote in 1990, the council had an approval rating of 71 per cent.[92]

Evidently, declining trust was not so much in the 'system' *per se* but in its housing provision. Indeed, barely 50 per cent of respondents in the Mori poll were happy with its housing provision – which placed Tower Hamlets second from bottom in Mori's table of councils.[93] Moreover, in a Harris Research Centre poll taken shortly after the BNP's election victory, 58 per cent of local respondents thought that in terms of council services, non-white people were treated more favourably that whites. It also found that people in social classes C2DE – those most dependent on council services – were particularly hostile to immigrants.[94] These feelings were especially strong amongst established working-class residents on the Isle of Dogs; of BNP voters, 60 per cent had lived on the Isle of Dogs for 21 years of more.[95] From the foregoing, then, if Eatwell's model is to pass muster then it clearly requires more thought. But that said, the central importance of the legitimation variable still holds true. And most of all, as we have suggested, it is this that provides the key to understanding the BNP's electoral breakthrough in Tower Hamlets.

The false dawn

In May 1994, as local elections approached, the BNP not only hoped to hold its seat, it also expected to have all three of its candidates elected, thereby obtaining a majority on the Isle of Dogs Neighbourhood Committee and access to an annual budget of £23 million. But this, for Tyndall, would only be the beginning. The twin obstacles of credibility and media 'silent treatment' would thence shatter.[96] Across the country, as the BNP established itself as a significant force in British politics, dozens or even hundreds of seats would subsequently fall to

BNP candidates. Before long, the party would be destined for Westminster. In his mind's eye, this was an easy vision for Tyndall to conjure up. The reality, however, was quite another matter. Due to an extraordinary mobilisation of the Labour vote in the Millwall ward – turn-out was 67 per cent, exceptionally high for a local election – the British National Party lost its only council seat.[97] Although the party made a good showing elsewhere in London, particularly in the neighbouring borough of Newham where BNP candidates came within 65 votes of being elected, losing its seat in Millwall was a bitter blow.[98] When it came to it of course, the 1990s would not sweep the BNP to power. On the contrary, it brought an internal power struggle in which, as Tyndall would find to his cost, his tenure as party leader would reach its inglorious end.

Yet notwithstanding the party's defeat in Millwall, in terms of the BNP's overall electoral performance, the year 1994 was actually its most successful to date. At the May local elections, the BNP put up 29 candidates and they averaged 13.17 per cent of the vote.[99] Thus, for Eddy Butler, 'Compared with results achieved by nationalist candidates in the recent past, our votes were nothing short of phenomenal.'[100] But this electoral success passed all too quickly. John Tyndall may have succeeded in retaining his deposit at a parliamentary by-election at Dagenham in June 1994 – the first time that an extreme-right candidate had saved a deposit since the NF's Martin Webster at West Bromwich in 1973 – but the seeds of the BNP's decline had already been sown. We need only track back to the weeks following Beackon's electoral victory the previous year to find the source of the BNP's emergent ills. At that moment, the Tower Hamlets branch first fell victim to Combat 18.

This group had started life in 1992 as the BNP's bodyguard, a strong-arm outfit under the nominal control of the BNP's chief steward, Derek Beackon. 'But in C18, the BNP had weaned a monster it could not control', as the investigations of *Searchlight*'s Nick Lowles reveal.[101] The brothers Charlie and Steve Sargent were its leading figures, both of whom were committed neo-Nazis. Indeed, the name C18 was deliberately chosen in respect to their spiritual leader – the '1' and '8' corresponded to the first and eighth letters of the alphabet, 'A' and 'H', and stood for Adolf Hitler. But not satisfied with merely providing the BNP with muscle, the Sargents had political aspirations too. Drawing upon the ideas of US neo-Nazis, the likes of Harold Covington[102] and William Pearce[103] in particular, C18 rejected the electoral road and instead advocated an uninhibited course of action against its 'racial enemies' where violence would occupy a central part. 'Whatever it takes' was C18's slogan, and in its magazine *The Order*, C18 inveighed against the BNP's 'moderate' electoral approach and called on its supporters to either quit the BNP or else try to take over the party from within.[104]

In the immediate aftermath of Beackon's electoral victory, the harvest of new recruits to the Tower Hamlets branch was largely comprised of 'red-blooded' types. These recruits were easily swayed by the aggressive promise of C18, and through the use of violence and intimidation C18 destabilised the local branch. According to one BNP activist, 'Within a couple of weeks of winning the seat in Millwall, the local branch of the BNP had been destroyed from within.'[105] This it has to be said probably overstates C18's initial impact: it did not stop local BNP activists canvassing the Isle of Dogs at least three times a week in the run-up to the 1994 elections.[106] Nonetheless, the effect, as Tyndall recollects, was 'a most unwelcome outbreak of grumbling, disaffection and desertion of many of our members – and nowhere more so than in East London, where the triumph had occurred. For a time this baffled us'.[107] And whilst the national leadership struggled to come to terms with it all, the damage was being done at the grassroots. Towards the end of December 1993, a circular proscribing C18 was despatched by Tyndall; but little was done to enforce it. Part of the problem was that C18 had no 'official members' and, besides, Tyndall was keen to reassure the 'Nazi fraternity' that the BNP remained true to the faith. Yet C18 was becoming a major thorn in the leadership's side. This was brought home in early 1994 when both Eddy Butler and Tony Lecomber found themselves the victims of violent assaults perpetrated by a top C18 activist. Butler, the mastermind of the 'Whites for Rights' campaign who had since been promoted to National Elections Officer, was slashed across the face with a knife.[108]

Eager to cash in on growing demoralisation within the BNP's ranks following the loss of its one council seat, C18 then established its own political wing – the National Socialist Alliance (NSA) – in June 1994. This was in fact a network of groups that stressed the futility of electioneering and endeavoured to undermine the loyalty of existing BNP members. Accordingly, in addition to physical attacks, the BNP leadership also found itself subject to a written onslaught. In this war of words, examples of C18's anti-BNP propaganda included such memorable accusations as the BNP welcomed transvestites and Jews as party members, and that Tyndall had supposedly used special party funds to purchase a yacht at his local marina.[109] And as these shots were being fired, in its Tower Hamlets fiefdom the BNP's electoral performance suffered. At a series of 'make or break' local council by-elections over the course of late 1994 and early 1995, a succession of candidates, with Beackon included, all failed to pass the 20 per cent threshold. With party activists increasingly pulled away by the more 'stimulating' activities of C18, the commitment to electioneering was flagging. At one by-election in Bethnal Green the BNP could only muster four people for its canvass team.[110] By late 1995 the BNP vote in Limehouse in East London had dropped to only 6.5 per cent.[111] With no more local elections scheduled in London for some three years and against the background of the Labour Party's rising popularity, Tyndall resigned the party to difficult times ahead.[112] Not surprisingly, its membership haemorrhaged. By the middle of 1995 C18 was boasting that some three-quarters of the BNP's young London activists had switched their allegiance to C18/NSA, and numerous BNP branches had also defected.[113] Meanwhile, membership of the BNP had possibly fallen to as low as 700 of which only 400 were fully paid-up members.[114]

Though late in the day, Tyndall finally went on the offensive. In a lengthy *Spearhead* article in September 1995, 'Doing the Enemy's Work', he maintained that following the BNP's victory in Millwall, C18 had been 'created' by the State security services in order to wreck the BNP.[115] The same claim was made in an anonymous 'blue' booklet circulated to all BNP branches at the same time.[116] In truth, Tyndall's suspicion was based on two considerations. The first was timing: 'It hit us just at the moment when we were poised to capitalise on our first election victory.'[117] The second was the fact that C18 had so far eluded prosecution despite having advocated a policy of violent 'direct action', instructed its readers on how to prepare bombs and openly incited racial hatred with its talk of shipping 'all non-whites back to Africa, Asia, Arabia, alive or in body bags, the choice is theirs'.[118] Therefore, what Tyndall saw in C18 all pointed to a state conspiracy. This might seem far-fetched but if, according to Nick Lowles, MI5 had 15 informants inside the BNP in the early 1990s and if, as a later *World in Action* television documentary would reveal, Charlie Sargent had been a probable Special Branch informant, there was certainly more to C18 than met the eye.[119]

There was another aspect to Tyndall's offensive against C18, however. In an attempt to counter C18's claim that it was diluting its policies, Tyndall set about trying to make the BNP appear more hard-edged. With this in mind, he secured the services of William Pearce as guest speaker at the BNP's annual party rally in November 1995.

Pearce, author of influential far-right bestseller, *The Turner Diaries*, and leader of the US-based neo-Nazi National Alliance, was one of C18's chief mentors. Naturally, this was a major coup. Of far greater significance for Tyndall over the longer-term, however, was the presence of another leading hardliner at this party rally. Popular with a number of local BNP branches, particularly its Croydon branch, this hardliner had been a key figure on the British far right in the 1980s. The man in question was of course Nick Griffin who Tyndall had recently admitted into the BNP fold in part to attract back those former activists who had deserted the BNP for the ranks of C18/NSA. Over the short-term, Tyndall's manoeuvres delivered some results; a number of NSA branches reverted to the BNP. But C18's influence did not lessen until an internal feud within the C18 leadership, which started at the end of 1996, split the NSA asunder and alienated many of its one-time supporters.[120]

Manoeuvring towards the leadership contest

In August 1995 Tyndall committed the party to contesting 50 seats at the next general election.[121] On the face of it, this was a curious decision. The party was in chaos. Apart from the disruption caused by the ongoing conflict with C18, another savage blow came when John Gummer, the Secretary of State for the Environment, upheld Bexley Borough Council's ban on the BNP using its bookshop as a headquarters. This meant that no BNP literature could be distributed from these premises, its public telephone number was lost and it was also forced to operate its administrative functions from a network of locations.[122] With the party in such turmoil, why commit to an audacious 50-seat campaign particularly when in 1992, in more favourable times, the BNP had only managed to fight 13 seats? To fully understand this decision, we need to see it as a last-ditch attempt by the leadership to enthuse and unify the party. Without it, the party would languish and probably disintegrate. As Eddy Butler recalls, 'A nation-wide campaign that served to unify the Party would promote central authority. The effort required to mount the fifty-seat campaign served this purpose perfectly.'[123] But as far as its ordinary members were concerned, this reason lay hidden. What was communicated to the grassroots was that recruitment was of the highest priority. Thus, writing in *Spearhead* in January 1996, Tony Lecomber stated that the reason behind the 50-seat campaign was that: 'We want recruits and we want them in big numbers.'[124] But even this objective should be read in terms of its ongoing struggle with C18 – as a way of 'making up' for membership outflows. Provided that 50 candidates could be found, not only would there be free broadcasting time across all four terrestrial channels, the BNP would also benefit from the free distribution of nearly two million election addresses. Hence Lecomber optimistically predicted that that the party would receive thousands more enquiries than it did in its first trawl for members in 1983.[125]

But the long run-up to the 1997 general election occasioned some serious muttering in the ranks, and the future course of the party increasingly became a bone of contention. This was a sign of rising intra-party divisions between those seeking political respectability and those, like Tyndall, who insisted that the drive for acceptability would lead the BNP down the path to oblivion. Of those who advocated a more 'respectable' form of politics, Michael Newland, the party's press officer, Eddy Butler and Tony Lecomber (who had recently 'reformed' since being released from prison following an attack on a Jewish teacher) were the main spokespersons. This triumvirate had all absorbed the lessons of Millwall and increasingly looked towards the examples of the French National Front and the Austrian Freedom Party as models for a 'new', modern and respectable 'Euro-Nationalism'.[126] But following the failure to convince the leadership of the need to use the forthcoming general election to introduce a change of strategy, Butler and Newland briefly resigned from the party in early 1996 convinced that it needed a new leader. Their destination was the Bloomsbury Forum, a far-right discussion group on the fringes of the Conservative Party. This included former Monday Club members like Richard Bowden and Adrian Davies who took their political inspiration from the French far right.[127] Consequently, Lecomber was more or less left as the lone voice in the party pending the launch of *Patriot* in early 1997. This was a 36-page magazine, edited by Lecomber, which became the primary vehicle for the 'moderniser' faction drawing contributions from Butler and Newland amongst others. Its financial backers almost certainly came from the Bloomsbury Forum, which according to Mike Newland had been discussing the possibility of a new party since 1995 but now looked to reform the BNP instead: 'The fact that a party so disadvantaged by its own tactics and image could win a council seat pointed to an obvious conclusion. A properly run party free from Nazi cranks could do far better.'[128]

At the opposite end of the spectrum – though he now supported the electoral road – was Nick Griffin. Ever since the failure of the 'political soldiers' and his estrangement from one of its offshoots, the

International Third Position, Griffin had been in political exile. In 1994, however, he started his political comeback with an approach to Tyndall expressing his interest in the work of the BNP.[129] Tyndall was hesitant not least because he feared that Griffin had one eye on the party leadership (quite literally, since he had recently lost an eye in an accident in France). Throughout 1995 Griffin had built up support within the party using *The Rune* as his mouthpiece, ostensibly a publication of Surrey BNP. Its Croydon branch, a branch that included many former activists from Griffin's 'political soldier' wing of the NF, produced it. With gathering support for Griffin within the party, there was a change of heart and in March 1996 Griffin was invited by Tyndall to take over as clandestine editor of *Spearhead*.[130] What Tyndall saw in Griffin was an ally whom he could use not only in his struggle against C18, but also as a counterbalance to those within the party who sought to jettison the BNP's more extremist baggage.

For several years Griffin obliged and played the part. In *The Rune*, Griffin opined that the

> electors of Millwall did not back a Post-Modernist Rightist Party, but what they perceived to be a strong, disciplined organisation with the ability to back up its slogan 'Defend Rights for Whites' with well-directed boots and fists.[131]

Meanwhile in *Spearhead*, Griffin launched an attack on the 'spiral of sickly moderation'. Avoid this, Griffin argued, otherwise the BNP would 'finally drop the inconvenient commitment to compulsory repatriation just before its last members totter off to rejoin the Tory Party'.[132] Instead of 'populism', Griffin called for a more forthright commitment to the 'revisionist struggle', in other words, more direct involvement by BNP activists in Holocaust denial.[133] By this stage, denying the Holocaust had become Griffin's favourite occupation: 'The Holocaust Lie is already dead – historically, legally and scientifically', Griffin declared in *The Rune*.[134]

Another one of his favourite (and certainly not unrelated) bugbears was Jewish conspiracy. A booklet, *Who are the Mind-benders?* part-written by Griffin was unveiled by the BNP in early 1997.[135] Its aim was to draw attention to what the BNP thought was an undemocratic and dangerous concentration of Jewish influence in the British mass media. Thus, in *Mind-benders*, Griffin took the reader through a veritable feast of Jewish names in the British media industry, and even drew attention to the particularly 'sinister' trend of the blonde female Jewish presenter

– Dani Behr and Gaby Roslin no less.[136] For the time being, however, this made it possible for Tyndall to hold on to power. Playing one faction off against the other, Tyndall could claim that he was steering the 'sensible middle course' between 'the politics of the nutty fringe, with its mental and spiritual isolation from mainstream society' and those that pursue 'elusive moderation' which 'always leads to compromise, alienates loyal fighters, dilutes crusading ardour and attracts only people who are useless for any hard struggle or radical change'.[137] Consequently, as the May 1997 general election approached, Tyndall's grip on power was still intact.

Nonetheless, the party's prospects failed to revive, and as disaffection grew, so Tyndall's position became increasingly precarious. In the first place, some £60,000[138] was invested on fighting over 50 seats at the 1997 general election, but little was obtained in return. Across the country, BNP candidates captured an average of only 632 votes (or a paltry 1.35 per cent).[139] There was little engagement between candidates and their local communities and, even in East London, campaigning was distinctly low-key. Although two deposits were saved in this area, Tyndall with 7.26 per cent and Dave King with 7.5 per cent, the latter undoubtedly benefited from voter confusion since he shared the same surname as Oona King, the winning Labour candidate. But if votes were always a secondary concern, recruitment was just as depressing. In its July *Members' Bulletin*, Tyndall claimed that its campaign had brought in between 2,500 and 3,000 enquiries, but this was no different to 1983 even with the advantage of more than two million free election addresses and a more professionally produced party political broadcast.[140]

Predictably, few enquirers became members. One problem was organisation. The closure of the headquarters in Welling, as the BNP admitted, was 'felt with particular severity during and just following the recent general election'.[141] But most were probably dissuaded when Nick Griffin's plans for the British far right were exposed on *The Cook Report*, a documentary screened by ITV shortly after the general election. In this programme, which did much to damage the post-election credibility of the party, Griffin was shown talking over dinner with TV reporters disguised as representatives from an independent fund-raising committee associated with the *Front National*. It was clear from this exposé that Griffin was scheming to take over the BNP. Moreover, he was intent on merger with the 100 or so remaining members of the National Front in order to create a new group, the British National Front.[142] Yet against all the odds, Griffin survived this episode. He quickly turned the affair on its head, claimed that he had quickly cottoned on to the reporters and everything he said was said merely to string them along.[143] Griffin promptly declared his loyalty to Tyndall and amongst the paranoia of the far right he managed to disentangle himself from this embarrassing situation. 'I did not believe him for a second', Tyndall (disingenuously?) claimed later on.[144]

So, as 1997 gave way to 1998, Tyndall was still not done for. Though he was now 64 years old, a life of temperance and exercise meant that he felt more like a man of 34 and he refused to give up.[145] But as the party took further backward steps, his political career was now on borrowed time. At local elections in May 1998, the BNP fielded five more candidates than in 1994 but its average vote fell from just over 13 per cent to a derisory 3.28 per cent. In Tower Hamlets, its average share of the poll slumped by almost 50 per cent.[146] Since the party lacked numbers on the ground, campaigning was minimal. Even in Tower Hamlets, no material was put out until just three days before the election when a video containing footage from the 1997 general election broadcast alongside footage that was locally shot and geared towards the East End, was hastily put through letterboxes. But, evidently, this was all to little effect. Together with these election results, overall party membership painted an equally depressing picture. In 1994, the party had an estimated membership of 2,000 but though it had recovered somewhat from its mid-1990s low, estimated membership was still only 1,100 in 1998.[147] Yet even this figure was probably inflated. As late as 1999, those members from 1996 who had not renewed were still counted as 'members' in the party's statistics.[148]

Within four years, the BNP had gone from thinking it was on the verge of a major electoral breakthrough to the point of stagnation. It was now clear to all apart from Tyndall and his diminishing band of diehards – Richard Edmonds, John Morse and the like – that he had run his course. As for leadership contenders, Griffin and Lecomber were the two most likely candidates. But as it turned out, Lecomber aligned himself with Griffin and became Griffin's 'unofficial' campaign manager. This all seemed rather odd given that both men had previously held no brief for one another. It may be that Lecomber felt he was the lesser of Griffin. As a Cambridge graduate from a relatively privileged and cultured background, the son of a right-wing Tory councillor, Griffin clearly had more gravitas and self-confidence. Yet because Griffin had thus far been an arch-critic of the 'modernisers', naturally there had to be more to it than that. Indeed, what happened during the course of 1998 holds the key to this curious twist. Like the proverbial leopard, Griffin changed his spots.

A number of factors seem to account for this. Firstly, at Harrow Crown Court, on 1 May 1998, Griffin was given a nine-month prison sentence, suspended for two years, for incitement to racial hatred arising from his writings in issue 12 of *The Rune*.[149] Griffin had no prior convictions but he now faced a custodial sentence if he returned to such open, uncompromising displays of ideological extremism. This was clearly a disincentive. Meanwhile, a close association had been struck up between Griffin and Dr Mark Deavin. Deavin, whose father had been a member of the National Front in the 1970s, had recently studied for a PhD at the London School of Economics under the supervision of Dr Alan Sked, then leader of the UK Independence Party (UKIP). During the mid-1990s Deavin had joined the UKIP and had sat on its governing executive. But in 1997, when Deavin's connections with Griffin were exposed, Sked had Deavin expelled. Now working openly with the BNP, although he was never a member of the leadership, ran a branch or stood as a candidate, it was Deavin who encouraged Griffin to adopt a more moderate line in the style of France's *Front National*.[150] Thirdly, in April 1998, there was an infusion of new-blood activists from the West Midlands branch of the National Democrats – a party formed when Ian Anderson's faction of the NF renamed itself in the mid-1990s. This strengthened the hand of the BNP's 'moderate' wing and, according to Newland, Griffin could see in which direction the wind was now blowing.[151] He was keen to run with the pack and developed a close working relationship with these activists, people such as the 'dynamic' husband and wife team of Steve and Sharron Edwards, who like Eddy Butler stressed the need for local community-based campaigning.[152] A further factor was Griffin's desire to win support from the rural constituency, in particular disaffected Conservatives. Thus, he sought to prioritise 'countryside' policies and looked to create the impression that BNP supporters were not some 'dangerous extremists' from the urban working class.[153]

In November 1998, in a hugely symbolic act, the Janus-faced Griffin rushed to the defence of Michael Newland who on the popular James Whale Talk Radio show, had backed away from a forced repatriation policy. 'NICK GRIFFIN says the "extremists" need to grow up', was how his *Spearhead* article started in its support for Newland's comments. Significantly, Griffin recommended that the party should drop its commitment to compulsory repatriation – a policy move that he had ridiculed less than three years earlier.[154] By launching a stinging attack on those hardliners who saw this move as a 'sell out', Griffin was now all but certain of the support of the 'modernisers'. Emboldened by this, and fearing a change to the BNP constitution, in February 1999 Griffin announced his intention to contest Tyndall for control of the party.

For the first time in 17 years, the question of who runs the British National Party was to be put to its membership. Tyndall was taken aback. He now found himself 'searching for words' to describe Griffin's perfidious behaviour.[155] But in truth, Griffin's challenge always had an air of inevitability about it. That Griffin would be Tyndall's successor had been rumoured within BNP circles ever since his return from political exile. The only real question was the timing and means of succession. More often than not, the practice on Britain's far right had been for changes in leadership to occur by schism and/or by forcing incumbents out. Tyndall was well-versed in this custom having relied on both methods in the past. Within the BNP's constitution, however, provision had been made for a leadership election by postal ballot.

To start with, Griffin had to win Tyndall's trust. Only then could he switch allegiance and align himself with the party's dominant faction. By the end of the 1990s, not only had Griffin achieved this undertaking but the party's leadership was also there for the taking: in some 40 years of far-right political activity, the summit of Tyndall's electoral achievements had been one local by-election victory. This was a modest return from a long-service political career and, in any case, the inspiration for Millwall had come from elsewhere. But instead of Millwall serving as the springboard for future electoral success, the party's development went into reverse. It soon became racked by an internal crisis wrought by Combat 18 and Tyndall took months to respond to this threat. Though the BNP did manage to contest over 50 seats at the 1997 general election, its recruitment campaign proved deeply disappointing. Moreover, when it returned to the local electoral arena in 1998, its vote had collapsed, particularly in its East London strongholds. As his former comrade, John Bean writes, 'John Tyndall was both its greatest asset and its greatest drawback. His persistence, rock-like reliability and leadership had kept the movement going, but with almost imperceptible growth since its 1982 foundation'.[156] Tyndall may have been a rousing speaker, but his tactical intelligence left much to be desired. By the late 1990s patience with him was wearing thin. Tyndall's standing was now at its lowest ebb, and with the new millennium fast approaching, his time had finally run out.

4
Fascism on the Fringe: The Ideology of Tyndall's British National Party

'Fascism was Italian; Nazism was German. We are British. We will do things in our own way; we will not copy foreigners'.[1] In the question and answer section of its 1992 election manifesto, this was how the British National Party defended itself against the accusation that it was a 'fascist' or 'Nazi' party. Meanwhile, the party's propaganda handbook – *Spreading the Word* – offered guidance for those activists on the doorsteps who might otherwise be tongue-tied when confronted with the awkward question 'Are you Nazis?' Answer an emphatic 'no', the handbook recommended, and since mainstream politicians like Enoch Powell have been called 'Nazis' for raising 'quite moderate objections to immigration', maintain that the word 'Nazi' has become a meaningless term of abuse.[2] For sure, since the words 'fascist' and 'Nazi' are all too frequently used in order to smear political opponents, they have been stripped of much of their meaning. Nonetheless, we will resist the temptation to disparage or remove them from the pages of our study. On the contrary, as we lay bare the extent to which the British National Party's political ideology over the 1982–99 period assumed a distinctly fascist form, we will insist on their correct usage. Moreover, since this provides the yardstick against which we can measure Nick Griffin's later programme of 'modernisation', this chapter provides an all-important background context to the latest phase in the evolution of the British National Party.

That Britain's electoral right-extremists should dissociate themselves from the labels 'fascist' and 'Nazi' hardly comes as any surprise – if they did not, they would repel the vast majority of their potential voters. Hence, instead of the phrase 'British fascism', the preferred expression in the lexicon of Britain's contemporary electoral extreme right is 'British nationalism'. This is a far more 'legitimate'-sounding term altogether.

We need only peruse Tony Lecomber's review of Mike Cronin's edited volume *The Failure of British Fascism* (1996) to bear this out. Almost immediately, the reader is brought to his 'particular gripe' that the word 'fascist' is bandied about the book, 'Not even as a term of abuse, but seemingly as statement of fact. Apparently, according to academia, there is no such thing as a non-fascist racial nationalist. Even democratic nationalists are accorded this term, which is plainly silly.'[3] Yet Lecomber is clearly doing us a disservice. Many academics would accept that racial nationalists could be 'non-fascist'. Besides, if Lecomber is implying that the British National Party under John Tyndall could be described as 'democratic nationalist', then he is surely stretching the limits of credibility too far. But before we pin down the nature of the BNP's ideological beliefs, we need to negotiate a number of theoretical obstacles first. To begin with, since the terms 'fascist' and 'Nazi' are so tied up with the concept of the extreme right, our analysis will start by locating the theoretical parameters of right-wing extremism.

Conceptualising right-wing extremism

Conceptualising the extreme right let alone fascism is no easy task. For a start, the fact that authors make use of varied terminology only adds to our confusion. A cursory glance at the specialist literature reveals a clutch of other terms in play such as radical right, ultra-right, insurgent right, far right, fascism, neo-fascism, neo-Nazism, national populism, new or neo-populism.[4] Frequently, this cluster of terms is used interchangeably; at other times, strict conditions apply. Thus, we have Peter Merkl and Leonard Weinberg using the terms 'radical right' and 'extreme right' as one and the same, as does Hebert Kitschelt in his comparative study.[5] Elsewhere, Hans-Georg Betz has argued that the concept of right-wing extremism – with its fundamental rejection of democracy and of individual equality – fails to appreciate the true nature of the contemporary right in established Western democracies. He prefers to use the term 'radical right-wing populism' when making reference to more 'moderate' far-right organisations like the French National Front and Austria's Freedom Party.[6] By drawing such a distinction between 'radicalism' and 'extremism', Betz more or less corresponds to a practice established in Germany. Here, 'radicalism' is said to fall short of seeking a full or partial elimination of democracy whilst 'extremism' is totally hostile to the democratic order.[7] But some writers, such as the Italian Franco Ferraresi, have argued that the term 'radical right' should only be used to describe the most 'radical sector' of the right-extremist field, that is to say, those who advocate the use of illegal political means.[8] In truth, the term 'radical right' (which has been deliberately avoided in this study) only serves to confuse the distinction between moderation and extremism. On the moderation–extremism continuum, 'radicalisation' merely describes the relative process of shift. Thus it makes sense to speak of Thatcher as a right-wing 'radical' and yet she was hardly a right-wing extremist.

There is, as Cas Mudde says, 'a broad consensus in the field that the term right-wing extremism describes primarily an ideology in one form or another'.[9] Yet the form that this ideology takes cannot be reduced to a uniform type that is identical in every case, as Paul Hainsworth has observed.[10] Instead, the extreme right should be viewed as a broad 'political family' which possesses an ideology of common constituent parts. In terms of actual practice and emphasis, however, it is subject to significant variation. When approached in this way, it then becomes possible to tease out various ideological distinctions and nuances. But to begin with, we need to identify what it is that constitutes the ideological 'core' of right-wing extremism. At this point, it makes sense to follow the lead of Mudde who uses a literature review and a rate of recurrence technique. What this means is that Mudde selects those ideological features that are repeatedly mentioned by at least half of the authors of 26 separate definitions of right-wing extremism. Adopting this approach, the core defining features of right-wing extremism turn out to be: (ultra) nationalism, racism, xenophobia, anti-democracy and the strong state. Consequently any group that matches this ideological profile can be regarded as extreme right.[11]

Without doubt, there are various methodological problems with this approach, not least ranking the different ideological characteristics in terms of their relative importance. But be that as it may, it seems almost certain that ultra-nationalism occupies the central point of the archetypal right-wing extremist's political universe. In the hands of far-right demagogues, as Roger Griffin defines it, nationalism is key since it provides the 'legitimation of hatred directed at "foreigners" (xenophobia) and of discrimination on the grounds of ethnicity (racism), both of which axiomatically deny the universality of human rights and thus generate "illiberal nationalism"'.[12] Therefore, even within the core of right-wing extremism, it is possible to make out the 'hub' of ultra-nationalism as well as its 'spokes' – racism, xenophobia, anti-democracy and the strong state. Moreover, from this point on, it also becomes possible to sub-divide the extreme right into at least two branches or 'ideal types'[13] of thought.

Once positioned according to relative ideological extremity, it is the 'revolutionary' right that occupies the most extreme point on this far-right scale. Here we enter the realm of generic fascism, which takes ultra-nationalism to the revolutionary extreme. Within this domain, we also find the full array of generic fascism's ideological sub-types, which in contemporary times would incorporate both neo-Nazism and neo-fascism. In both cases, the prefix 'neo' denotes revival or revision of the original but in new forms. Whilst neo-Nazis tend to be mimetic and cling to the world-view of interwar National Socialism, neo-fascists are said to 'have either introduced original themes or cultural idioms into major interwar permutations, or reject them altogether in the name of entirely new rationales', as Roger Griffin has already informed us.[14]

Naturally, there will be objectors to this theoretical sketch. For a start, there are those who might still hold on to the outdated view that fascism is not a generic concept.[15] Yet all fascisms, including *both* Nazi Germany and Fascist Italy, were based on revolutionary ultra-nationalism. Others insist that if there is a generic fascism, then it was locked into a specific epoch, and that right-wing extremism today is 'essentially different' to its interwar manifestations.[16] Whilst differences naturally occur over time, fascism's ideological core has nevertheless remained the same. Then there are dyed-in-the-wool Marxists who find any thought that fascism can somehow be considered 'revolutionary' hard to accept.[17] Obviously, fascism in practice 'reacted' against the Enlightenment tradition and did little to destroy class relations, but this does not mean to say that it did not offer a radically alternative future. The words of George Mosse are particularly apposite here: 'A revolution from the political Right is as possible as one from the political Left, once revolution is defined as the forceful reordering of society in the light of a projected utopia.'[18] There are also those who, despite its vicious hatred of liberalism and the fact that historically fascists have tended to collude with the mainstream right, misplace fascism in the 'centre' albeit a 'revolutionary', 'extremist' or 'authoritarian' centre.[19]

Our second 'ideal type' is essentially reformist rather than revolutionary. It seeks to restore strong, ultra-nationalist government and reassert traditional values such as law and order, authority, community, work and family. In an earlier article, I referred to this type as the 'authoritarian nationalist' right,[20] though perhaps a more appropriate description of its manifestation today is the 'national-populist' right, that is to say, an 'electorally friendly' and 'respectable' branch of the extreme right that occupies the political space between fascism and the mainstream right – the French National Front, the Austrian Freedom Party, the Italian National Alliance are frequently held up as examples of this 'ideal type'. Where ideologically, the 'national-populist' right remains opposed to the 'system', especially its mainstream parties and its 'political class', it rarely (at least openly) questions the legitimacy of democracy and moreover, through its identification with ordinary people, it defines itself as part of the 'mainstream'. 'It is of the people but not of the system', as Paul Taggart says.[21] In the real world, however, there is the very finest of lines between these two 'ideal types': neo-fascists are undoubtedly drawn to ostensibly non-fascist 'national-populist' parties, whilst at the same time neo-fascist organisations frequently construct a false front in order to cloak themselves in the 'respectability' that this second 'ideal type' offers. As we shall see, Nick Griffin's BNP is a classic case in point.

Fascism: the revolutionary ideology of the extreme right

On returning to the subject of fascism, we arrive back at what is, *par excellence*, a definitional and theoretical quagmire. As any student will confirm, in the muddy waters of generic fascism it is all too easy to become mired in a morass of competing theories and definitions. Nonetheless, a lifeline has been thrown by a new generation of historians and political scientists who by approaching their subject as a search for an ideological 'fascist minimum' have defined fascism in terms of a 'revolutionary' form of ultra-nationalism. Whether this approach constitutes a 'new consensus' in fascist studies or whether Roger Griffin, its leading advocate, has manufactured such a 'consensus' does not interest us here.[22] Rather, our concern lies with the British National Party's ideology. And, by adopting a methodological approach to fascism that is ideologically driven, we can equip ourselves with the diagnostic tools that are required to subject the BNP's ideological universe to serious critical examination.

But as soon as fascism is defined solely as an ideology, it draws flak from those writers who insist that fascism's ideas cannot be decoupled from its wider practice. Hence, David Renton's cry from the heart that fascism should not be seen simply as an ideology. For Renton, the 'formal pronouncements of any leaders should be weighed against their practice'.[23] Moreover, Renton believes that 'Mussolini, Hitler and Oswald Mosley were highly opportunistic leaders', and 'their parties have been characterised more by the emphasis on action rather than by an adherence to key ideas'.[24] Likewise, a call has been made by Robert Paxton for theoretical work on generic fascism to focus on the ways in which it has manifested itself in history rather than treating fascism simply as an 'ism', a body of thought on par with conservatism, liberalism and socialism. For a time, as Paxton says, such was fascism's political expediency, he was 'tempted to reduce the role of ideology in fascism to a simple functionalism'. However, his approach has now softened: he is willing to admit that ideas 'count in fascism' even if they 'count more at some stages than at others'.[25]

So at what stages do fascist ideas matter? In Paxton's five-stage 'functional' model of fascism, from its creation as a political movement to its radicalisation or entropy as a régime, fascist ideas most obviously count when the movement is created (stage 1). However, once 'rooted' in the party system (stage 2), ideological deviation can occur as fascist leaders seek tactical alliances with the conservative right. For Paxton then, we cannot define fascism according to its first stage, because 'examining one limb of course, may mislead us about the whole beast'.[26] But whilst it cannot be denied that fascist leaders frequently surrendered ideological principles to political expediency, fascist movements were not unique in this regard. Moreover, we must not let Mussolini's legendary opportunism overshadow Hitler. Domestic fascism in Germany rarely behaved in such a compromising manner. What is more, Paxton's model is derived from the experience of interwar Europe and as such tells us nothing about contemporary manifestations of fascism. Indeed, when fascism is abstracted into an ideological 'ideal type', how it then reveals itself in reality will not necessarily follow set patterns. This clearly makes nonsense of Paxton's claim that ideologically based definitions of fascism are somehow 'static'.[27]

More often than not, individual theorists of generic fascism have their own product to sell and Roger Griffin has certainly been accused of overselling his.[28] Nonetheless, from the range of ideologically-based definitions on offer, over a decade since it made its first appearance, Griffin's product still remains the most attractive – if only in heuristic terms. Of his main rivals, Roger Eatwell follows close behind with his single-sentence definition of fascism as a revolutionary ideology, an attempt to create a *'holistic-national-radical Third Way'*.[29] However, in constructing these four-point core annotations, Eatwell rather clumsily end-loads his definition on the 'Third Way', an interpretation of fascism as 'neither capitalism nor communism'. Yet in truth, within fascist ideology, the 'Third Way' was often an ill-defined concept.

Corporatism may have been its most frequently stated intention, but Hitler's ideas in the area of political economy were rather vague. In fact, fascists often conceived the 'Third Way' in 'spiritual' rather than economic terms whereby an exaggerated nationalism bordered on a 'civic religion' – a way to rise above the 'decadent' materialism of both Marxism and capitalism. As a result, the 'Third Way' describes more 'an attitude to life' and so, when looked at from the inside out, as George Mosse has done, 'Fascism was a revolution, but one which thought of itself in cultural, not economic terms.'[30]

Others, too, such as Stanley Payne, have defined fascism as a revolutionary ideology. However, Payne 'factors-in' unnecessary, historically contingent external features such the *Führerprinzip*, mass mobilisation, and a positive valuation of violence, military values and war.[31] In so doing, his definition necessarily restricts fascism to the 1919–45 epoch. What is needed, however, is an abstracted definition of fascism that stands outside of time and place. In Roger Griffin's definition of fascism, we have this: a theory of fascism that not only allows for a myriad of different permutations, but which also does not impose any time ceiling on us.

Significantly, the core of Griffin's 'ideal type' is located in the 'energising' myth of 'palingenesis' – a word that has certainly gone the rounds within the academic circles of fascist studies. For those unfamiliar with its etymology, this is a Victorian term derived from the Greek *palin* again, and *genesis* birth: a regenerative idea of rebirth or renewal, a new start after a prolonged phase of perceived decadence, decline or crisis.[32] Thus, at its core, fascism's vision is of a radically new beginning or 'new order' (like the phoenix rising from the ashes), a revolutionary vision of a vigorous reborn nation growing out of an old decaying, decadent and diseased system. For Griffin, then, fascism takes on a 'palingenetic' form of populist ultra-nationalism which seeks the rebirth of the nation through a radical social, moral and political revolution: 'Fascism is a genus of political ideology whose mythic core in its various permutations is a palingenetic form of populist ultra-nationalism.'[33]

According to Griffin, the fascist mind is also energised by a closely related sub-myth of the herculean 'new man'. This is a mythical aspiration for a strong, honourable, heroic, vitalistic *homo fascistus* – a selfless, rejuvenated and perfectible member of a new national community. On this point, Griffin is clearly in debt to the earlier work of Mosse who detected the 'new man' 'about whom all fascists talked'.[34] But perhaps the most striking aspect to fascism's palingenetic ultra-nationalism is its ruthless monism – the negation of 'contradistinction' within the national community. Fascism thus seeks to destroy all-pervasive 'decadence' and so tends towards 'totalitarian' control over political, economic, social and cultural life. But this is not to say that we should drop Griffin and give way to academic models of totalitarianism.[35] As these merely describe the external features of a régime, they tell us little about the ideological bases of fascist doctrine.

All the same, Griffin's research into the nature of fascism hardly constitutes the 'last word' in fascist studies. It is, of course, in the nature of paradigms that they shift. Indeed, there are elements to his definition that should be treated with some caution, as Eatwell and others have already noted.[36] For a start, ultra-nationalism is not an easy concept to define, though Griffin is clearly using 'ultra' as a prefix to nationalism in order to underscore fascism's fanatical opposition to liberalism. As for 'populism', this tends to describe a political style rather than a strict ideological trait and so Griffin seems to fall into the familiar trap of 'externalising' his own definition. Moreover, the idea of 'palingenesis' or 'rebirth' is not as distinctive as it first sounds: it can be detected in other movements, whether on the right or left. With these problems preying on one's mind, it would surely be tempting to let go and slip back into the morass. But despite that, we will hold fast with Griffin; that he currently offers the most heuristically useful theory is beyond doubt. In any case, since all three defining features are supposed to run together, all we do is overstate these problems when we deliberately single them out in isolation. With our theoretical outline finally in position, we are ready to make the next step. The journey into the ideological heart of Tyndall's British National Party can now commence.

In search of revolutionary rebirth

> By joining the British National Party you are in fact joining a movement that is revolutionary in its objectives in that it aims at the total transformation of the British body politic and British society.[37]

Sure enough, as the first section of the BNP *Activists' Handbook* makes clear, the BNP under John Tyndall saw itself as a revolutionary party. This is 'a party unlike the other parties', it proudly proclaimed.[38] And what marks the BNP activist out is that he resembles a 'member of a guerrilla army operating in occupied territory' forced 'to contend, as such movements must, with the hatred of the old world of politics that it has been created to replace'. In other words, expect to be treated like a political pariah, the handbook said, but you 'should regard it as a badge of honour – to be worn proudly'.[39] Becoming an activist with the BNP was no soft option. This, clearly, was no message for the faint-hearted.

Shut out from the 'old world of politics', mainstream political life was seen by Tyndall's British National Party as little more than a sordid racket run by a mafia of self-interested 'party gangs'. But in fact, its hostility towards Britain's political class operated on a far wider canvas. As Tyndall said, this 'political rot' is 'only a part of a much more general rot' where Britain's 'entire national life is in the grip of degenerative forces, which barely leave one small area of affairs unaffected, as they run amok like maggots invading a diseased carcass'.[40] Just as earlier generations of fascists whether home-grown or otherwise had tormented themselves with the fear of impending national dissolution, frequently conjuring up morbid images and biological metaphors, so Tyndall followed suit. He also saw in Britain a state of deadly sickness and decay. Though the source of contamination lay elsewhere, the pathogen is as one would expect:

> At the heart of the sickness is the doctrine of liberalism, which has atrophied every healthy national instinct for survival and growth. This doctrine of decay and degeneration contaminates almost every aspect of our national life – not only in the field of politics but also in those of religion, education, philosophy, the arts and much else.[41]

What the BNP held in view filled it with dread: Britain is in perpetual crisis heading towards total collapse. This abject failure is rooted in its 'degenerate' liberal-democratic system and Britain is dying, sliding ever downwards to an apocalyptic crash. 'There is a cancer in the body of the nation and liberalism is that cancer', despaired Tyndall. Yet there is still hope: its 'consequences will be terminal unless rapid surgery is used to remove it. We are at the Eleventh Hour: we do not have long left'.[42] A classic dialectic of pessimism and optimism no less and, as Thomas Linehan has previously observed, this everywhere 'characterised fascist ideology in its more mature palingenetic form'.[43]

With Britain in chaos, Tyndall's BNP saw itself as the revolutionary force that would lead the British nation to heroic rebirth, springing forth a new utopian future from the ashes of a diseased and decadent liberal-democratic past. Writing in *New Frontier*, just months prior to the BNP's founding, Tyndall maintained that as far he was concerned, 'only a government with revolutionary powers and a revolutionary will is going to be equipped to do all that is necessary'; he even stated that policies 'will not be rejected merely because they have earned the epithet "fascist"'.[44] In similar vein, the BNP's election manifesto in 1983 promised that 'a revolutionary spirit and method must pervade not only the economy, but the whole apparatus of government and national leadership, indeed the whole of society'.[45] But it is in the first edition of Tyndall's *The Eleventh Hour*, originally published in 1988, that we perhaps see the clearest example of Griffin's 'fascist minimum':

> If we are seriously to grapple with the chaos of the present day and formulate a creed and movement for national rebirth, our thinking must begin with an utter rejection of liberalism and a dedication to the resurgence of authority. As such it must entail the embrace of a political outlook which is, in relation to the present, **revolutionary**.[46]

Nor do we need to look far for the myth of the 'new fascist man' either: 'We must dispel the idea that Britain can be led by ordinary people. What we need are **extraordinary** people, people of a type that our political system and climate do the utmost to discourage.'[47] And, as Tyndall further insisted: 'it is within the individual that this renewal must begin. No revolutionary change in society can occur except through every person aspiring to that change first undergoing a revolution within himself'.[48] What this entailed was the embrace of the whole new 'attitude to life' that sets fascism apart:

> It will be recognised from what has been written that the doctrine being put forward is much more than just political. It embraces every aspect of the life of the nation and its members, for nothing less than a total reformation of personal, as well as national, values can bring about the renewal that we need.[49]

> This means an adjustment, where necessary, to new habits of living as well as to new values. It means a wholesale rejection of our contemporary civilisation, with its worship of the deformed, the diseased and the decayed, and the quest for a new order of truth and beauty, built by a higher breed of people.[50]

What bearing was all this supposed to have on its party activists? The leadership urged them to live 'life in a way that serves as a microcosm of that kind of country we wish Britain to become in the future'.[51] On a practical level, this meant regular exercise, tobacco and alcohol in moderation and a healthy diet. It also recommended that its activists ration their viewing of television, to read books instead and to avoid degenerate 'popular music', 'designed to be mentally and spiritually crippling'.[52] Musing on this subject in *Spearhead*, Tyndall even suggested that BNP members 'should stand straight and not slouch, walk proudly and not apologetically, talk in clear and strong tones and not with the lisp of the creep and cringer'.[53]

To save Britain from collapse, Tyndall's BNP believed that a battery of extreme measures was called for. The first step to deliver Britain from catastrophe was to remake the entire political system. In *The Eleventh Hour*, Tyndall declared that the BNP did not identify itself with any precise proposals for constitutional change,[54] however the party had previously set out its plans for 'strong' and 'effective' government elsewhere.[55] Investing the office of Prime Minister with full executive powers was deemed essential, and the people would also directly elect the Prime Minister for an indefinite period of office, the BNP proposed. Under such a system, stress was placed on the charismatic leader, an exceptional person that could be entrusted to mobilise the nation in a 'co-ordinated' campaign for national rebirth. But surely this would mean dictatorship? Not so, argued Tyndall's BNP. This is not a dictatorship, it said, when the Prime Minister could be dismissed constitutionally through a parliamentary vote of no confidence and subsequent national election.[56]

Yet in truth, parliamentary government would have found itself all too quickly emasculated. That Tyndall's BNP wanted to put an end to the 'antics' of 'fraudulent' and 'decadent' political parties was obvious. The present party system was lambasted as inefficient, corrupt and a sham in which political parties spurned the national interest in a disgraceful scramble for votes. Elections were, for that reason, dismissed as little more than 'squalid contests of bribery and corruption, with the parties toadying to every selfish whim on the part of the voter'.[57] Under a BNP government, therefore, electoral contests would have been carried out on a non-party basis – each candidate would stand as an individual bearing no party label. And so, by removing political parties from the political arena and taking Tyndall's desire to socially engineer the 'new man' into account – strong, self-reliant, imbued with a will to work and above all else, devoted to the nation – those elected to this 'national parliament' would hardly be inclined to act as a shield against illiberal dictatorship. Thus, as one student has rightly sensed,

Tyndall's 'view of "popular participation" involves the establishment of a system wherein the participants would, ultimately, be rendered politically impotent'.[58]

As for the British National Party's place in all this, it is not clear. Indeed, even in the series of 'sub-parliaments' that the BNP proposed, there seems to have been no place for the party as all representatives would be elected on the basis of an occupational franchise. In point of fact, much of this yearning for an occupational franchise (instead of an area franchise) had Mosley's stamp on it. The need for government to bypass the 'ignorance' of the masses by only allowing people to vote for candidates from their own occupations, had been an integral part of the Mosleyite canon.[59] Yet it need hardly be added that this anti-democratic thinking also repeats classic fascism in the wider sense too. The hunger for the end of corrupt parliamentary plutocracy, the rejection of pluralist representative democracy is all too familiar: 'The old system of party warfare must come to an end, and political forces within the nation must be coordinated together in a mighty effort of national reconstruction', the BNP declared in 1987.[60]

That the BNP should use the word 'co-ordinated' here is indeed ominous. Under the Third Reich, the 'co-ordination' or *Gleichschaltung* of society was the euphemism used to describe the ruthless suppression of dissent. Quite simply, for national rebirth to occur, there can be no difference of opinion – all sectors of society must work in the same direction, all must labour towards the same goal. Hence, the 1992 election manifesto pledged to weld the entire nation 'into a single and solid community, dedicated to a common patriotic purpose'.[61]

For the ultra-nationalist project to succeed, liberal-democratic 'decadence', that is to say avarice and self-interest, must be eliminated. This called for a systematic programme of moral regeneration. As a result, Tyndall's BNP was monistic, holding out the promise of moral leadership and a new moral order – a resonance of the 'ethical state' that Italian fascist philosophers, like Giovanni Gentile, had espoused.[62] This moral revolution would have entailed a draconian crusade against all things 'decadent': against drugs, violence, sexual deviants, pornography, crime, corruption, ineptitude, and so on. The party's explicit allegiance to fascism may have been mute, but it did not pull any punches when it declared that: 'We are pledged to wage war against all those influences that are making for the disintegration of our society' and what this amounted to was an open-ended commitment 'to take whatever measures are necessary to being about the wholesale clean-up of Britain'.[63]

Of its bid to 'clean up' Britain, much in fact paralleled historic fascism. To 'decontaminate' British society, the BNP promised to create a national youth movement, enforce a complete eradication of 'trendy' left-wing influences in the classrooms and the universities through arbitrary dismissal, and place the mass media, which according to the BNP constituted 'an enemy fifth column in the heart of Britain, promoting doctrines conducive to national disintegration',[64] under the control of British citizens of 'indigenous British ancestry'. The government would strictly monitor the media and whilst the BNP promised to allow all shades of opinion to be aired, it would draw the line at views that were inimical to British interests.[65] Under Tyndall's BNP, feminism would have been stamped out, 'we should depart from the concept of the career woman as our national and social ideal' but instead 'encourage our womenfolk to regard home- and family-making as the highest vocation of their sex'.[66] As for culture, Tyndall's BNP promised to challenge and eliminate artistic modernism and, through the allocation of funds to cultural projects shaped by British national and cultural character, establish a 'truly' British culture shorn of all liberal 'decadence' and 'depravity'. Clearly, this 'cleansing of society' should not be seen as a form of moral ultra-conservatism close to the protestations of Mary Whitehouse. Rather, it was a 'total' overhaul of society in accordance with meeting the revolutionary objectives of national rebirth.

The racial fascism of the British National Party

> 'We are 100 per cent racist, yes.'—Richard Edmonds to *Guardian* journalist, Duncan Campbell (February 1993)[67]

It goes without saying that within fascism, the union between ultra-nationalism and racism has been a recurring feature. However, racism has clearly been more intrinsic to some fascisms than others, and at this point it is customary to draw the distinction between German National Socialism and Italian Fascism. Yet even British fascism has shown some variety where 'race' has been concerned. Indeed, in most academic discussions of British fascism, those influenced by 'scientific racism', such as Arnold Leese have been frequently differentiated from those, such as Oswald Mosley, whose racism had a more ethnocentric and cultural feel to it. Significantly, when we uncover John Tyndall's BNP, what lay at its core was a racial nationalism that was more in debt to Leese, Hitler and to 'biologically racist' ideas of Nordic supremacy than to Oswald Mosley.

When John Tyndall's political career is tracked, that this should be so is hardly surprising. One only needs to keep in mind the application forms for the 1960s British National Party which asked the applicant to declare that he is of pure 'Northern European racial ancestry'[68] and the later National Socialist Movement, which featured the following 'race' declaration: 'I, the undersigned, am of pure British or kindred Northern European racial ancestry', to see where Tyndall's true sympathies lay.[69] Indeed, ever since the early 1960s, if not earlier, Tyndall's belief in 'biological racism' had remained deeply entrenched.

For Tyndall, then, the British 'race' was formed from several 'tribal' branches of the North European or 'Nordic' tree and, as such, was 'until recent migrations, one of the most homogenous of all the larger populations of the world'.[70] In this respect, Tyndall borrowed heavily from Arnold Leese who had earlier claimed a racial hierarchy in which Anglo-Saxon or Nordic peoples reigned supreme.[71] There is thus, in Tyndall's eyes, a 'pure' British 'race' and it is this racial entity that forms the bedrock of the nation: 'By "we", we mean of course the Anglo-Saxon and Celtic peoples whose unique blend of Northern European stocks gave Britain her greatness and her genius', the party's 1997 general election manifesto clarifies.[72] Thus, Scottish and Welsh nationalisms are dismissed as bogus nationalisms since they seek to divide the British racial stock. But more than that, Tyndall also remained true to his earliest writings that the Nordic 'white' race is inherently, that is to say genetically, superior. That his words in this regard became less candid over time is the likely consequence of his prosecution under 'race relations' legislation. Following his most recent court case, Tyndall therefore lamented in *The Eleventh Hour* that 'anyone henceforth who ventures to suggest in public, either in speech or in writing, that one race may not be equal to another is on "dangerous" ground'.[73]

On nationalism, Tyndall's thinking is intrinsically racial: 'Race, and not geographical location, is the cement that binds nations'.[74] In Tyndall's crude Social Darwinist world-view, 'nation-races' rise and fall according to their relative homogeneity and survival instinct. The problem with Anglo-Saxons, Tyndall argued, is that despite their natural superiority they possess a weak survival instinct having fallen victim to the 'self-destroying ideology of liberalism'.[75] Moreover, the spread of liberal ideology was said to be the diabolical work of Jews. The 'Jew knows himself to be the inventor of Democracy', Tyndall had proclaimed in 1962, because 'maximum freedom of operation is an essential rule. The Jew must be "tolerated"; he must be free from "prejudice", if his work is to succeed'.[76]

Between the British and the Jewish 'race', Tyndall drew a sharp distinction: Jews have a passionate devotion to their own racial survival and so promote liberalism in order to weaken non-Jewish peoples. As part of this 'conspiracy' to subvert and destroy the British 'race-nation' from within, Tyndall believed that Jews were responsible for multiracialism and, by implication, the mass immigration of non-European 'races' into Britain after the Second World War.[77] In the early 1960s he was frank about this:

> As Democracy tamely allows droves of dark-skinned sub-racials into our country, the Jew cleverly takes advantage of their presence to propagate the lie of racial equality, thus gradually encouraging their acceptance into European society, with the ultimate results of intermarriage and race-degeneration that he knows will follow.[78]

Naturally, in recognition of the offensiveness that the dissemination of such views might cause, the BNP's election material toned down its anti-Semitic colours. When, in the 1960s, Tyndall had declared that 'Jewish influence, in politics, and commerce, in morals and culture' was 'perhaps more than any other single factor responsible for the organised filth and corruption that has infected our society',[79] the British National Party specifically attacked 'Zionists' rather than the 'ordinary Jew'. Nonetheless, as we shall see later, there was still 'a definite **Jewish Question**' as far as Tyndall's BNP was concerned, 'which no patriotic Briton can avoid facing if he is to get to grips with the forces undermining our country and obstructing its rebirth'.[80]

On 'race', the cornerstone of BNP policy under Tyndall – as it had been all through the 1970s in the National Front – was the repatriation of all 'non-whites'. What was envisaged was a two-part programme of resettlement. In the first place, a period of voluntary resettlement, followed by a second period of compulsory repatriation. In carrying out this policy, Tyndall's BNP would have offered resettlement grants and predicted that the entire process would take 10–20 years to complete.[81] Of those of 'mixed-race', little was said although the implication was that such offspring would be classed as 'non-white' and hence subject to repatriation. Though Tyndall admitted to feeling 'deeply sorry for the child of a mixed marriage', he felt 'no sympathy whatsoever for the parents who brought that child into the world'.[82] And, even if the party did not openly state this, Jews would have undoubtedly found themselves placed in this 'non-white' category too. In a less guarded moment in the 1960s, Tyndall had let the cat out of the bag:

> Citizenship of the State, and hence participation in the life of the nation, should be denied to all those of alien race, including the large coloured and influential Jewish communities, who should be eventually repatriated to their countries of origin or to other countries suitable for settlement by them.[83]

Alongside repatriation, Tyndall's BNP also looked to improve the quality and quantity of the 'race'. In *The Eleventh Hour*, Tyndall wrote:

> 'Liberal' dogma forbids us, on pain of the worst conceivable ostracism (including the attachment of the well-worn epithet 'nazi') even to consider the introduction of a policy of genetic improvement as a means of breeding out the worst, and procreating the best, strains in our population.[84]

At this moment, we surely cannot fail to miss the disturbing parallels with the racial-hygiene measures practised by the Nazi régime. And, as in Nazi Germany, this eugenics policy would have had both 'positive' and 'negative' sides to it. If Tyndall's BNP had come to power, social welfare benefits would have been readjusted to provide various incentives to those most racially fit, whilst penalties and deterrents would have been imposed on those at the opposite end of the scale. What's more, Tyndall also raised the possibility that criminals might find themselves subject to compulsory sterilisation:

> At the same time, I shall not shirk proposing that there are elements in the population which, if not deprived of life themselves, should most certainly be deprived of the faculty and right to give life to future generations in whom criminal tendencies of the very lowest kind might be reproduced.[85]

In furtherance of the regeneration of Britain's 'racial stock', Tyndall's BNP also committed itself to the prohibition of homosexuality. Abortion, too, would be outlawed except for cases of rape or when the life was 'unworthy of life', that is to say, when the child would be physically handicapped or when the well-being of the reproductive mother was put at risk.[86] And even if, as Martin Durham's work has previously shown, on the subject of eugenics, 'not everyone spoke with one voice' in the party,[87] all its members agreed on the inviolability of the 'race'. Where 'race' ultimately defined the nation, so the battle to save the 'race' becomes the most important battle of all, as Tyndall wrote: 'for if that is lost we will have no nation in the future'.[88]

On the Jewish question

If, at the level of political agitation, opposition to non-European immigration was the issue that most defined Tyndall's British National Party, what lurked behind it was an ingrained belief in Jewish conspiracy. For the most part, the party's reading of this conspiracy corresponded to the classic conspiracy text, the *Protocols of the Elders of Zion*, which Hitler (and many others, including Henry Ford) had taken as fact.[89] But as far as John Tyndall was concerned, as we have already seen, it was A.K. Chesterton that had first brought this Jewish 'world conspiracy' to his attention during the 1950s. What Tyndall has since divulged is that 'Chesterton's view, which is at the same time both the most factual and the most balanced, is the one to which I myself subscribe'.[90]

As Chesterton had understood it, the 'supreme headquarters for the overthrow of the West and the conspiracy to control the World' was located in Wall Street in New York.[91] From here, Jewish international financiers attacked national sovereignty by spreading internationalist doctrines – communism and finance capitalism – as the twin instruments 'with which to subdue and govern, not the British nations alone, but all mankind'.[92] Moreover, Jews were supposedly responsible for subverting the Empire and British spirit, for promoting 'the idea of integrating peoples of disparate racial stocks'[93] and for creating supranational forms of government (the European Economic Community, for example) in the lead up to their 'One World Federation'. Chesterton was therefore convinced: 'World Jewry is the most powerful single force on earth.'[94]

Without doubt, conspiracy theory followed Tyndall throughout his political career. During the early days it was expressed in the bluntest possible terms. From the 1970s onwards, however, coded references to 'Zionism' appeared more frequently as Tyndall sought to deflect the charge that he was attacking Jews as a racial group. Nonetheless, during the mid-1970s, as we saw in our first chapter, Tyndall would let his guard drop. And if more recently the tone became less shrill, Tyndall still averred that there were 'three definite strands of fact': that internationalism has become the dominant global ideology, that conspiratorial forces are at work in Britain and that there is a great deal of 'circumstantial evidence' to suggest that Jewish power is behind it all.[95]

Of particular concern to Tyndall's BNP (and hence the party put it in bold type) was the supposed power of Jews in the media industry: '**very few people in Britain are aware of the huge influence over the mass media exercised by a certain ethnic minority, namely the Jews**'.[96] What results is a daily diet of 'degeneracy', 'blatently one-sided' treatment of the 'race' issue and the frequent denunciation of parties, like the British National Party, as 'dangerous extremists'. With Jews controlling public opinion, 'A poisonous virus is thriving in the heart of Britain', *The Enemy Within*, a BNP pamphlet published in 1993 warned. It is being 'financed by the licence fees paid by the British viewing and listening public'. Therefore, 'Something must be done about it – or it will destroy our country utterly and irreparably.'[97] And even if the BNP claimed that it wished no harm of Jews, the fact that Tyndall's BNP regularly chose York for its annual 'Remembrance Day' rally, the scene of a bloody pogrom against Jews in the 12th century, smacked of insincerity. When interviewed by BBC Radio York in November 1987, Tyndall had informed listeners that York was chosen because it was the historic site of English resistance to 'alien money-lenders hundreds of years ago'.[98]

Though Tyndall fully subscribed to Chesterton's conspiracy theory, it should also be added that his version went beyond it in one important respect. Tyndall grafted Holocaust denial – an important component in the propaganda arsenal of contemporary right-extremists – on to it. With the electoral progress of the far right since the Second World War having been stymied by its own historical legacy, if doubt could be thrown on Nazi Germany's historical record, a major stumbling block could be removed to right-extremism's future political success. But Tyndall also read the Holocaust in conspiratorial terms. For Tyndall, it was a way to induce sympathy for the plight of Jewish people and thus facilitate their objective of world domination: 'Cast your eyes about the historical section of any large bookshop and you are almost certain to see an ample selection of books dealing with the sufferings of Jews', and then 'Do the same thing in a public library and you will have the same experience', Tyndall suggested.[99]

To be fair, the party's show of Holocaust denial fluctuated, and in all probability it followed strategic concerns. Thus, in the late 1980s and mid-1990s, first in distributing *Holocaust News* and then by giving Nick Griffin free rein to propagate Holocaust denial, Tyndall used it insofar as it could appeal to hardliners. However, he refused to commit himself to Holocaust denial in *The Eleventh Hour*,[100] and yet when interviewed by *The Guardian* in June 1962 Tyndall had already dismissed the Nazi genocide as a 'Jewish fabrication': 'Hitler roped in the riff-raff and put them in camps. Some of them may have died of starvation, but there was a food shortage', Tyndall absurdly remarked.[101] Moreover, when there was a prospect of success at the ballot box, Holocaust denial was also conveniently buried. Thus, in *Spreading the Word*, party activists were instructed to reply to the question 'Do you deny the Holocaust?' with the following:

> The BNP has no position on the 'Holocaust' at all because, true or untrue, it is a subject that belongs to Germany and German-occupied Europe half a century ago rather than to Britain today, and the BNP is concerned only with matters that relate to Britain today. The 'Holocaust', in other words, is none of our business.[102]

And yet, all of this was called into question by the various publications offered by the BNP book service. In 1994, for instance, many Holocaust-denial tracts were featured, including such 'classics' as *The Hoax of the Twentieth Century*, *The Leuchter Report* and *Did Six Million Die?*[103] What is more, as *Searchlight's* investigations have revealed, the party also gave its support to David Irving's 'revisionist' activities. In July 1992 it provided security for an Irving seminar in London.[104] For many, such shows of support were instinctive and they continued into Griffin's reign: a number of party activists turned up at Irving's ill-fated trial proceedings in the spring of 2000.[105]

'Neither capitalism nor socialism': the British National Party and the new economic order

In its attack on the philosophies of capitalism and socialism, Tyndall's British National Party rejected the view that it felt was common to both: that man's material welfare should be the first priority of politics. 'Politics must lead, and not be led by, economic forces', Tyndall said.[106] The alternative to *homo economicus*, in the BNP's understanding, was a revolutionary new society (inhabited by *homo fascistus*), a society of the 'Third Way' in which economics merely served as the means to an end. Thus, in a rare philosophical interlude, the 1997 election manifesto insisted that economic progress 'should not be the principal aim of a community of people; that aim should be the increasing moral, spiritual, mental, physical and racial betterment of that people itself: its evolution upwards towards ever higher life-forms'. Seen from this perspective, the role of economic development is to assist the revolutionary process of national rebirth; the danger is that 'economics not subject either to wisdom or control can corrupt and destroy a people'.[107] Accordingly, economics must become the servant of the nation, not its master.

Within the pages of *Beyond Capitalism and Socialism*, a pamphlet written by Tyndall in the 1970s, this alternative doctrine was rather unimaginatively titled 'Economic Nationalism'. At its root, we find a simple dictate: 'all forces of industry and commerce, whether they belong to the private or public sector, must be controlled and regulated in the national interest'.[108] It follows, then, that the state must play an active role in the economic life of the nation. Unsurprisingly therefore, since it disregards national boundaries, neo-liberal economic philosophy, with its *laissez-faire* principles of free trade and the free movement of capital, is anathematised. From the very start, as revealed in the very first section of its constitution in 1982, the British National Party took exception to *laissez-faire* economics and 'international monopoly capitalism'.[109] All through Tyndall's leadership, the party remained steadfastly opposed to liberal capitalism despite the electoral success of continental counterparts, organisations like the French National Front and Austria's Freedom Party, which had seemingly departed from the ideas of earlier generations of right-wing extremists by endorsing free-market capitalism.

Having taken his cue from his ideological mentor, A.K. Chesterton, (Jewish) 'Money Power' is the driver behind international capitalism, according to Tyndall:

> It is this excessive power possessed by an unelected *élite*, distinguished only by its success in the commercial jungle, and the corresponding diminution in the authority of the political leadership which should stand over it, which has accounted for the evils of what we know as 'Capitalism'.[110]

The nexus of this 'Money Power' supposedly stretched to Britain amongst the 'self-serving' institutions of the City of London. Hence, Thatcher's free-market economic 'revolution' was derided as illusory since it failed to challenge the 'deeply entrenched interests which over the decades have constantly resisted change: the interests of the City, of International Finance, of the Stock Market and of Usury'.[111] What

Tyndall's BNP proposed was a 'real revolution' that would reconstruct Britain's entire financial system. Private bankers would be prevented from lending money in excess of that held on deposit, and this would free Britain from 'financial usury' (code for Jewish 'money-lenders'). With the creation of all new money becoming the sole prerogative of government, so the monetary system could be turned into a national resource, the BNP claimed, 'controlled according to national needs'.[112]

Although Tyndall's BNP stood firmly opposed to free-market economics, in capitalism it still identified certain strengths. For Tyndall, in true Social Darwinist style, capitalism with its encouragement of individual enterprise, offered the most natural environment for born leaders to emerge. Nonetheless, in order to protect the national interest, strict limits had to be placed on individual ambition. Consequently, planning and control must be brought to the fore, and in this regard Tyndall also saw a strength in socialism: 'there is in socialism the virtue, that, at least in theory, it stands for the replacement of the economic free-for-all' and in its place, the 'regulation of economic forces by the state in the interests of the whole'.[113] In view of that, the party's economic revolution wished for a radical synthesis of the best parts of two diametrically opposed economic doctrines.

In taking us beyond capitalism and socialism, the BNP envisaged a reconstituted economy anchored in national self-sufficiency. The long-term goal of autarky – a central feature of historic fascism – was seen by Tyndall's BNP as the way forward if Britain was to cut itself free from the international economic system and take its economic destiny into its own hands. Thus, the state had to reassert economic sovereignty and take the lead in bringing all economic sectors under British ownership. At the same time, domestic production had to be protected from overseas competition. Naturally, this necessitated a future outside the European Union but Mosley's alternative postwar Europeanism had long been scorned. For Tyndall, Europe contained non-Nordic 'races' and thus Mosley's clarion call for 'Europe-a-Nation' rang hollow.

Rather than the European Union, Tyndall's BNP put forward a new form of trading association with the 'White Commonwealth' countries, namely Australia, New Zealand and Canada. In reality, however, what this concealed was Tyndall's neo-imperialist and white supremacist aspirations. Not only would Britain play the hegemonic role in this 'White Commonwealth', but this organisation would also promote the 'interests, development, mutual prosperity and security' of the 'Anglo-Saxon-Celtic-Race', as Tyndall revealed.[114] That said, the party claimed to have 'retired from imperialism'. It had no intention of recreating the

Empire, it insisted: 'We have no interest in trying to recapture India or the myriad of other non-white colonies that formerly were our responsibility and our burden.'[115]

Yet in *The Eleventh Hour*, Tyndall was at odds with the 'official' party line. In a surreal moment, he openly called for the European 'recolonisation' of Black Africa. 'As these words are written', Tyndall acknowledged, 'it does not need a lot of imagination to envisage the screams of protest that will sound forth'.[116] Therefore, not by chance, we discover their absence from the party's election programmes. While he clearly bemoaned the loss of Empire, Tyndall acceded that Britain's 'sphere of interest' in Africa should be modest. Only those 'territories previously known as Northern and Southern Rhodesia, together with possibly Kenya and Uganda, should be the limit of our claim'.[117] A 'limited' African policy is the way to lessen the probability of future European wars, Tyndall suggested, as this will satisfy competing demands for 'living room', an unfortunate turn of phrase with its resonance in Hitler's policy of *lebensraum*. At any rate, it all provides further confirmation of the Social Darwinist world-view that underpinned Tyndall's thinking. In his mind, expansionist urges are part and parcel of the process by which 'nation-races' struggle for survival. It is therefore only natural that the most 'superior' of the 'nation-races' exploit their racial 'inferiors'.

For all its imperialist undertones, the party claimed (understandably for electoral reasons), that its economic programme was based on the contemporary Japanese model. In Japan, it saw an example of a dramatically successful postwar economy rooted in national protectionism – at that time, the envy of the world. Yet in reality, much of the party's economic policy actually drew its spirit from the prewar past and, in particular, from fascist corporatism. Unfortunately, those eager to point to Tyndall's Nazi credentials have often overlooked this fact. Yet even when Tyndall's National Socialism was at its most candid, he wanted to see British industry brought under the aegis of the Corporate State.[118] Clearly this was one policy not copied from Nazi Germany; on the contrary, the party's 'New Charter for Industrial Relations' recalled earlier experiments under Italian Fascism and also bore resemblance to the blueprint for a corporate Britain that had been put forward by Oswald Mosley.

What Tyndall's BNP pledged, then, was a radical restructuring of the industrial relations system whereby all trade unions and all employers' associations would be amalgamated into a single national body, in other words, a 'corporate' body. Under this system, strikes or management breaches would become illegal as all adjudications by that body would assume the status of law.[119] 'As Nationalists, we do not recognise that there is an employers' interest or an employees' interest; there is only a national interest', the BNP stated in its founding principles.[120] But if the historic example of Fascist Italy serves as any guide to practice, had Tyndall's BNP ever come to power, such a system would have been used to discipline the labour force and, where adjudications took place, they would have invariably favoured capital since the BNP remained committed to the maintenance of a private-enterprise economy albeit within the parameters of national economic policy.

But be that as it may, we are concerned not with the likely outcomes of such a policy but with the ideological vision that drives it. There can be no doubt that in its formula for ultra-nationalist rebirth, what the British National Party aspired to was an economic revolution. On offer was a strident rejection of *laissez-faire* economics, a radical overhaul of the financial system, a single-minded push for national self-sufficiency, neo-imperialism, and a desire to rise above divisive class conflict through corporatist structures. What all this foresaw was not some 'tinkering' with the prevailing system, but a 'total' transformation of British economic life – the onset of a new, post-liberal economic order.

Conclusion: a contemporary British fascism

So what is 'fascism'? It is a word of Italian origin used to describe the programme carried out in Italy by Mussolini between 1922 and 1943. It is not part of our language and we do not need it.[121]

Contrary to what John Tyndall said above, fascism is not a concept trapped in time and place. Nor should his claim that it did not feature in the party's language detract us either. What our investigations reveal is that once the ideology and policies of the British National Party are measured against our theoretical 'ideal types', all the evidence suggests that the British National Party under John Tyndall's leadership was fascist. Between 1982 and 1999, during the whole time that Tyndall was leader, there was a 'palingenetic' myth of populist ultra-nationalism at the party's ideological core. Here was an organisation on the British political fringe – a party that wanted to turn itself into a national mass movement – that called for national rebirth through a 'total' political, social and economic revolution. Since its destruction of liberalism was intended to be *permanent*, what Tyndall's BNP had in mind was wholesale transformation, a root and branch overhaul that reached into the four quarters of society. In promising to strike 'at the very heart of the sanctified decadence that represents 20th century liberalism', no stone was to be left unturned.[122] And even if the word 'fascism' was not mentioned, in marking out liberalism for destruction, such language was hardly the language of the reformist, authoritarian or 'national-populist' right. For sure, this was a revolutionary right intent on overthrowing pluralist, representative democracy and replacing it with an illiberal system of totalitarian control. And yet, incredulously, Tyndall still insisted that his party repudiated 'what most perceive to be the central feature of fascism: the intolerance of dissent and the forcible imposition on people of policies that run contrary to their will'.[123]

In actual fact, in terms of its particular permutation, the party's barely hidden allegiance to biological racism and Jewish conspiracy theory does suggest that 'neo-Nazi', the most extreme sub-type of contemporary fascism, is the most appropriate epithet. However, Tyndall's BNP was more than crudely mimetic. Roger Griffin suggested in the 1990s that the BNP is among a cluster of parties, which 'turn their back on any indigenous fascism,[124] but this is simply not the case. As we have seen, Tyndall was also indebted to a range of indigenous sources: A.K. Chesterton and Arnold Leese for the most part, but also Oswald Mosley, the most likely inspiration for some of the party's more corporatist-style beliefs.

It is clear, then, that deep fascist roots, including indigenous ones, nourished Tyndall's political psyche. His political career, spanning over 40 years, saw him pass through an array of right-extremist organisations. Moreover, regardless of some cosmetic changes, his ideology remained the same from start to finish. Unsurprisingly, therefore, like the National Front before it, Tyndall's British National Party found itself tagged with the fascist label (and deservedly so). And yet, in the face of such an objectionable public image, Tyndall continued to lead the party down the blind alley. Even though some efforts were made to present a more acceptable public face – 'fascism' was denied, anti-Semitism was toned down, public displays of fascist trappings were generally disapproved – little serious effort was put in to revamping the party's image:

> Trim this policy and trim that policy. Smooth this edge and polish that edge. Jettison our 'extremism' and assert our 'moderation'... and the legions of activists and voters just waiting for a new party with such an impeccable gloss will come flooding towards us. How great it would be if things were that simple![125]

As ever, 'the main deterrent to greater progress is not our public 'image', Tyndall opined, 'but our perceived political impotence resulting from no representation in parliament, or on councils'.[126] But after so many years of political failure, the future that Tyndall suggested was more of the same: further setbacks as the party patiently waited on the wings for the moment when some mythical pendulum swung its way back and brought with it a people ready to vote for the revolutionary politics of the extreme right. Yet as Tony Lecomber understood it, in contemporary liberal-democratic societies, when people vote, they ordinarily do not vote for a revolutionary form of politics.[127] Only in the most exceptional circumstances, such as in the aftermath of the First World War, could this ever happen. Where Tyndall went wrong was to even imagine that an occurrence of events in contemporary Britain could take place where the masses would flock to an open, full-bloodied revolutionary form of ultra-nationalism. This was to indulge, in the well-chosen words of Roger Griffin, 'not so much in counterfactual speculation as political science fiction'.[128]

5
New Millennium New Leader: Nick Griffin and the Modernisation of the British National Party

Towards the end of September 1999, the result of the British National Party's first ever leadership election was announced. On the basis of an 80 per cent turnout, Nick Griffin had succeeded in winning 1,082 votes cast in a postal ballot of the party's membership. With the incumbent, John Tyndall, having received only 411 votes or just 30 per cent of total membership, Griffin had easily got the better his opponent.[1] In their hour of decision, amongst a clear majority of the party's members, Griffin had obviously hit the right note. Where previously he had been Tyndall's second-in-command, now he could finally take charge. In having obtained such a decisive vote, Griffin also possessed a clear mandate 'to stamp his own style and vision on the party', as an internal bulletin declared to its members.[2]

However, it need hardly be added that all through his right-extremist career, there had been notable variations in Griffin's political style. If more recently, as we have seen, he had become 'a man committed to respectable politics and electioneering', in other words, an out-and-out 'moderniser', erstwhile comrades in the International Third Position remember Griffin in a variety of former guises, be that as 'a conservative, a revolutionary nationalist, a radical National Socialist, a Third Positionist' or 'a friend of "boot boys" and the skinhead scene'.[3] What all this ideological inconsistency might point towards over the longer term is of course open to debate. But for the moment at least, Griffin's objective was to transform the internal culture of the British National Party – to 'modernise' it and 'normalise' it as a legitimate political party.

Shortly after declaring his intention to contest Tyndall for leadership of the party, Griffin laid out his blueprint for the future direction of the BNP in the spring of 1999. His mouthpiece was Tony Lecomber's magazine, *Patriot*. An opportunity would soon present itself for radical nationalists in Britain, Griffin forecast, when the material and psychological gains of the postwar consumer society are thrown into reverse by the onward march of 'globalisation' – defined by Griffin in terms of growing ethnic and racial diversity, increasing European integration and the harmful effects of global capitalism. Looking ahead, Griffin prophesised that during the next few years the 'dark horsemen of the globalist apocalypse will visit more and more of this land', extending their reach beyond those run-down 'sink' estates that are already haunted by 'poverty', 'malnutrition', 'insecurity' and 'despair'. In Griffin's thoughts, the BNP could become a beacon of hope not only for the dispossessed white working class, but also a potential saviour for those in the traditional middle class, of so-called 'Middle England', who would become increasingly disoriented and frustrated by the process of globalisation. Thus, the future of the party lay in bringing together town – the voters of the old 'left', neglected by New Labour – with country – those of the old 'right', disillusioned by the decline of the Conservative Party.

Yet there is no point in the British National Party idly waiting in the wings for this crisis of globalisation to occur, Griffin warned. In the first place, the masses may not perceive it as such and, besides, 'even if a sudden lurch into a full-scale Slump does prompt a popular rejection of the existing order', it is by no means 'inevitable that the British National Party would automatically become the political beneficiary'. To take full advantage of this impending crisis, it must therefore concentrate on transforming itself from its current status as a political pariah into a respectable mainstream party with both 'mass movement potential' and 'electability'. This called for a far-reaching programme of party 'modernisation' through which the BNP should adapt itself to present conditions, adopt modern methods and a modern vocabulary. And two basic principles should govern this modernisation programme, Griffin thought – 'responsibility' and 'professionalism'.[4]

Responsibility

On 'responsibility', Griffin now spoke with a different voice. The days of attacking the quest for 'respectability' as 'a hunt for fool's gold' had gone.[5] In their place, Griffin spent his time weighing into the culture of 'careless extremism' within the party: 'If we seriously want to be elected', Griffin said, 'the very first step is to look at the things we do, or condone, which make us unelectable'.[6] Hence, when contesting elections, notwithstanding scrutinising the past records of the party's prospective candidates for potential embarrassments, the party's message should be kept simple and presented in a non-threatening form – 'in the least controversial way possible'. Yet Griffin quickly reassured his readers that this exercise would be purely cosmetic – merely a case of remarketing the same product. Thus the party would not sell-out on its ultimate revolutionary objectives; in other words there would be no surrendering of core ideology. The point that needs to be made is that for Griffin, it all boils down to political expediency and short-term tactics:

> Politics is always the art of the possible, so we must judge every policy by one simple criterion: Is it realistically possible that a decisive proportion of the British people will support it? If not, then to scale down our **short-term** ambitions to a point at which the answer becomes 'yes' is not a sell-out, **but the only possible step closer to our eventual goal**.[7]

It is therefore hard to escape the conclusion that, as far as Griffin was concerned, fascism would always remain the party's ultimate objective: 'Of course, we must teach the truth to the hardcore', but 'when it comes to influencing the public, forget about racial differences, genetics, Zionism, historical revisionism and so on', Griffin insisted.[8] Instead of presenting the party as a revolutionary alternative to the system, 'we must at all times present them (the electorate) with an image of moderate reasonableness'.[9]

On this point, Griffin merely followed another's lead. Mark Deavin, in a *Spearhead* article the previous year, had already called on the British National Party to adopt a 'flexible communication strategy', which in form was pretty much indistinguishable to that of the National Front in France. One reason why the FN had cultivated a 'moderate and less abrasive image', Deavin explained, was through its use of non-threatening political discourse that 'produces the *least amount of resistance* in ordinary French people'.[10] By implementing this strategy, first pioneered by the theoreticians of the French *Nouvelle Droite* in the 1970s[11] and eagerly pursued by Le Pen's past deputy and former chief strategist, Bruno Mégret, the FN had carefully avoided using racist language and had instead taken on terms such as 'racism', more often than not used to stigmatise the far right, turned them on their head – 'anti-white racism' – and used them against their opponents.[12] Therefore, in its struggle for political acceptability, Deavin recommended that the British National Party should take a leaf out of the FN's book and restyle its political language accordingly. This meant that the discourse of the old BNP should henceforth be dropped: 'In everything we say and do, through our total image', Deavin concluded, 'we must present ourselves nationally as the party of *Democracy* against Plutocracy, of *Freedom* against Euro-tyranny, of *Security* against Fear, and of *Identity* against Multi-culturalism'.[13]

A year later, Griffin simply reproduced what Deavin (who by this stage had severed his links with the BNP) had to say. The party, Griffin urged, should moderate its language and communicate its propaganda through these very same words: freedom (which covers opposition to the European Union and petty bureaucracy); democracy ('whereby the wishes of the majority of the people prevail on issues such as immigration and capital punishment'); security (from crime and from the 'chronic insecurity produced by globalism'); and identity (a term that 'raises all the issues connected with mass immigration' but not 'the negative Pavlovian conditioning which decades of brainwashing have associated with the word "race"'). All four of these terms – he took the credit for identifying them in 1998 – Griffin described as 'idealistic, unobjectionable, motherhood and apple pie concepts'.[14] What Griffin therefore urged was a rejection of the verbal extremism of the past (recall in the previous chapter the boast by Richard Edmonds that the BNP was 100 per cent racist) and a remodelling of the BNP's political style (if not its core ideology) on national populism. Hence, the claim to represent the mass of ordinary people, the opposition to bureaucracy, the demand for law and order, hostility to immigration and the call for the nation's cultural inheritance to be protected – all staple features of the style of contemporary national-populist parties.[15]

What is more, as Deavin had earlier advised, Griffin insisted that the party should challenge the terminology that all too often is used against it. 'It's time to use the weight of "democracy"'s own myths and expectations against it by side-stepping and using verbal judo techniques', Griffin declared.[16] Hence in May 1999, the back page of *Spearhead* affirmed that the BNP 'is *not* a racist party' and called on its readers to organise 'a political response to anti-white racism'.[17] As for fascism, Griffin's response was to use this term against those who 'hold the multi-racial state in such exalted worship', particularly those who seek to destroy the BNP's freedom of speech: 'the people who deny us the right-to-reply and to broadcasting time', those 'who organise frenzied mobs to try to: attack our election candidates, close down our meetings, and march on our premises with the stated intention of tearing them down brick-by-brick', those 'who order their political police to tap our phones, steal our computers and use *agents provocateurs* to sow dissension in our ranks'. Griffin asks: 'Are these tactics democratic? No. What are they? By any genuine understanding of the term they are, quite simply, **fascist** – And these people who employ such tactics are fascists'.[18] In reality, Griffin contends, it is the British National Party that is the 'democracy' party – it alone represents the true 'silent majority': 'Not only are we not 'anti-democratic'; but we are in reality the only democrats. We are the only people who say what countless millions think.'[19]

In 1998 the BNP had committed itself to contesting the European elections. As the party's new Director of Publicity, Griffin now had the political opportunity to put a policy and identity makeover to the test. These elections would take place the following year on the basis of Proportional Representation (PR), a type of electoral system common on the continent but hitherto denied to right-wing extremists in Britain. PR is typically said to favour minor parties and it was one reason why party hardliners had maintained that a pure electoral strategy was easier on the continent and therefore remained rather lukewarm to electoral politics. In order to qualify for free broadcasting time in England and Scotland, the BNP had to field a full slate of candidates – 71 in England and 8 in Scotland. This would incur obvious costs, £50,000 on deposits alone, but nonetheless Griffin saw the European elections as the essential first step in making the party acceptable to the voters of 'Middle England'. To party organisers, however, as in 1997, recruitment was made top priority.[20]

Significantly, Griffin drew up the strategy for the campaign. The ranks of disaffected Tories who had deserted the Conservatives in 1997 for the UK Independence Party and James Goldsmith's Referendum Party were his primary target. With them in mind, Griffin drafted the party's European election manifesto – *Freedom for Britain and the British*. In comparison with previous manifestos, invariably the work of John Tyndall, the tone was markedly different. References to 'revolutionary' change or British 'rebirth' had disappeared. We have copious occasions when the far more accommodating word 'freedom' was used instead: it appeared in every single sub-title. A mere fleeting reference was made to the party's policy of repatriating non-whites. In any case, following Griffin's recommendations, the BNP no longer insisted that the repatriation of non-whites should be compulsory.[21] All of this was clearly a bid to widen the party's base of campaigning beyond the straightjacket of 'race'. This continued a strategic shift that Griffin had first piloted in

1998 when the party had branched out to run anti-paedophile and pro-farming campaigns in a number of different localities.[22]

Furthermore, Griffin was assigned the task of designing the party's full-colour election leaflet, which as a consequence of standing more than 25 candidates, the Royal Mail posted out free of charge. The verso of this 'Save Our Sterling' election address saw the party's opposition to the European Union articulated under the four sub-headings of 'freedom', 'security', 'identity' and 'democracy'. On the front, mean-while, a 'voter-friendly' photograph of former National Democrat activists, Steve and Sharron Edwards, along with their three young chil-dren, occupied centre-stage.[23] The inclusion of a young family on the party's election leaflet, which was delivered to millions of homes across the country, had been a popular choice amongst leading party activists.[24] As for its TV broadcast, this was innocuous too. It featured both Tyndall and Griffin, and it was interspersed with a selection of inoffensive 'sound-bites' from 'ordinary' party members – a mother (Sharron Edwards), a farmer (Terry Cavill, South Wales Organiser), a van driver (Chris Jackson, North West Organiser), a pensioner (Griffin's mother) and a computer communications consultant (Simon Darby, the former National Democrat activist).[25]

In contesting the 1999 European elections, Griffin's prescription for respectability was therefore given its first trial run. Yet during the middle of the election campaign, cold water was thrown all over the party's attempt to repackage itself. On 25 May 1999, four days after the party's TV broadcast aired, the association with violent neo-Nazism reemerged when the *Mirror* newspaper exposed a link between the London nail bomber David Copeland and BNP leader, John Tyndall. In April 1999, Copeland had planted bombs in Brixton, Brick Lane and Soho, and the bomb that had exploded in the Admiral Duncan, a gay pub in Soho, had resulted in three deaths.[26] It turned out that Copeland had been active with the British National Party for a short period following the 1997 general election and had been photographed alongside Tyndall in Stratford, East London. The reproduction of this photograph on the front page of the *Mirror* almost certainly helped the public see through the mask of respectability that the BNP had donned.

Moreover, the fact that the party also found itself crowded out by the more mainstream UK Independence Party and the Euro-scepticism of the Conservative Party resulted, not surprisingly, in an ill-fated cam-paign. When it came to it, the party's share of the vote amounted to a pitiful 1 per cent, even less than its 1997 general election result. It seems that as much as £100,000 was wasted on contesting this election – around one pound for every one vote.[27] One activist complained that 'It would have been more cost effective if we had given £250 to every new member recruited during the campaign.'[28] If these figures are correct, the party probably recruited not more than 400 new members in the wake of its European election campaign. Tyndall's claim that as a result of the 'huge public interest' that its Euro-election campaign generated the party 'is now stronger than it has ever been and bids to grow even more'[29] was clear wishful thinking. In September 1999, during the BNP leadership contest, party membership still stood at a paltry 1,353.[30]

Yet to some extent, the picture painted by these European election results is misleading. Admittedly, in local elections in May 1999, several party candidates had actually polled relatively well. On closer inspection, the party's best results were obtained in Sandwell in the West Midlands, not a rural shire but a deprived urban district in the heart of the Black Country. Here, in Tipton Green and Great Bridge, Stephen and Sharron Edwards had polled 17.17 per cent and 12.94 per cent of the vote respectively.[31] The key to their success had been local community campaigning, modelled as Steve Edwards said, on the experience of local Liberal Democrats. Whilst still activists in the far-right National Democrats, this husband and wife team had distributed over 30,000 leaflets in a 12-month period, campaigning on local issues such as policing, housing, education, speed limits and environmental concerns. 'Within months', Steve Edwards recalls, 'three large residents associations who had rejected the main parties came to us for help'. The result was that 'Our local helpline was "red hot". My wife Sharron, our secretary, was working flat-out liaising with Sandwell Council on behalf of local residents.'[32] Evidently, when local activists targeted their efforts at rendering a service to people in their own community, the party could nurture legitimacy. As in Millwall, most progress was made when the party established contact with local residents and concentrated its efforts on local campaigning and target wards. For Eddy Butler, therefore, the lesson was obvious: avoid 'jumping straight into the big elections' because by doing so, you will miss out on the intervening stages.[33]

Professionalism

We now arrive at 'professionalism' – the second of Griffin's requirements (though by forcing a leadership contest on the eve of a

European election campaign, Griffin was not necessarily a practitioner of what he preached). A will to win was not enough, Griffin said, the party will never progress 'by continuing at our present 'adequate' level – monthly magazine, monthly paper, a range of A5 leaflets'.[34] The party had to equip itself with 'power-winning' machinery and the first stage, Griffin maintained, was to infuse a range of preexisting initiatives with fresh blood.

One such initiative was the party's Media Monitoring Unit, launched in 1998. Its aim was to force the media (typically the local media) to retract from labelling the party as 'fascist' or 'Nazi'. In reality, however, it proved a relatively insignificant operation not least because this 'unit' was more or less run single-handedly.[35] The party's embryonic training programme was another existing project that Griffin wanted to see brought to maturity. Aside from improving the quality of grassroots activists beyond recognition, Griffin hoped that this initiative would deliver a layer of two-dozen or so 'middle-managers' that could push the party's 'modernisation' effort forward. On this point, Griffin once more took inspiration from the French National Front, which boasts a National Training Institute for its party activists. Also singled out for an upgrade was the party's website. As I have pointed out elsewhere, Michael Newland launched this in the autumn of 1995, but it lacked sophistication.[36] For Griffin, the Internet offered an unparalleled opportunity. Not only could the BNP use this medium to bypass the mainstream media and its (Jewish) 'gate-keepers', but it could also create a sense of belonging amongst party members particularly since the party had abandoned more traditional forms of 'collective' street activity in the mid-1990s, such as set-piece rallies and marches.[37]

The Internet, then, would assist with both the recruitment and retention of party members. For sure, as we have seen, membership turnover had been a perennial problem for the British far right. More recently, over the period 1996–99, party members had been dropping-out at a rate of 20 per cent.[38] If the party is going to finally put the 'plug in the metaphorical nationalist membership bath', members need to feel valued, Griffin stressed: 'The new recruit must be made welcome, kept informed and made to feel an important part of his or her party.'[39] Thus Griffin also pointed to the importance of regular members' bulletins and good quality membership cards. He recalled how, as a teenager in 1975, he had almost failed to renew his subscription to the National Front because the previous year he had been so disappointed with the modest return on his subscription – a card and two bulletins. Another way to make members feel more involved,

Griffin suggested, was to undertake a regular 'skills audit' of the party membership. And in so doing, the full talents of the party membership could be harnessed and its potential for growth maximised.

As for party structure, decentralisation was proposed, but this idea was not new to Griffin. When radicalising the National Front in the 1980s, the principle of decentralisation featured highly.[40] Each section of the BNP should have its own dedicated contact number for queries and complaints, Griffin suggested; he even proposed a party ombudsman to whom party members could turn if their complaints were left unsatisfied. A further item on his list was a leadership 'Think-Tank', an advisory council that would meet every few months. This would offer new proposals and advice to the party Chairman although Griffin would have no return to NF-style 'rule by committee'. Hence, the Chairman would retain the constitutional right to ignore its advice. As a matter of urgency, with Tyndall still effectively holding the 'purse-strings', Griffin also implored the party to appoint a national treasurer and to organise a fund-raising team. If the party is to 'reach into new areas and with new techniques', it clearly required money and all of this made prudent financial management vital.[41]

A final area for development, which again took its cue from the French National Front, was Griffin's plan to create a series of satellite organisations. What Griffin had in mind here was in fact a 'counter-society' or 'counter-culture' formed from a series of semi-autonomous party associations or 'circles' that would extend the party's influence amongst various segments of the population. A whole series of such 'circles' had been formed by the National Front in France, amongst businessman, farmers, women, war veterans and so on.[42] Likewise, Griffin's idea was to form an analogous network of party-linked operations. Their intended function: to 'build bridges' with different social groups and so make the party more 'approachable'.

The development of such a network had already been set in motion in 1998 when Griffin had launched 'Land and People', a farming-cum-environmental circle that was intended to 'provide a "halfway house" for members of the public who aren't quite ready to commit themselves to joining the BNP proper'.[43] However, its achievements proved modest – *Searchlight* reported that its coordinator had abandoned it altogether in 2000 after becoming disillusioned with its lack of success.[44] Of greater significance was the establishment of a support group amongst British expatriates based in Falls Church, Virginia, in the United States. Mark Cotterill, who between 1978 and 1992 was the National Front's south-west organiser, was the 'Griffinite' who set up the American Friends of the BNP (AFBNP) in January 1999. This could not be so casually dismissed. Some observers have suggested that the AFBNP contributed significant funds to the party's European election effort.[45]

In the meantime, on British soil, West Midlands branch secretary, Sharron Edwards fronted 'Renaissance' – the party's new 'family circle'. This group organised a 'family fun day' in the West Midlands in July 1999 aimed at promoting the British National Party as a respectable organisation that warmly welcomed ordinary families rather than the 'street gang' of old. When driving home from this social event 'with the children asleep in the back of the car', Griffin claims to have had 'a glimpse of the British National Party of the future'. What he had seen on this day was 'unsmearable, positive, attractive – and successful'.[46] Yet if truth be told, it was the *Front National* having an effect on Griffin yet again. In 1998 he had visited the French National Front's *Fête Bleu, Blanc, Rouge*, a social event first held in September 1981 as a '*contre-fête*' to the more popular festival organised by the Communist Party daily, *L'Humanité*. Griffin wanted to imitate it and therefore proposed building on the BNP Family Day by staging a weekend 'Red, White and Blue' festival the following year. And with video and Internet coverage of such an event, Griffin thought, more could be done for 'normalising' the BNP than a 'thousand marches or tub thumping rallies' could ever do.[47]

Slinging mud and electing the leader

With the blueprint for the party's future having been laid out, Griffin now had to negotiate the leadership election itself. Unlike Tyndall, however, he did not wait until after the European election campaign before he made his start. Whilst Tyndall came across as complacent, Griffin was prepared to steal a march on his opponent. During the European election campaign, in a bid to drum up support, Griffin toured the branches. Campaign leaflets and a cassette tape were used to boost Griffin's campaign,[48] while Tony Lecomber, the BNP's north and east London regional organiser, lobbied on Griffin's behalf in the capital.[49] Meanwhile, *British Nationalist* and a number of local bulletins and newsletters voiced their approval of Griffin's candidature.[50]

Everywhere, Griffin was supported by *Patriot* magazine. Intent on seizing the occasion, its summer issue saw Griffin's promotion drive in full swing. His photograph not only featured on its front cover (along with the caption 'New Millennium New Leader'), but on seven other occasions inside the magazine as well. A further helping hand from *Patriot* came with the publication of *Moving On, Moving Up*, Griffin's sleek election brochure. This was posted out to party members in September, and in it Griffin's team claimed that he had already won the backing of 85 per cent of party organisers and 80 per cent of party activists.[51] The brochure featured a series of ringing endorsements from leading figures in the party – Tony Lecomber, Michael Newland, Derek Beackon and Mark Cotterill amongst others. But for Tyndall loyalist, John Morse, this was 'the standard advertiser's trick of promoting a product by claiming that everybody is buying it'.[52]

Whilst the brochure remained respectful to Tyndall as the party's 'elder statesman', the various contributors went into raptures over Griffin – his eagerness to bring fresh ideas to the party; his youth (aged 40 as opposed to Tyndall's 65 years); his intellectual qualities (a Cambridge graduate rather than the current office-holder who had left Beckingham and Penge Grammar School with a modest three O-levels); and the fact that Griffin's image was not tainted by a series of highly compromising photographs. Bruce Crowd, the party's south-west regional organiser, drew attention to this fact in particular when asking: 'How many members and voters have been lost over the years by photographs of JT in his neo-nazi uniform?' This exasperated Crowd, 'I am sick and tired of trying to explain the unexplainable and excuse the inexcusable to new members, enquirers and people on the doorstep.'[53] As a further reminder, a picture of Tyndall, aged 28, dressed in his Spearhead paramilitary uniform was juxtaposed with a photograph of a smartly dressed Nick Griffin on a National Front demonstration, aged 22.

The fact of the matter, Griffin said, is that the public 'will never support a party which has about it anything which gives credibility to the inevitable media smear of "Nazi"'. For Griffin, 'such irresponsible and impractical extremism remains the political kiss of death as far as 98 per cent of people are concerned'.[54] But these comments smacked of sheer hypocrisy. Here was a former 'Strasserite Nazi' and one-time 'pedlar of the Mr. Gaddafi's "Green Book"',[55] attacking Tyndall for having an 'extremist past'. It is no wonder that, as soon as the Euro-election campaign had ended, Tyndall hit back.

After failing to persuade Griffin to call off his challenge, Griffin was sacked as editor of *Spearhead* in July 1999. Tyndall along with staunch supporter John Morse then availed themselves of numerous pages in *Spearhead* in order to badmouth their opponent. In the first place, by encouraging internal division, Griffin was berated for having desta-

bilised the party and for having undermined its post-election recruitment efforts. This, for Tyndall, had demonstrated a negligent disregard
for the interests of the party. Attention was also drawn to the incon-
sistencies in Griffin's political past whilst Griffin's attempts to rewrite
his political career in *Patriot* were ridiculed. As we have seen, Griffin
stressed the need for careful financial management, but with the intention of damaging his credibility on this issue, Tyndall exposed the facts
about Griffin's bankruptcy: in 1994 Griffin had been declared bankrupt
at Welshpool and Newtown County Court in mid-Wales with debts of
£70,000 resulting from a failed business venture. Tyndall also revisited
the embarrassing episode of the *Cook Report* in 1997 and the claim on
the 'sole copyright' of 'every useful BNP innovation in recent times'
that Griffin had staked was laughed at. There was even the suggestion
that Griffin's challenge was part of a state conspiracy to wreck the
party. At this point, reference was made to a report in the *Daily Express*
earlier in the year that alleged that Scotland Yard and MI5 were plan-
ning a covert operation to break up far-right groups such as the British
National Party.[56] Yet potentially the most damaging revelations came
from outside the party. In early September, Martin Webster in a four-
page magazine, *Loose Cannon*, claimed that he and Griffin had started a
four-year homosexual relationship in 1976 that had continued
throughout Griffin's time at Cambridge – a story given credibility by
Searchlight magazine. Of course Griffin, who dismissed it as a sad
attempt by Webster to settle old scores, denied the story.[57]

If Tyndall thought that all this mud-slinging would prompt party
members to reconsider their positions and see off the challenge of Nick
Griffin, he was sadly mistaken. Tyndall committed two serious blund-
ers, and in so doing his anti-Griffin offensive badly misfired. First of all,
when Lecomber and Newland had questioned Tyndall why he had
never produced a set of audited accounts in the party's history, Tyndall
informed a gathering of party members in the West Midlands that he
had burnt them in order to protect the identity of the party's donors.
Under Tyndall, the offices of Chairman and Treasurer had been combined in one man (though constitutionally, they were supposed to be
kept separate). This ensured that no-one could ruin the organisation
through financial recklessness, but there was little in the way of trans-
parency. One party member from Northumbria had left Tyndall a substantial legacy in 1991 – a property worth £100,000 of which the rental
income was £10,000 a year. Though it was supposed to benefit the
party, Lecomber suspected that it had become Tyndall's personal property.[58] Secondly, in a leaked letter, Tyndall had promised reprisals

against Griffin's supporters should Griffin's leadership challenge fail. Griffin, meanwhile, promised no recriminations and therefore could pose as the 'unity' candidate.[59]

At its root, however, Tyndall's real problem was that he offered very little to capture the imagination of the party's rank-and-file. To put it bluntly, they had grown weary of him. Since Tyndall had largely run the BNP as his own personal fiefdom, too much depended on one man. He might have claimed that his record as head of the party during the 1990s was 'one of considerable *success*',[60] but the reality, aside from one local council by-election victory in 1993, was a track record of dismal failure. For many, if Tyndall were elected, the long-term aim of turning the British National Party into a major political force would remain as remote as ever. Tyndall's record effectively sealed his fate. Even dragging the leadership contest into the gutter failed to rescue it. Not surprisingly, therefore, despite some damaging revelations, Griffin retained the backing of the party's leading regional organisers. Support remained solid in the West Midlands and parts of the east Midlands, north and east London, the north-east, south-west, Scotland and Wales.[61] And so, following the close of ballot on 27 September, there were no surprises when Griffin easily outpolled Tyndall and captured 62 per cent of the vote. The British National Party would therefore go into the new millennium with a new leader. However, as the October 1999 members' bulletin stressed, though the party leader may have changed, as always, the cause (that is to say, racial nationalism) would remain the same.[62]

Griffin takes charge

Naturally, coming so far behind Griffin was a crushing blow for Tyndall. Yet he accepted defeat with equanimity and the transfer of power occurred in an orderly fashion. 'I have no plans to launch any "new party"', Tyndall declared, but he didn't want to be pensioned off either.[63] He would remain a party member and *Spearhead* would continue to support the British National Party. As for Tyndall's most loyal supporters – Richard Edmonds (national organiser) and John Morse (mid-south organiser) – they also followed Tyndall's lead and resigned their party posts. Meanwhile, the election of Nick Griffin brought with it the promotion of key 'modernisers' to a string of new party offices. Tony Lecomber was made Director of Group Development whilst Michael Newland, an accountant by profession, was appointed National Treasurer. The Advisory Council was also established comprised of the National Chairman and his deputy (Sharron Edwards), the party's national officers (Treasurer, Administration, Information Technology, Group Development, Media Monitoring, Stewarding) as well as all the regional organisers from the party's main regions (West and East Midlands, North-West England, Yorkshire, Scotland and Northern Ireland). Moreover, as Griffin promised, the party's administration was swiftly decentralised. A series of regional 'think-tank' meetings also took place in the weeks that followed. These meetings were sold to party members as a consultation process but they were almost certainly used by Griffin as a means of tightening his hold over the party.

Needless to say, Griffin had to see to it that Tyndall no longer represented a threat. Consequently, during the course of the next few months, Griffin progressively fenced him in. From when *Spearhead* had first launched, over the winter of 1964–65, it had taken pride of place on Britain's far right as Tyndall's mouthpiece. Thus, as Griffin saw it, if distribution of this magazine could be curtailed, Tyndall's influence would surely wane. Therefore, sample copies of *Spearhead* were no longer included in the information packs that were sent out to those people who enquired about the party. In the past, Tyndall's main source of new subscriptions for his magazine had come via this route. *Spearhead* was also dropped from the party's revamped website and, furthermore, branches were instructed to give priority to selling the party's new magazine – *Identity*. This was unveiled at the start of the new millennium and numerous party branches cancelled their standing orders to *Spearhead* as a result. But Tyndall was determined to fight back. He formed 'Friends of *Spearhead*', a new support group independent of the party, and in order to ensure the magazine's survival members were asked to donate £10 a month.[64] However, with sales of his magazine on the decline and with his erstwhile supporters no longer in positions of responsibility, Tyndall's prospects for a political comeback looked thin. Instead he had to console himself with sniping at Griffin from the sidelines.[65]

True to his original intentions, Griffin quickly devoted his energy to repackaging the party's hard-line message in terms that ordinary voters would find comfortable. As part of this project, the party's new magazine, *Identity*, first appeared as a bi-monthly in January 2000. According to its editorial, the name 'Identity' was chosen to reflect the 'new, modernist nationalism to which the British National Party is now firmly committed', in other words, a type of non-threatening nationalism where the party's primary purpose becomes 'the preservation of the identity of the traditional inhabitants and cultures of Britain'. The far more contentious term 'race' would henceforth disappear: 'Our demand to preserve that identity threatens no one; it raises no alarming or debatable questions of superiority or inferiority.'[66] Though this was presented as Griffin's latest serving of ingenuity, it was surely no coincidence that the title of the French National Front's bi-monthly, first launched in April 1989, was also *Identité*.

In order to further accommodate itself to the need for greater public acceptance, the title of the party's newspaper was also changed from *British Nationalist* to *The Voice of Freedom*. Unlike its earlier incarnation, it was taken to newsprint in order to look like a professional, mass distribution newspaper. Five or six years earlier, Tony Lecomber and Eddy Butler had first proposed this idea to the party Chairman but it had not been acted upon by Tyndall, who thought that since the BNP was such a reviled party he would not be able to find any printers that would be prepared to handle its newspaper.[67]

Having given its media a face-lift, it was not long before the BNP had to contend with a fresh round of electoral contests. Priority was given to the London mayoral elections, which had been dominating the headlines following the decision by the maverick Labour MP 'Red' Ken Livingstone to stand as an independent. With mayoral candidates entitled to free postal delivery of their election addresses, and since 'the capital gets you noticed politically so it was a good idea for the party to stand',[68] the British National Party threw its hat into the ring. One does not need to look hard for the reasons why Griffin approached Michael Newland to stand as the party's candidate for mayor.[69] Newland was not only a life-long Londoner, but more importantly, he was an articulate professional who unusually for a British National Party activist had a squeaky clean image.[70]

In return for £20,000 (the cost of Newland's nomination as well as the cost of his election address in the official election booklet), five million electors in London received a copy of the party's election address. Thus, as Tony Lecomber points out, in many cases the party 'reached areas that hadn't seen nationalist, let alone BNP literature for more than twenty years'.[71] This was obviously a bonus for the BNP – given its meagre resources, it would have had difficulty covering all 14 constituencies with a traditional door-to-door leafleting campaign. Whilst the official election booklet formed the centrepiece of its campaign, the party also distributed 120,000 'calling cards', which were left on parked cars, and 'loud-speaker' vans toured each London borough.

As for the election address itself, this was co-written by Newland and Griffin.[72] In the official election booklet, it stretched over two pages and its very inclusion, next to the election addresses of the main-stream candidates, almost certainly brought the party a degree of respectability. On its first page, Newland and Griffin decided to focus on crime, public transport, opposition to 'multicultural indoctrination' in schools, 'equal rights', that is to say opposition to 'positive discrimi-nation', and finally the promotion of family values. Meanwhile, on the second page, a sizeable portion was devoted to 'bogus' asylum-seekers – an issue that, as we shall see, was becoming more overtly politicised as the mainstream parties responded to a wave of sensationalist reporting in the tabloids. If the results of one polling organisation are to be believed, 14 per cent of voters had identified asylum-seekers as their chief concern in the lead-up to polling day.[73] Indeed, in the very first issue of *Identity*, the BNP promised to concentrate on this issue in the months ahead. Yet throughout, the BNP remained guarded: 'We are not opposed to individual immigrants', it claimed. 'What we oppose is the destruction of the traditional identity of the British people in our own homeland'. This, it maintained, was 'not a matter of 'racism' or 'hate' against other peoples'. In truth, the party's racism was merely being repackaged. Pseudo-democratic language, whereby the wishes of the majority should prevail, now became the order of the day: 'We ask for our culture, freedoms and our traditions to be respected, and for the majority to have the right to run our country as they wish.'[74]

Unlike its 1999 European election campaign, the party did not come in for any damaging revelations this time around. Unable to find any dirt on Newland, the media largely fell silent. Aside from the *Evening Standard* putting his biographical details on its website and running an online poll, the press almost entirely blanked Newland's campaign. In the event, Newland polled 33,569 first-preference votes and 45,337 second-preference votes, suggesting that of the 1.75 million who voted, close to 80,000 Londoners would have supported a BNP mayor. This worked out at over 5 per cent across London, whilst the figure in East London approached 9 per cent (or possibly as much as 13 per cent of the white vote). Nor should we forget that at the same time, in elections to the Greater London Assembly, the BNP also presented a party list of six candidates. This list polled 47,670 votes or 2.87 per cent, thereby meeting the target of 2.5 per cent that was required to retain the party's £5,000 deposit. In the June 1999 European elections, the BNP had taken a little under 18,000 votes from Londoners. Within 11 months, albeit on a higher turnout, its support had increased significantly.[75]

In point of fact, this upturn in electoral fortunes found resonance in isolated pockets elsewhere. Outside London, on 4 May 2000, there were elections to more than 3,000 local council seats. The BNP targeted just 16 local council wards, with the West Midlands being the region where the party concentrated most of its efforts. Here, the party's average vote increased from 6.8 per cent to 10.8 per cent. Not surprisingly, the best score was obtained in Sandwell's Tipton Green ward where the BNP had established its 'Helping Hand' team, assisting local people with neighbourhood concerns. Steve Edwards, who presented himself as respectable, traditional family-man fought a tireless campaign on local issues – crime, housing, litter, opposition to 'positive discrimination' measures and so on. His share of the vote increased from 17.2 per cent in 1999 to 23.7 per cent. Another encouraging performance was recorded in Dudley's Castle and Priory ward where Simon Darby doubled his vote from 8.1 per cent to 16.1 per cent. Meanwhile, in Burnley, the party established itself on the local political landscape for the first time. As late as May 1999, there had been no local BNP organisation in Burnley – in fact, there had only been two paid up members in the town. Following a leaflet drive, and a subsequent meeting which attracted some 20 supporters, Simon Bennett along with Steve Smith founded the Burnley branch in August 1999. Smith recalls:

> In the early days we picked a ward, Fulledge Ward near Turf Moor, and leafleted it three times in nine months. Simon then stood as BNP candidate in Fulledge in May 2000 and polled 20% of the vote. That result set us on our way and we haven't looked back since.[76]

Elsewhere, one candidate was also returned unopposed. John Haycock, who had joined the party in 1995, became a parish councillor for Bromyard and Winslow in Herefordshire. He was the first BNP councillor for over six years.[77] However, he failed to attend any council meetings for six months and was later disqualified.[78]

Soon after, in July 2000 the party notched up another notable electoral gain. At a local council by-election in Bexley, a district of Kent, the party's candidate Colin Smith (south-east London regional organiser) polled 26.2 per cent of the vote in the North End ward. Smith, a former British Movement skinhead in his teens, ran an energetic campaign. His canvassers, at all times immaculately dressed, leafleted the ward at least three times a week in the run-up to polling day. Whilst local community issues did feature, the focus of his campaign was almost exclusively on the asylum-seeker issue. According to the BNP, the local Tories were guilty of hypocrisy. Although local Tories campaigned for a tougher approach, the BNP claimed that the Conservative-controlled council was simultaneously intent on housing asylum-seekers in the poorest and most deprived parts of the borough (such as the North End ward) rather than traditional middle-class Tory areas such as Sidcup and Old Bexley. As it turned out, Smith outpolled the Tory candidate by 42 votes.[79]

By the look of things, under the guise of the asylum-seeker issue, the ghost of Enoch Powell was returning to haunt mainstream political life. During the 1970s Powellism had opened up legitimate political space for the National Front, but when Margaret Thatcher had made a bid for the racist constituency in the late 1970s this space had been reoccupied by the Tories. Thereafter, the 'race' issue was removed from the arena of national political debate even if by means of successive pieces of restrictive legislation, the Conservatives were still generally seen as the toughest of the mainstream parties on the 'race' issue. Instead of challenging the Tories, however, the Labour Party merely shadowed them. In consequence, 'race' was not subject to party competition. Thus, notwithstanding rhetorical outbursts from lone Tory MPs over the years (such as Norman Tebbit, Winston Churchill and Nicholas Budgen) along with various instances where the grassroots of mainstream political parties made a play for the racist vote at the local level (as in Tower Hamlets), 'race' as an issue remained beyond the pale. This was the case down to the spring of 2000 until the Conservative Party leader William Hague re-politicised the 'race' issue by turning asylum into a central plank of the Tories' May local election platform.

Every so often, this 'conspiracy of silence' amongst Britain's political elite drew scathing comment from the tabloid press. For instance, the *Mail* rushed to the defence of Tory MP Winston Churchill for having had the 'courage' to break the 'race taboo' when, in a speech he had given in Bolton in May 1993, a stand against the 'relentless flow' of Muslims had been taken.[80] Yet, invariably, frontbench Tories would distance themselves from such outbursts, just as Edward Heath had isolated Enoch Powell. Nonetheless, in order to force them on the political agenda, parts of the right-wing press would still try to stoke up the contentious issues of 'race' and immigration. For instance, in the lead-up to the 1992 general election, the *Daily Mail* and the *Sun* both campaigned against 'bogus' asylum-seekers and raised the spectre of a 'flood of bogus refugees' should Labour be elected.[81] And, whilst 'race' may not have been overtly politicised during the 1997 general election campaign, the *Daily Mail* in particular had stigmatised migrants as 'bogus', 'scroungers' and 'cheats'.[82] All the same, it was towards the end of the 1990s before the rate of tabloid coverage on the asylum issue grew appreciably. And on this occasion, mainstream politicians joined in the cry of the tabloid scaremongers.

But what brought about the national media's growing obsession with this issue? One obvious factor was the year-on-year increase in the number of asylum applications. In 1996 there had been 29,000 asylum claims but by 1999 this figure had increased to 71,000.[83] Nonetheless, the overall quantity of asylum applications still remained relatively low, with Britain placed eighth amongst European countries in terms of asylum-seekers per head of population.[84] A second factor was provincial press coverage, particularly in places such as Dover where local newspapers had become increasingly frenzied in their attacks on asylum-seekers. One editorial from the *Dover Express* (1 October 1998) had described asylum-seekers in terms of 'human sewage'. Indeed, when analysing 161 local newspaper reports collected over the course of October and November 1999, the Audit Commission found that in only 6 per cent of the cases did local journalists report on the positive contribution made by asylum-seekers.[85] More often than not, the national press followed the provincial lead, and as the tabloid dailies competed with one another for readers, so by the spring of 2000 the headlines had become ever more intemperate and sensationalist: 'Time to kick the scroungers out' (the *Sun*, 15 March 2000); 'Get out Scum!' (*Daily Star*, 4 April 2000) and 'Hello Mr Sponger...Need any Benefits (*Daily Star*, 27 April 2000).

On 15 March 2000, the editor of the *Sun* had called a pusillanimous William Hague to account for having failed to launch a campaign 'against beggars and fake asylum-seekers'. A month later, in a speech to the Social Market Foundation, William Hague answered his critics. Common cause was now made with the tabloids; all new asylum-seekers should be placed in secure units, he declared, and he further recommended the creation of a new agency that would seek to eject from Britain all rejected asylum applicants. As he toured the shires and a number of seaside constituencies in order to urge local Tory candidates to maximise political capital out of the asylum issue, Hague claimed that asylum-seekers were costing the British taxpayer £180 million and that old-age pensioners were now receiving less money than refugees. For Conservative strategists, as they succumbed to the temptations of electoral expediency, this move made sense. Indeed,

Daily Telegraph journalist, Janet Daley, saw 'race' and immigration as the 'big idea' through which Hague could make a serious challenge to Labour at the next general election. Seen from this angle, with the Keynesian economic consensus having already been destroyed by Thatcher, William Hague's opening gambit formed part of a wider attack on the prevailing left-liberal social consensus. Some radical critics have even detected a conspiracy by the right-wing press: according to this perspective, the right-wing tabloids deliberately orchestrated Hague's demonising of asylum-seekers in order to undermine the results of the Macpherson Inquiry.[86]

Whatever the truth may be, the way Labour Cabinet Ministers reacted – by stressing how 'tough' they were on immigration and by making repeated references to 'bogus' asylum-seekers – made sure that tabloid-style anti-asylum rhetoric went unchallenged. The screen through which the public viewed asylum-seekers was therefore shaped according to how the tabloids had originally framed this issue. And so, instead of countering xenophobia, hostile attitudes towards asylum-seekers became more socially acceptable. This, in turn, threatened to set off latent prejudices towards other ethnic minorities. Bill Morris, general secretary of the Transport and General Workers' Union, thus attacked the Home Office for having 'given life to the racists'.[87] With the mainstream parties trying to outdo one another on the asylum battleground, the British National Party, with its language of 'moderation', now started to manoeuvre itself into position. This was a defining moment, as Nick Griffin remarked to one *Guardian* journalist in the May of 2000: 'The asylum seeker issue has been great for us...It's been quite fun to watch government ministers and the Tories play the race card in far cruder terms that we would ever use. This issue legitimises us.'[88] Griffin was right. At this instant, legitimate political space was being created for his party at a time when, through its programme of modernisation, the BNP had already taken steps (albeit cosmetically) to narrow the distance between itself and the generally accepted norms of the liberal-democratic society.

Modernisation de-railed?

Yet inside a matter of weeks, just as it was gearing itself up to take full advantage of this more favourable political climate, Griffin's modernisation programme looked certain to hit the buffers. At a meeting of the party's new Advisory Council held on 26 August 2000, Michael Newland had his membership suspended for three months whilst

Deputy Chairman Sharron Edwards and her husband Steve Edwards were expelled from the party altogether. For all his talk of professionalism and unity, Griffin was now at loggerheads with a clutch of influential party activists. Within a year of taking over the leadership of the party, Nick Griffin's British National Party gave the impression of being ready to implode.

The suspension of Newland and the expulsion of the Edwards's had ostensibly occurred as a consequence of a number of disciplinary offences. Newland had supposedly revealed details of the party's financial affairs to non-Advisory Council members and had spread rumours that Griffin had been drawing from party funds in order to finance an extension to his family home. Meanwhile, the Edwards's were charged with more serious offences: circulating a petition implying financial irregularities on the part of the leadership, calling both an unofficial Advisory Council meeting and Organisers' meeting and stealing the party's membership list. For Griffin, this was an attempt by a faction of 'ultra-Tories', buoyed up by the Bloomsbury Forum, to hijack the party from within. For sure, Newland and the Edwards's now wanted Griffin out. It soon became clear to them, Newland said, that Griffin was intent on running the party like Tyndall – 'in the old manner as a fiefdom'.[89]

With activists in the West Midlands, the party's strongest region, demanding that the Edwards's be reinstated forthwith, Griffin had little choice but to accede to their wishes. Nonetheless, the olive branch that Griffin extended to them at a special 'unity' meeting at a local leisure centre in the West Midlands left a particularly bitter aftertaste. Rather than allowing Sharon Edwards to stand as the party's candidate at the forthcoming West Bromwich West parliamentary by-election, Griffin insisted that he would stand instead. But with supporters of the Edwards's refusing to canvass for Griffin, the leadership was forced to rely almost totally on the election address delivered by the Post Office. Left with no other option, Griffin had to experiment. An electronic copy of the electoral register was purchased and some 50,000 electors were split into lists of men, women, first-time voters and Asians. A full-colour leaflet was sent to all women, a red-white-and-blue leaflet to all men, a short-run leaflet to all first-time young voters and a sample of 1,200 Asian voters were sent a 'neat' but 'cheaply produced message' strictly for publicity purposes. As we have seen, some 23 per cent of those who had voted in Tipton Green in May 2000 had backed Steve Edwards, but when it came to it, Griffin could only muster 4.2 per cent of the vote (just 13 more votes than Steve

Edwards had polled). On what should have been favourable terrain Griffin's result was clearly a setback. But he was quick to make his excuses – Tipton Green only accounted for one-seventh of the entire parliamentary constituency and, besides, since local party activists had gone 'on strike', Griffin had been denied a team of canvassers. But to make matters worse, at a parliamentary by-election in Preston, the party's north-west regional organiser Chris Jackson had polled less than Griffin – he had obtained a derisory 1 per cent of the vote.[90]

As the feel of internal crisis grew more palpable, the party looked all set for a takeover. Griffin had suffered a major blow to his authority and results in West Bromwich and Preston only served to damage his credibility further. As the party ranks destabilised and no issues of *Identity* appeared for a number of months, Griffin's leadership looked destined to end. However, even if the air was thick with rumours, a leadership challenge never manifested itself. Both Newland and the Edwards's held back. Rather than taking Griffin on, his rivals launched a new party in December 2000 instead – the Freedom Party (following the Austrian model).[91] According to Newland, by this time he had decided along with the Edwards's and a number of activists from the Bloomsbury Forum (Eddy Butler, Adrian Davies), that reforming the BNP was no longer a viable option. But outside its West Midlands base, this new party failed to attract many defectors, and even within the West Midlands it was significant that Simon Darby, West Midlands regional organiser and a close colleague of the Edwards's opted to remain with Griffin. Possibly no more than two-dozen BNP supporters defected.[92] One key problem was that the Freedom Party had no obvious leader – it intended to govern itself by a system of committee rule which, as Griffin pointed out in the party's *Members' Bulletin*, had 'repeatedly led the nationalist movement into a blind alley of faction-alism and division'.[93] Furthermore, in every respect the new party was merely a splinter group for ultra-Tories. 'We do not have any undercurrent of smirking Hitler fans, which is still there below the surface in the BNP', Newland proudly declared.[94] But as such, it held no appeal to those hardliners that remained within the BNP for whom Tyndall was still their potential savour should Griffin fail to make any impact at the forthcoming general election.[95]

With the grab for the leadership having failed to materialise, Griffin started 2001 anxious to put his modernisation programme back on track. Consequently, the first few months of 2001 saw a flurry of new initiatives: *Identity* was redesigned and reappeared as a monthly magazine, described by January's *Members' Bulletin* as the party's best-ever magazine (though to be honest, it was more a case of style over substance);[96] Land and People was reactivated and the party also launched a new circle – 'FAIR' or 'Families Against Immigrant Racism'. This was intended to function as a support group for 'white people and communities who are the victims of discrimination and racism, and to provide a counter-balance to the huge number of organisations pushing the interests of non-whites and foreigners'.[97] Yet to tell the truth, these initiatives merely papered over the cracks. The acid test for Griffin's political future would be the general election though he moved quickly to scale down party expectations: 'it's neither the time nor the place to press for a BNP breakthrough', he declared, 'it would be a piece of political folly to throw too much into that contest'.[98] But as we shall see, the June 2001 general election proved to be the most successful ever for the British National Party. In fact, its success was unparalleled in the entire history of right-wing extremism in Britain. Not surprisingly, before the close of nominations on 30 June 2001, John Tyndall quickly despatched a letter to party headquarters. His proposed leadership challenge had been withdrawn.[99]

How then are we to react to Nick Griffin's modernisation programme? One response might be to dismiss it of any real substance. If we take the term 'modernisation' at face value, surely we lack historical perspective? In a glance back to the 1970s, we find the National Front trying to pass itself off as a respectable political party with reasonable policies. Even if in this respect, its efforts left much to be desired, we have to acknowledge that the NF cloaked itself in a mask of contrived respectability and also offered the British public populist solutions. Furthermore, during the early 1990s, as we have seen, the BNP paid more attention to becoming 'voter-friendly', and certain activists, such as Eddy Butler, were willing to embrace more 'forward-thinking' ideas.[100] In this sense, there is nothing particularly 'modern' or 'new' about Griffin's political strategy.

Admittedly, all this cannot be denied. However, it is important to bear in mind that Griffin had taken careful note of the many failures of both the old-style NF and the BNP: the problem of Tyndall's political past, the 'march and grow' tactic which invariably resulted in clashes with anti-fascist opponents and placed the far right outside the cultural norms of liberal-democratic society, the threat the far right posed to ordinary voters, the policy of compulsory repatriation, the fact that the NF and BNP had frequently described themselves as 'racist', the prevailing culture of 'careless extremism' – activists like Eddy Butler were generally atypical of the BNP membership as a whole for whom unconventional political activity (hence the growth of Combat 18) continued to hold strong appeal. What is more, Griffin did not look to the example of domestic forerunners but took his inspiration from elsewhere, that is to say, the recent examples set by more successful 'national-populist' parties in continental Europe – in particular, the French National Front. It therefore seems right to speak of modernisation especially since, as we have seen, Griffin's programme also carried a commitment to professionalism, a commitment that has been somewhat lacking on Britain's postwar far right.

In the sharpest of contrasts, the French National Front had succeeded in constructing broad political and social legitimacy, something that on the journey from the political fringe to the mainstream no far-right party could do without. In many cases, therefore, in order to further the party's quest for legitimacy, Griffin simply lifted elements from both the political style and organisational features of the *Front National*. Yet Griffin also made it clear that the party's ideological core was not for compromise: 'for like you, I do not intend to allow this movement to lose its way'.[101] With its revolutionary ideology now buried beneath the surface gloss of 'Freedom, Democracy, Security, Identity', Griffin intended that it should remain there for the foreseeable future. But on this point he was anxious to set minds at rest – it was after all merely a case of short-term political expediency: 'As long as our cadres understand the full implications of our struggle', Griffin reminded his readers, 'then there is no need for us to do anything to give the public cause for concern'.[102]

6
Into the Political Mainstream? The 2001 General Election and After

With an average vote of 17.3 per cent across the seats contested, and some 13 council seats won, the local elections of May 2003 brought the British National Party a level of electoral success hitherto unknown on Britain's far right. During the 1930s Mosley's British Union of Fascists had managed to win just one council seat, whilst in the 1970s Britain's largest postwar fascist organisation, the National Front, had failed to secure election to any office.[1] On 2 May 2003, almost a decade after its solitary win in Millwall, the British National Party could lay claim to no fewer than 16 councillors. It had now outperformed all its predecessors by far. The jewel in the crown was the East Lancashire town of Burnley where it had come second to Labour and formed the official opposition. As the *Lancashire Evening Telegraph*'s headline writer put it, with right-extremists holding a grand total of eight seats in the town, Burnley had become the 'BNP CAPITAL OF BRITAIN'.[2] But such attention-grabbing headlines can be deceptive. Of all the seats that were up for election in May 2003, the BNP only managed to win one-tenth of 1 per cent. Nonetheless, even if its influence proved local rather than national, the electoral ground that it had captured was undoubtedly significant. As a result, the party found itself tantalisingly close to a national electoral breakthrough – an opportunity that it expected to seize in 2004 when, at the same time as elections to the European Parliament and the London mayoral elections, entire councils would be up for election in a raft of metropolitan districts across the country.[3]

The small upturn in the British National Party's electoral fortunes, it should be recalled, was already underway in 2000. For the most part, this was occasioned by the interplay of three factors: the asylum issue and the mainstream politicisation of 'race', cultivating the appearance

of moderation, and grassroots community politics in isolated pockets
Though momentarily disrupted by internal dissent, by the start of 2001
the British National Party had returned to normality. As it stepped back
onto the treadmill of electoral politics, its progress gathered pace. At
this instant, an advantageous turn of events in the north-west of
England imparted fresh momentum. The party broke new ground in
Oldham where at the 2001 general election Nick Griffin polled 16.4 per
cent of the vote at Oldham West and Royton – the largest vote ever for
a far-right candidate in a parliamentary election in Britain. Meanwhile,
Oldham organiser Mick Treacy gathered 11.21 per cent in the neighbouring seat of Oldham East and Saddleworth. All told, some 13,250
people in the borough had marked their cross against British National
Party candidates.[4] What is more, this breakthrough was not confined
to Oldham. Elsewhere in the region, local organiser Steve Smith polled
11.35 per cent of the vote in Burnley – the party's second-best result.[5]
Therefore, when we take the recent electoral rise of the BNP and map it
out, it follows that the focus of our attention inevitably falls on the
north-west of England.

Oldham, Burnley and the 2001 General Election

Our starting point is the end of January 2001, when the head of
Oldham's police division, Chief Superintendent Eric Hewitt, voiced
concerns about the rising number of attacks by Asian youths on
white men in the town. For some six to seven years, Oldham had
been the worst division in Greater Manchester for racial violence.[6] Of
572 racial incidents recorded over the course of the previous year,
60 per cent of victims had been white.[7] This represented more than a
twofold increase on the figure that Hewitt had previously made
public in 1999 – 250 racial incidents in one year, with the majority
involving Asian-on-white violence.[8] But since these figures were presented without context, they were deceptive. Ethnic minorities in
Oldham comprised 11 per cent of the population and were still six
and a half times more likely to be victims of a racist attack.
Underreporting of racial crime amongst the ethnic minority population was also common.[9] Had Hewitt an axe to grind? Were these
figures released in order to subvert Macpherson? At first glance, the
evidence lends itself to such a conspiratorial reading. On closer
inspection, however, care must be taken. What his critics fail to
mention is significant: Hewitt had attended the Stephen Lawrence
Inquiry; he was also personally involved in setting up Operation

Catalyst – a series of positive recommendations by Greater Manchester Police in response to the Macpherson Report.[10] Nevertheless, Hewitt was still at fault. The release of these figures was insensitively done particularly when the town's daily newspaper, the *Oldham Chronicle*, with its largely white readership seized on the issue of Asian-on-white crime, brought it starkly to the fore and so unwittingly prepared the ground for the intervention of the far right.[11]

In Oldham, Nick Griffin caught sight of his political opportunity early on. Notwithstanding the fact that the local press provided the BNP with most of its ammunition, the general lie of the land also looked promising. Here was a town with a socially segregated ethnic minority population principally of Pakistani and Bangladeshi origin, spatially concentrated in a handful of Oldham's neighbourhoods. Historically, little social interaction had existed between the Asian and white communities, and as a result the communities remained deeply divided. Everyday racism came with the territory. A low-wage economy, relative deprivation, a distrust of local governance and a fear of crime were other staple features of the local socio-political landscape.[12] The fact that the party had recently reestablished a branch in the area was further conducive to the needs of the moment. Under Tyndall, the BNP could boast a local unit in Oldham but its profile had been distinctly low-key, and towards the end of the 1990s it was reported that the party had no members in the town at all.[13] Activity did resume with local elections in May 2000, however. The town's Hollinwood ward was contested and the BNP candidate polled a creditable 9.72 per cent of the vote.[14] Consequently, in terms of building party organisation in Oldham, Griffin did not have to start entirely from scratch.

In February 2001, after speaking out against the building of a mosque in the predominantly white Chadderton district of the town, the local press caught attention of the party's Oldham organiser Mick Treacy.[15] The following month, the BNP held its 'North of Britain Spring Rally' at the Bowling Green pub in Oldham.[16] Immediately afterwards, in an early bid to capitalise on the publication of Hewitt's figures, and recalling its 'Rights for Whites' agitation of the early 1990s, BNP activists demonstrated in support of 'Equal Rights for Oldham Whites' outside the town's police station. Nick Griffin was in attendance and led the demands for a clampdown on Asian attacks against whites.[17] As Griffin later revealed, 'we were in Oldham, working in the local community and in defence of white rights, months before the rioting began'. This was no accident but 'the result of a recognition that circumstances were combining in the town to provide us with a great opportunity'.[18]

Intent on creating a political opening for itself, party activists were increasingly drawn to Oldham especially when, throughout March and April 2001, inter-racial tensions were brought to boiling point. In the first place, a series of attacks by Asians on lone whites continued to grab the headlines. 'This has got to stop', the *Oldham Chronicle* cried out following an assault on a 16-year-old white youth by a dozen Asian teenagers in early April.[19] Within days, however, an Asian man had viciously assaulted Walter Chamberlain, a white 76-year-old grandfather. Though his family was ill at ease with the attack being described as racist, the story made the national newspapers and many dyed-in-the-wool opponents of multiculturalism subjected Chamberlain – a D-Day veteran – to martyrdom. His badly beaten face featured prominently on local BNP leaflets and talk of 'no-go' areas for whites, going the rounds for some time, was now rife. This was given further credence by the broadcast media. Just two days before the attack on Chamberlain, BBC Radio Four's *Today* programme broadcast from Oldham claiming that young Asians were establishing 'no-go' zones for whites.

In the meantime, the rival National Front further stoked it up by proposing to march through the town. Hankering after a violent response from the local Asian community, one BNP defector suspected that someone in the BNP was deliberately issuing NF press releases threatening to march in Oldham. The BNP could then distance itself from the violent extremism of the NF and pass itself off as a respectable and legitimate defender of the local white community.[20] This is certainly a possibility. Griffin was keen to raise the temperature but the BNP had dropped the confrontational 'march and grow' tactics of the past. Instead, the party adopted a more subtle approach. On 23 April – St George's Day – party activists flew a number of St George's flags from lampposts in the town knowing that they would be removed by the Council as a distraction to drivers. Inevitably this occasioned criticism of the Council in the letters page of the local press.[21] It was also on this day that Griffin announced his intention to stand in the Oldham West and Royton constituency. An obvious publicity stunt, it won prominent exposure in the *Oldham Chronicle*.[22]

At the end of April, some 450 Stoke City football hooligans ran amok in an Asian district of Oldham, and in the ensuing weeks tensions boiled over. Following repeated incursions by outside agitators, for the most part NF activists from Birmingham and London, and a series of clashes between Asian and white youths at a predominantly Asian school in the town, racial friction in Oldham finally exploded into serious disorder. On 26 May the fuse was lit when groups of white youths, including hardened C18 activists, BNP supporters and racist football hooligans congregated in various pubs in Oldham intent on provoking a violent backlash from local Asians.[23] After an early evening skirmish, hundreds of Asian youth took to the streets in Glodwick – the centre of the town's Pakistani community – and ran riot. A series of running battles between the police and Asian youth ensued. Petrol bombs were hurled, missiles were thrown and vehicles were vandalised and set alight. The police described the scene as 'carnage' and it was dawn before the streets were cleared.[24]

From then on, the violence tapered off. In the days that followed, where disturbances flared, they were now sporadic.[25] But in one notable incident, the *Chronicle*, seen by the Asian community as racist, had its offices firebombed.[26] The managing director of the newspaper's parent company immediately threw out any suggestion that its reporters had let racism shape their coverage.[27] Admittedly, in the interests of promoting inter-ethnic dialogue the newspaper had earlier called for a ban on the NF's proposed march through the town,[28] but even so, by accentuating Asian-on-white attacks, the *Chronicle's* reporters had helped set an agenda that was singularly edifying for the extreme right. They also gave the impression that certain parts of Oldham, predominantly Asian areas, were receiving a disproportionate slice of local funding. Moreover, its letter pages were replete with correspondence, often anonymous, that expressed frank opinions about Asian attacks on whites, and about the Asian community in general.[29] History informs us that where readers' letters disseminate racist opinions, they can help set local agendas. Racist correspondence in the local press in Smethwick in Birmingham in the late 1950s and early 1960s, for instance, almost certainly contributed to the election of the Conservative Peter Griffiths in 1964 following a campaign that has since achieved notoriety for its vulgar 'If you want a nigger for a neighbour, vote Labour' slogan.[30]

Revealingly, the *Chronicle* had not one single ethnic-minority journalist on its editorial staff,[31] and the British National Party's monthly, *Identity*, had even carried a sympathetic interview with one of the *Chronicle's* principal journalists.[32] Thus, in the lead up to the Oldham riots, it is hard not to overdo the significance of the *Chronicle's* reporting. It spread the mentality of white victimhood and redefined racism as 'anti-white racism', and in so doing it meshed with the discourse of the BNP and therein gave the British National Party's call for 'Equal Rights for Oldham's Whites' both legitimacy and credibility.

When white racists had gathered at Oldham's Britannia pub on 26 May, Nick Griffin – earlier canvassing in the town – was placed at the scene. Yet on the day, it is not clear whether Griffin pulled the strings. His stopover at the Britannia was brief, and when threatened by two leading figures of C18 he bid a hasty retreat.[33] On the other hand, it would be naïve to think that Griffin did not intend to reap the benefits from any violent Asian backlash. But he had obviously drawn lessons from the past and so everywhere presented the British National Party as a scrupulously respectable organisation. In this regard, the encroachment of other extremists from rival organisations played directly into his hands. The BNP had nothing to do whatsoever with the NF, he argued. The NF was a separate organisation, a law unto itself, whereas the BNP was only trying to give the ordinary people of Oldham a political voice and thereby defuse the potential for violence. Local BNP activists were merely canvassing the area using conventional, law-abiding democratic methods, Griffin maintained.[34] Accordingly, he told the *Chronicle*: 'We're not here to put others down or cause trouble, all we want is a fair deal for own people: equal rights for whites!' And the *Chronicle* further obliged by taking Griffin's claim to have 'worked to reposition the party in the mainstream of British political life, dumping old-style confrontational tactics' at face value.[35]

As soon as distance had been established between the BNP and the openly confrontational NF, and having convinced many of its potential electors that it was in Oldham to campaign for justice, the party set itself on a course of intensive doorstep campaigning. It bussed in some 50 activists from across the country, targeted largely white wards and distributed thousands of leaflets. Its literature blamed local 'Muslims' for the riots, claimed that the main parties were ignoring ordinary whites and repeated the accusation that non-white areas received preferential treatment. There were some noticeable innovations in campaign methods too. These included a 'voice of the people' CD in which people explained why they were voting for the party, and an advertising trailer which raised further interest in the party's election literature by calling on people not to read the BNP's 'green leaflets' (the colour 'green' chosen to symbolise Islam). A dedicated space was also given over to Oldham on the party's website.[36] Meanwhile the canvassing of the main political parties was lacklustre. With the doorsteps largely abandoned by the mainstream, the BNP filled the void. And while the *Chronicle* did finally call on its readers to 'resoundingly reject' the British National Party's 'odious policies', the party encountered little in the way of sustained anti-fascist opposition.[37]

Once again, as in Tower Hamlets in the early 1990s, by promising to restore the lost birthright of local white residents, by demanding that whites were no longer treated as 'second-class' citizens, the party was able to tap into a deep vein of popular racist resentment. With tensions continuing to fester in the immediate wake of the riots, and with Oldham's Labour MPs having signed up to the Commission for Racial Equality's pledge not to politicise 'race' at the general election, the British National Party offered a large number of disaffected and disenfranchised working-class voters in Oldham an alternative political voice. As one in six of Oldham's voters turned to the BNP, Labour's vote fell. In Oldham West for instance, it dropped by 7.6 percentage points. This was a greater fall than that experienced by the Conservative candidate.[38]

Taking a broader view, it is tempting to blame Conservative rhetoric on immigration for casting a dark shadow over Oldham. This, for instance, was the opinion of Simon Hughes, Liberal Democrat Home Affairs spokesman.[39] At the Conservative spring conference, William Hague had spoken of Labour turning Britain into a 'foreign land'. That same month, at a local by-election in Beckton in London's East End, the BNP had polled 17.2 per cent of the vote despite running a virtually non-existent campaign. In a moment of biting wit, 'The Tory party's 14-pint skinhead has unwittingly become the BNP's second-best recruiting sergeant', Griffin remarked with some justification.[40] Still other Tories joined in. On 27 March, Conservative MP John Townend blamed 'coloured immigration' for rising crime; a month later, he criticised the government for turning the British into a 'mongrel race'. For sure, against this background, with racism becoming more socially and culturally acceptable, Westminster politicians contributed to the British National Party's Oldham breakthrough. But we should be careful not to make too much of this. During the 2001 general election campaign itself, asylum and immigration issues were soon sidelined as both tax and public spending came to dominate the concerns of the major parties.[41]

In keeping with the 'ladder strategy' – mastering each level of electoral politics before moving up to the next – Griffin's objective in contesting Oldham at the 2001 general election was to lay the foundations for the May 2002 council elections.[42] More generally, this thinking underpinned the party's decision to target a mere 33 constituencies in June 2001. Rather than dispersing its efforts across the country, the goal was to prepare ground in key areas of support so that come May the following year, the party stood a realistic chance of winning a handful of local council seats. The results of the 2001 general election certainly offered good reason to support this strategy. Despite contesting fewer seats than in 1997, the party's total vote increased by more than one-quarter. In the seats contested, the BNP averaged 3.9 per cent of the vote.[43] It had polled over 10 per cent of the vote in three constituencies and scores above 5 per cent were obtained in two further seats.[44] As we have seen, Griffin's original expectations for the 2001 general election had been modest but the party's prospects had been 'transformed' by its success in Oldham, the self-satisfied leader of the BNP could declare: 'New credibility, new growth and new opportunities will all follow as surely as night follows day.'[45] Reflecting on the British National Party's shock result in the town, the *Oldham Chronicle* believed that it had been the size of the party's mandate that had brought it local political legitimacy.[46] Yet it had missed the obvious point. With no local legitimacy – the most important variable in extreme-right electoral breakthrough – the party would never have achieved this result in the first place.

So far our concentration has been on Oldham. But in terms of getting its people elected, the British National Party would find that Burnley – the other area in which it polled over 10 per cent in June 2001 – offered the richest soil. There is, of course, much that holds Burnley in common with Oldham: a traditional textile and manufacturing base that is in long-term decline, a low-wage economy, relatively high levels of socio-economic deprivation, and high crime rates, reportedly the highest in East Lancashire.[47] A significant ethnic-minority community also resides in the town – some 7 per cent of the population. Matching Oldham, Burnley's ethnic minorities are chiefly Pakistani and Bangladeshi in origin, and they also conform to a similar pattern of spatial concentration. In Burnley's case most populate the Daneshouse ward, which is one of the town's smallest and deprived wards.[48] Here ethnic minorities comprise close to 50 per cent of the area's residents. What is more, like Oldham, Burnley was also the scene of 'race riots' during the summer of 2001. Yet its disturbances occurred over the weekend of 23–24 June, that is to say, more than two weeks *after* the British National Party's candidate Steve Smith had already struck a respondent chord with many of the town's voters at the 2001 parliamentary election.

As we noted in the preceding chapter, the British National Party had no organisation in Burnley before Steve Smith joined its ranks in May

1999. But within nine months of holding its first meeting in the town, it had already announced its arrival on the local political scene. It should be recalled that the party's vote of 21.5 per cent in the Fulledge ward in May 2000 was surpassed only by the party's performance in Tipton in the West Midlands. And even if an additional BNP candidate, contesting the town's Gawthorpe ward, polled less impressively at 5 per cent, this was still an impressive return from a 'standing start', particularly as the party also encountered some early opposition.[49] In April 2000, the town's borough councillors, with unanimous cross-party support, had signed an open letter warning voters in Burnley that the British National Party was 'no ordinary political party' and was 'dedicated to spreading the ideas of Hitler and the Nazis'.[50]

If sensationalist reporting of Asian-on-white crime had opened the door to the BNP in Oldham, at the base of its success in Burnley was popular resentment at 'positive discrimination'. Most crucial of all was the perception that the Asian community in the Daneshouse ward received preferential council funding. Racially motivated violence was not a particularly salient issue in Burnley; most criminal activity that was reported in the local press related to drugs, theft or vandalism.[51] The issue of 'positive discrimination', on the other hand, had taken a hold on the town after the local Independent Group, especially its leader Councillor Harry Brooks, a former Labour Party member, had raised a hue and cry about spending disparities between Daneshouse and the town's other wards.

The Independents had briefly taken control of Burnley Borough Council in May 2000, which was the first time that Labour had lost control of Burnley council for some 30 years.[52] According to one local Labour Party official, the town's press had consequently 'elevated' Brooks 'to almost cult like status'.[53] Assisted by the *Burnley Express*, Brooks drew public attention to the fact that the Daneshouse ward was the major beneficiary of public monies. In so doing, he stirred up resentment from white residents in neighbouring wards and made racism appear respectable. Unintentionally – Brooks later came out against the BNP[54] – he softened up mainstream electoral ground for the far right. Moreover, when no Independent candidate came forward to contest the 2001 general election, this political space was left open for the British National Party to fill.

It need hardly be added that the party's relative success in Burnley was also determined by its ability to seize the occasion. The fact that the local Independents had cleared the way was a stroke of luck. But neither should we forget that Burnley, like Oldham, was not impervious to the effects of the ongoing immigration debate within the national political arena. Nonetheless the party still had to make sure that its potential voters were not frightened away. Hence Steve Smith called particular attention to his local patriotism (he owned the Burnley Heritage Centre)[55] and to his charitable work. A photograph of Smith handing over a cheque to the Burnley branch of the Royal British Legion adorned his election leaflet.[56] Moreover, Smith ensured that his 'moderate' platform mirrored that of Brooks: he concentrated his attack on 'positive discrimination' and demanded that grant allocations should be targeted towards deprived neighbourhoods in Burnley's predominantly white districts. As for raising the party's local profile, innovations in campaigning style were also in evidence. A mobile display board was brought into play and a 'Vote BNP' banner was also draped from a mill chimney in the centre of the town.[57]

Despite a call by the local clergy to vote against the BNP and protests by the Anti-Nazi League, Smith still polled over 4,000 votes.[58] Indeed, as past experience shows, within local arenas where 'race' is politicised such an outcome was not entirely unforeseeable. And with 'not a race riot in sight', Burnley had thus provided the party with its 'best natural vote' of the 2001 general election.[59] Like Oldham, most of its support had come from disaffected former Labour voters; in Burnley, Labour's vote dropped by 8.6 per centage points.[60] Yet soon enough Burnley also experienced its own racial disturbances.[61] Although these were not directly inspired by the BNP, its level of support at the general election earlier in the month almost certainly fanned the flames. Naturally the BNP denied all responsibility; it held local Muslims to blame instead and claimed that Asian-on-white violence had sharply increased since the disturbances.[62] In this way, the argument that whites were the real victims of multiculturalism was given greater potency. And looking forward to the upcoming council elections in 2002, local BNP activists expected to reap the political benefits sooner, rather than later.

Courting the media, winning votes and getting elected

As regards its quest for broad political legitimacy, the party's relationship with the mainstream media provides us with another important yardstick. Where previously the BNP had either been largely ignored or else denounced as fascist thugs, now it was becoming increasingly 'normalised' under the glare of media publicity. More and more, the party drew the broadcast media and in particular the BBC towards it. On 26 June, in the wake of the disturbances in Burnley, Nick Griffin appeared on the BBC's *Newsnight* programme. The daunting Jeremy Paxman supplied the questions, but rather than being overwhelmed Griffin returned a polished performance.[63] A few days later, speaking to some seven million listeners, Griffin also featured on BBC Radio Four's highly respected *Today* programme. The programme's editor, Rod Liddle (a former member of the Socialist Workers' Party no less) set no store by the policy of 'No Platform', the code of practice that enjoined the media to act as gatekeepers. Its recent origins date back to the 1970s when it had been taken up in order to prevent racist and/or National Front propaganda from gaining a voice in the mainstream media. With the support of the National Union of Journalists, it had become a rule of thumb ever since.[64] 'The only way to expose what the BNP is actually doing is by interviewing them', Liddle countered, 'You don't combat that sort of racism or that sort of extremism by sticking your head in the sand.'[65] True to his word, *Today*'s exchange with Griffin was not easy on the ear. Listeners to the show were informed of Griffin's description of one Liberal Democrat MP as a 'bloody Jew whose only claim to fame is that two of his grandparents died in the Holocaust'.[66]

The following month, as racial disturbances spread to both Bradford and Stoke, Griffin featured on ITV's primetime *Tonight* programme. On this occasion, attention was drawn to Griffin's 'career racism' and to the many criminal convictions of numerous party members.[67] Then, in August, he was cross-examined by Tim Sebastian on BBC News 24's *Hardtalk* where he was immediately confronted with his denial of the Holocaust and his previous conviction for incitement to racial hatred.[68] But despite everything, the very fact that the BNP had been granted access to the mainstream media in the first place meant that the traditional 'No Platform' policy had been compromised. Areas of the media that had hitherto been closed to right-wing extremists now opened up. In this way the broadcast media helped 'normalise' the British National Party even if the claim that the BBC had become, as Bill Morris put it, 'the house journal for the BNP' was somewhat overdone.[69]

On 24 August, the party returned to the headlines when it was revealed that a campaign aide to Iain Duncan Smith (IDS) was none other than Edgar Griffin, the father of party leader Nick Griffin.[70] There is a fair chance that a BNP insider leaked this information to the press in order to wreck Iain Duncan Smith's leadership challenge, open the way to a Ken Clarke victory and thereby drive disaffected right-wing Tories into the arms of the British National Party.[71] It goes without saying that if this was the plan then it came to nothing. Moreover, the very fact that Edgar Griffin was immediately axed from the Iain Duncan Smith campaign team and forced out of the Conservative Party indicates that although the BNP may have been 'normalised' to an extent, as far as its acceptance into the realms of the political mainstream was concerned, there was still a good deal of distance left to travel.

Nonetheless, a further boost to the party's fortunes shortly followed. By inducing a popular anti-Muslim backlash, the terrorist attacks on New York and Washington in September 2001 came at a most opportune time. In the immediate aftermath of '9/11', numerous cases of anti-Muslim violence, verbal abuse and attacks on property were reported across Britain. Meanwhile, media attention fell on the potential 'enemy within', that is to say those Muslim extremists who declared themselves willing to wage an Islamic war against the West.[72] Since some of these individuals had originally come to Britain seeking asylum, the two issues became increasingly confused. From now on asylum-seekers became potential terrorists.[73] This all provided further grist to the BNP mill, and with Britain's political leaders calling for restraint Griffin was determined not to let the occasion pass. In no time at all the party had intensified its anti-Muslim campaign, and activists around the country were quickly supplied with tens of thousands of anti-Islam leaflets.[74] Furthermore, the BNP also saw an opportunity to play down its racism by approaching rogue representatives from the Sikh and Hindu communities with a view to forming a common 'anti-Muslim front'. The vehicle for this was the party's 'Ethnic Liaison Committee' – a project designed to organise joint activity with non-whites in order to cancel out the media image of the BNP as a racist party. Of the main media outlets, the *Today* programme ran the story but most considered it too sensitive.[75]

As the party launched its joint campaign against Islam, an unexpected opportunity to test its electoral mettle arose in its Burnley fiefdom. The resignations of three councillors triggered a series of by-elections in the town with two scheduled for 22 November 2001 and a third taking place a week later. Insofar as these elections provided a launch pad for May 2002, the results augured well. The party's average vote rose to 21 per cent.[76] This was particularly impressive since the Liberal Democrats had urged their supporters to vote Labour in order to stop the BNP.[77] Meanwhile, the Labour Party had distributed no less than five separate leaflets and local party activists had also called on the support of Deputy Prime Minister John Prescott and TV celebrity Tony Robinson.[78] Furthermore, between the by-elections in Trinity and

Lowerhouse wards and the by-election in the Rosehill ward, BBC screened an investigation into the party's dark side by the *Panorama* team. The claims made by Nick Griffin that the party had abandoned its racist, violent and anti-Semitic past were exposed as a sham.[79] The programme was also supported by its own dedicated website, and possibly more than 175,000 people viewed this site within 26 hours of the broadcast.[80]

If the *Panorama* team expected to deliver a knockout blow to the BNP, the effects were disappointing. The party claimed that the number of visitors to its website more than doubled whilst it also boasted that the programme had led to surge in recruitment.[81] What we know for certain is that, troubled by these revelations, Jim Cowell the party's candidate for Burnley's Rosehill ward stopped canvassing for support. Yet Cowell, who had joined the BNP some four months earlier, had a last-minute change of heart, and local organiser Steve Smith persuaded him to continue.[82] Because Cowell went on to poll 19.2 per cent of the vote, the damage inflicted to the party's local legitimacy by the *Panorama* exposé looks negligible. Then again, the BNP derived strength from the fact that the Rosehill ward included the Burnley Wood area, one of the most deprived parts of the town. This was also the stamping ground of Harry Brooks. It was his resignation that led to the by-election in the first place and so the BNP had particularly productive territory on which to even the score. A final point worth considering is that these results were garnered even though the BNP ran a low-key campaign that relied almost exclusively on local activists. In the November 2001 *Organisers' Bulletin*, a call had been put out for party workers to assist with its campaign in Burnley. But this was an afterthought. Griffin's main concern was to get the push for the 2002 local elections going as quickly as possible – some seven months before polling day.[83]

Whilst over 100 key party organisers and activists had attended the party's first 'Annual College' in October – an event designed to provide training in various aspects of electioneering and community politics – November 2001 saw the official opening of the party's 2002 local election campaign.[84] In its technical details we can see that Griffin clearly wanted to give the party a far more professional character. For sure they borrowed heavily from the community-based approach pioneered by the likes of Eddy Butler and Steve and Sharron Edwards, but one could not fail to notice the influence of Liberal Democrat electioneering techniques either. Whilst the party most obviously looked to model itself on 'national-populist' parties abroad, it drew inspiration from native soil too. A key backroom promoter of the strategy of community politics was new recruit Shane Sinclair – a former Liberal Democrat parliamentary candidate.[85]

To begin with, this strategy involved identifying an appropriate ward. For the moment the party expected to make electoral inroads in relatively deprived, white working-class neighbourhoods, abandoned by New Labour where the Tories and Liberal Democrats were weak and where the party's opposition to immigration and asylum-seekers and a tough stance on crime would chime with local residents. Ideally a charismatic candidate would front the campaign. What's more, the party considered it essential that its candidates root themselves in the local community. With this in mind activists were instructed to distribute a 'Helping Hands' leaflet. This was based on the Liberal-Democrat 'grumblesheet' tactic, although it was thought that since residents were asked what problems they would like to see BNP councillors sort out, it had a more positive twist. The candidate's profile could then be built up by using a local newsletter and by helping with local grievances and community campaigns (neighbourhood watch schemes, local residents associations, petitions to save local council facilities, and so on).[86] Where this happens, as we have seen, local legitimacy could be nurtured.

As for the finer grain of the election campaign itself, the November *Organisers' Bulletin* set out ready-made instructions detailing how electioneering in target wards should operate. Activists were instructed to obtain a copy of the electoral register, and any residents with foreign-sounding names should be avoided and where residents were addressed by their names, canvassing teams should appear polite and non-threatening. The first four months should be devoted to standard doorstep canvassing. Then, in stages two and three, the focus would be on the 'yes' returns. The 'yes' voters would be revisited with a new leaflet in March and re-canvassed in April. In the final stage – the eve of polling day – all efforts would be directed towards maximising 'yes' voter turnout.[87] As far as the decision to stand a candidate in a ward was concerned, responsibility was placed with the local branch itself. However, the guiding principle was to target only those wards with the greatest potential support. Since the party had scarce resources and lacked manpower, the feeling was that it could not possibly stretch itself across dozens of seats. For all its 'success' at the 2001 general election, membership stood at only 2,173 in November 2001. This represented a growth of 37 per cent on 2000 but it remained a paltry figure.[88] Nonetheless the BNP still managed to field 67 candidates in

May 2002 – its highest number in local elections thus far. However, only in its Oldham and Burnley strongholds did the party realistically expect to win any seats. Elsewhere, the prime objective was to garner a credible poll and so lay the foundations for future local electoral breakthroughs.

Consistent with a populist appeal to those ordinary white voters who felt disenfranchised, overtaxed and 'put upon', the party's 'mini-manifesto' promised local council taxpayers a major say in how their taxes were spent. There was a rider of course: no public monies would go to asylum-seekers or to local ethnic-minority organisations. It also made common cause with those who sought a hard-line policy on crime. 'Zero tolerance', the reintroduction of corporal punishment and the eviction of the families of 'anti-white racist thugs' were all promised. The party also vowed to regenerate sink estates, protect the local environment and provide decent services for 'local people'.[89] Traversing from place to place, however, there was often notable variation in emphasis. In Burnley for example, where local candidate Simon Bennett claimed that he had originally been 'cautious of aligning himself' with the BNP because of its bad press but that his investigations had found a 'modern, professional and much-changed organisation',[90] opposition to preferential funding for predominantly Muslim areas featured highly.[91] This was true of Bradford too.[92] But farther afield, the party's message on Wearside recalled the crude racism of the 1960s with its 'Vote Labour if you want asylum seeker neighbours' slogan.[93] In the West Midlands, meanwhile, the revelation that two local Labour councillors had links with the 'Tipton Taliban' – a group of young Muslims who had supposedly volunteered to fight in support of Bin Laden and the Taliban regime in Afghanistan – occupied centre-stage.[94]

At the grassroots, the nature of the party's electioneering revealed that a culture of professionalism was certainly filtering through. For the most part key target wards were systematically canvassed, particularly in Burnley and Oldham.[95] Following one canvassing sweep, a local BNP activist revealed that the issue of preferential funding still remained at the hub of its appeal in Burnley: 'As soon as we mentioned Labour's funding for Daneshouse, eyes were raised to the ceiling and common ground was found.'[96] The campaign in Burnley was also supported by a *Burnley Bravepages* website. The primary aim of this site was to further raise the party's profile in the town. To advertise it, some 10,000 calling cards had been distributed in local pubs and clubs whilst a *Bravepages* banner was positioned to catch the attention of passing motorists.[97] Elsewhere, special editions of local BNP newssheets appeared. In Sunderland for instance, *British Worker* homed in on disaffected white working-class voters who felt betrayed by New Labour. With a headline of 'LOOK WHAT YOU GOT FOR VOTING LABOUR', it concentrated its attack on council corruption, community collapse, Labour's failure to revive local manufacturing industry and also raised the spectre of thousands of asylum-seekers descending on the city.[98]

But it would be wrong to suggest that the party's electoral strategy had been honed to perfection. Part of the problem was its lack of organisers; another was mobilising its membership to carry out a protracted election campaign. Hence canvassing was patchy and few branches followed instructions to the letter. In its former fiefdoms in East London, for instance, canvassing was non-existent. Surprisingly, not one leaflet was distributed in Tower Hamlets. In truth, the BNP was in organisational disarray in the capital.[99] But even in its Oldham stronghold, preparations could have been more thorough. First, it only managed to scrape together enough candidates to fight five wards and then, when anti-fascists exposed the BNP's Oldham campaign director as a convicted rapist, local party activists were thrown off guard. In Bradford, meanwhile, a BNP residents' group – CARE (Caring About Ravenscliffe Estate) – saw its efforts marred by embarrassing election literature.[100] In his address to voters, the local BNP candidate, Arthur Bentley, told a tragic story of his youth, claimed that he could not find employment because of his political activities, that he was 'persecuted' by the police and that, as a result, he had 'little money, few clothes' and was forced to 'live a meagre existence'.[101] As one anti-fascist activist put it, 'Bentley's leaflets were so bizarre that we wondered whether we need to campaign at all.'[102]

Nonetheless, the party's election campaign was still more professionally organised than at any time in the past. Having received a wake-up call in June 2001, anti-fascists were alive to this fact. As a consequence, the BNP had to contend with a major counter-offensive particularly in its northern target areas. The anti-fascist campaign was the most intensive and organised for two decades; over 200,000 pieces of anti-fascist literature were distributed in the British National Party's target wards.[103] Events in France almost certainly helped galvanise anti-fascists too. On 21 April Le Pen had captured 17.2 per cent of the vote in the first round of the French presidential elections. This was the first time that a far-right candidate had won through to the second round in the entire history of the Fifth Republic. Not surprisingly, it sent a shockwave throughout Europe. In Britain, anxious to prevent the BNP enjoying a Le Pen-type success, the *Daily Express* and the *Mirror* both ran prominent anti-BNP campaigns.[104] With its eve of poll headline – 'Vote for Oldham, not divisive BNP' – the *Oldham Chronicle* joined the chorus of disapproval.[105] And although the *Burnley Express* remained neutral, it carried an exclusive interview with Tony Blair who urged the good people of Burnley to 'vote for any of the mainstream political parties to keep the BNP out'.[106]

All the same, the British National Party still won three council seats in Burnley.[107] An important credibility threshold was passed. Its average vote in the town increased to 28 per cent and the absolute number of votes it captured from the Burnley electorate more than doubled in relation to June 2001. In Oldham, even if no BNP candidates were elected, the party's share of the vote was up to 27.3 per cent. Elsewhere, the party polled 28 per cent in Town End Farm in Sunderland, and in the West Midlands it captured 26.09 per cent in the Castle and Priory ward in Dudley and 24.34 per cent in Princes End ward in Sandwell. Across the country, whilst standing over 50 candidates more than at local elections in May 2000, the BNP's vote averaged out at an alarming 15 per cent (when calculated using the best-placed candidate).[108] The fact that the BNP was gaining ground was thrown into sharp relief.

Generally-speaking where the party canvassed, it found most favour. As was shown in Millwall, establishing doorstep contact with voters was a proven strategy; thereupon, the party's legitimacy amongst would-be voters remained intact. The portrayal of the BNP as a party of criminals, thugs and Nazis – the stock-in-trade of anti-fascists – often jarred with what voters encountered on the doorsteps. This was particularly true if female candidates stood, Carol Hughes in Burnley for example.[109] Indeed, all the evidence suggests that the anti-fascist campaign did not divest the BNP of political legitimacy, nor did it erode the far-right vote. Its main achievement was to mobilise anti-BNP voters, particularly in Oldham and Burnley. Average turnout across the country was 32.8 per cent,[110] yet turnouts ranged between 41.9 and 49.2 per cent in Oldham and between 44.7 and 63.4 per cent in Burnley.[111]

When the party's vote was mapped, observers were surprised to discover that in some areas, such as Burnley's Cliviger and Worsthorne ward and Oldham's Royton North, the party had encroached on more affluent neighbourhoods. Although its core supporters remained solidly white working-class, one must avoid drawing over-simplistic conclusions about the social composition of the party's electorate. The point that needs to be made is that it was now drawing votes from across the socio-political spectrum. It seems likely that one key factor in attracting former Tory voters was the change of leadership in the Conservative Party. IDS ran a low-profile campaign and his reluctance to follow the lead of William Hague and exploit voter concerns about immigration and asylum probably occasioned an embrace of the far right in a handful of more prosperous areas. That these concerns were apparent is undeniable. By May 2002, MORI pollsters were finding that for 39 per cent of its respondents, 'immigration' was either the most important or one of the most important issues facing Britain today – second only to the National Health Service.[112]

As for New Labour, where previously it had tended to deny the BNP any publicity, its strategy now started to shift. Labour Home Secretary David Blunkett urged the mainstream parties to fight the BNP head-on.[113] But this did not mean ignoring immigration as an electoral issue. On the contrary, against the backdrop of the ongoing controversy surrounding the Sangatte refugee camp in France and the second reading of the new Nationality, Immigration and Asylum bill in the House of Commons, Blunkett chose to occupy BNP ground. On 24 April, he borrowed from Thatcher's 1978 phrase book[114] and declared that children of asylum-seekers were 'swamping' Britain's schools. But if Thatcher's comments had helped undercut support for the extreme right over two decades earlier, then Blunkett's copycat manoeuvre had the opposite effect. Rather than stopping its electoral rise, it gave the British National Party further legitimacy. What Labour strategists failed to see made all the difference. In the first place, they did not appreciate that with the tabloids railing against Labour over this issue, there was little trust in government ministers. Secondly, Griffin's BNP was not a carbon-copy of the 1970s National Front. This time around Britain's far right had comparatively more respectability, credibility and professionalism.

'The genie is out of the bottle'

Griffin was eager for the party not to lose any momentum. Neither did he want to see the party's recent labours undone by a return to the culture of 'careless extremism'. If the party were to progress any further towards the political mainstream, Griffin decreed, it had to do away with the 'Three Hs' – 'hard talk', 'hobbyism' and 'Hitler'. To put it another way, members had to steer clear of violence, football hooligan-ism, skinhead culture and Hitler-worship.[115] There could be no break in its quest for legitimacy, Griffin thought. He was not wrong. An ICM Research poll conducted during 7–11 May 2002 revealed that the BNP still had to overcome a major barrier to its public acceptability – 57 per cent of white respondents favoured a total ban on the party.[116] Meanwhile, in order to retain the support of the hard core whilst also hanging on to hundreds of new recruits, its bandwagon of electoral success had to keep rolling. After a string of local council by-elections in the summer of 2002 in which the party's performance ranged from a nugatory 2.1 per cent to a more respectable 10.2 per cent, a promising opportunity arose in October 2002 when voters in Stoke were asked to directly elect the city's mayor.

Stoke had a recent history of racial tension. Over 100 Asian youths had rioted in the city's Corbridge area in July 2001 following the rumour (in all probability spread by the BNP) that the National Front intended to march through the city.[117] As you might expect, the BNP threw its hat into the ring. But rather than Asian-on-white crime or preferential funding for Asian areas, it was opposition to asylum-seekers that formed the core of the party's campaign. Its mayoral candidate Steve Batkin – an unemployed 42-year-old former pipe fitter – was a long-standing BNP activist. He had contested Stoke at the 1997 general election and polled just 1.23 per cent of the vote, and at the 1999 European elections he had garnered 2.41 per cent; by June 2001 his share of the vote had increased to 3.77 per cent.[118] Through community campaigning – his 'helping-hands' team even lent pensioners a hand with their gardening – Batkin had fostered a degree of neighbourhood legitimacy. Not surprisingly he performed best in local council elections. In May 2000, in the city's Fenton ward, he won 9.3 per cent of the vote. Two years later, with 16.6 per cent of the vote, Batkin came within 70 votes of being elected in the city's Longton North ward.[119] As a result, expectations for a good showing at October's mayoral election were high.

In his election address, Batkin claimed that asylum-seekers were pouring into Stoke and that the city had become 'an adventure theme park for economic migrants'. He was pictured outside a local pub claiming that this once favourite local hostelry had now become a home for 'refugees from Afghanistan'. He also made secondary promises to stop the spread of Islamic fundamentalism, to clampdown on crime, paedophiles and racial attacks on whites. And in a final populist gesture, he pledged to forgo the mayoral salary of £70,000 and only draw the minimum wage.[120] Canvassing was problematic, however, not least because Batkin had the entire city to cover and, in any case, the branch in Stoke could only rely on a small number of activists. Consequently, during the last week of the election campaign, the BNP fell back on word of mouth and circulated rumours throughout the city. Apart from free driving lessons, mobile phones and taxis, asylum-seekers were said to be in receipt of £5,000 cheques from the Benefits Agency in order to purchase their own cars. A local post office was even said to have a special queue for asylum-seekers, which forced local residents into longer waiting times! Yet Stoke only had 4.8 asylum-seekers per 1,000 residents – a figure comparable to other cities such as Nottingham and Derby. But the perception that the city was 'overrun' by asylum-seekers was common.[121] This urban myth was easily put into circulation especially when asylum-seekers in Stoke were concentrated in five or six wards. Moreover, with British society fed on a diet of tabloid scare stories, the number of asylum-seekers in Britain was routinely overestimated. One poll found that Britons believed that their country was host to some 23 per cent of the world's asylum-seekers, when the true figure was put at a mere 1.98 per cent.[122]

Batkin took as many as 8,213 first preference votes, which represented some 18.67 per cent of the poll on a turnout of just 24 per cent. Not only had Batkin polled more votes than the Conservative and Liberal Democrat candidates combined, he had just fallen short of qualifying for the second round of voting. The party's vote was secured despite the fact that 20,000 anti-fascist broadsheets were distributed and that the election addresses were sent out several days after the all-postal ballot papers. Batkin claimed that the election had been rigged. He believed that thousands of people had voted before they had read the party's manifesto and that this had stopped him from winning the election.[123] For Griffin meanwhile, what Stoke had shown was that the 'BNP genie is well and truly out of the bottle and has no intention of ever returning'.[124]

This all started to ring true when towards the end of 2002 the British National Party won another local council seat. This time the victory came in the Mill Hill ward of Blackburn. Once again, luck played its part. During the summer, BNP activists had already established a presence in the town after objecting at plans to turn a local old-aged peoples' home into a hostel for asylum-seekers. In the run-up to polling day, BNP activists then systematically canvassed the ward. Opposition to asylum-seekers and calls to end alleged preferential funding for Asian areas were the party's twin campaign themes. Despite a plea by Prime Minister Tony Blair not to let the BNP in, carried on the front page of the *Lancashire Evening Telegraph*, Robin

Evans, a self-employed builder pushed Labour into second place by a margin of just 16 votes and took the seat with 32 per cent of the vote.[125] Griffin was in buoyant mood. His strategy was clearly paying dividends. The BNP now had four councillors. Moreover, over the course of 2002 party membership had increased by 60.5 per cent and total party income had grown from £144,743 to £228,136.[126] Even so, by comparative standards, the party still lacked strength. At 3,847, membership was far below the numbers the NF could boast in the 1970s. Nevertheless Griffin was right – now it was only a matter of time before the BNP would start winning council seats outside its breakthrough zone in the north-west of England.[127]

'We don't just win in Lancashire'

When the British National Party won its fifth council seat in January 2003, it occurred in Halifax, West Yorkshire. The party's candidate Adrian Marsden pushed the Liberal Democrats into second place in the Mixenden ward by a margin of just 28 votes. The BNP had collected 679 votes from a ward in which it had managed just 59 votes in 1999. Teams of canvassers tirelessly worked the streets and distributed no less than seven leaflets. Several of these even had different versions tailored for two different audiences: the deprived white working-class voters on the Mixenden council estate and more middle-class residents in outlying districts. The party also circulated a video in which Adrian Marsden could be seen talking about local issues. This was delivered to a limited number of homes chosen since they either contained large numbers of white voters or key opinion formers. A number of local publicans also screened the video to their customers. It was the party's most sophisticated local by-election campaign in its history.[128]

True to form, the focus of its election material was on the supposed influx of asylum-seekers, but political capital was also made out of the decision by local councillors to raise their allowances by 43 per cent at the same time as increasing council tax by 18 per cent. In the week before polling day, both the *Daily Express* and the *Mirror* ran anti-BNP stories. Anti-fascists also distributed leaflets that identified Marsden as a former C18 organiser.[129] Still, canvass returns remained steady throughout the campaign. Once more, the party's quest for legitimacy was underpinned by doorstep contact. Yet the party's success in Halifax derived as much from more general factors as from the professional organisation of the party's campaign.

Even if parts of the national press had come out against the BNP, this was only one side of the story. In the weeks leading up to the council election in Halifax, the tabloid 'crusade' against asylum-seekers grew to a new intensity. This followed the discovery of a lethal toxin in a flat that housed immigrants in North London and the related killing of a special branch officer at the home of North African asylum-seekers in Manchester. Now Britain's most popular tabloid, the *Sun* joined forces with the *Daily Mail* and *Daily Express*. On 20 January, it headlined with 'Asylum Meltdown' and urged its readers to 'Read this and get angry'. The *Mail* ran a series on 'Asylum Britain'; the *Express* congratulated itself with 'We told you so' and reproduced no less than 20 of its front cover pages on asylum-seekers. This was all to the good as far was the BNP was concerned. And with David Blunkett warning that on the issue of asylum, British society was 'like a coiled spring',[130] the stage was now set for the BNP to take a major step towards the mainstream.

Fielding 219 candidates, the May 2003 local council elections represented the party's most ambitious election effort so far. Determined to extract maximum advantage from a climate of public opinion dominated by the asylum-seeker issue, it felt confident that it could obtain strong electoral showings even in those areas where its activities were fairly low-key. However, as in 2002, it pushed hardest where it expected to win: Burnley, Oldham, Stoke, Halifax, Sandwell and Sunderland. The party had been looking 'to win five or six new seats in order to maintain momentum with a dozen being at the high end of expectations'.[131] As it happened, it won 13 seats. Over half were in Burnley (7) but wins were also recorded in Sandwell (2), Dudley (1), Halifax (1), Stoke (1) and Broxbourne (1) in Hertfordshire. Nationwide, the party captured 104,037 votes in all. Its average vote was 17.3 per cent. Were this showing to be repeated in the 2004 council elections, with entire councils up for election across a swathe of metropolitan districts (Oldham, Sunderland, Sandwell, Dudley, Bradford and so on) the party could expect to win dozens of seats. And as for the European elections in 2004, Griffin calculated that it could take five seats – the North-West, West Midlands, Yorkshire, East Midlands, and the South-East.[132] Tony Lecomber further extrapolated the figures. Since the BNP had only contested 2 per cent of local council seats, the party's potential constituency could now be in the order of five million voters – on a par with its more successful continental brethren.[133]

When digesting the electoral advance of the BNP at the May 2003 local elections, we can isolate a number of factors behind the party's localised success. The most obvious dynamic has been the reemergence of popular racism. That such racism continues to course through the veins of mainstream British society is clear. In 2000, the British Social Attitudes Survey found that a quarter of Britons still admit to being either 'very racist' (2 per cent) or 'a little racist' (23 per cent). Moreover, two-thirds believe that there are too many immigrants in Britain.[134] Whilst Britons have undoubtedly become more tolerant of multicultural society and overt forms of racism have become socially unacceptable (hence the BNP denial that it is a racist party), immanent racism has reanimated itself through a series of sensationalist media campaigns directed against asylum-seekers and the accommodation of anti-asylum rhetoric by mainstream politicians. This racism, albeit articulated through 'socially acceptable' forms of intolerance towards asylum-seekers, and heightened by post '9/11' insecurities, has provided the British National Party with its largest reservoir of support. In May 2003, Simon Darby, the party's successful candidate in Dudley, believed quite rightly that newspaper coverage of the asylum issue was the single most important driver behind the party's recent success: 'Issue after issue, day after day, asylum this, asylum that. So we now have the luxury of banging on people's doors with the mainstream issue of the day.'[135]

But there are complicating factors. If we take Burnley for example, the asylum issue played a secondary role. Following the disturbances in 2001, no more asylum-seekers were sent to the town. The popular racism that occasioned the party's success in Burnley was grounded far more in feelings of resentment towards the local Asian community and perceptions that the funding distribution between wards was unfair. We need only reflect for a moment on its May 2003 campaign slogan of 'Vote for a fairer Burnley'. This had little to do with asylum-seekers – its key demands were for a more equitable distribution of public monies, the return of ownership of communities to those who live in them, withdrawal of funding to the town's translation unit and the creation of a special unit at Burnley police station to deal with 'anti-white' racism.[136] Likewise in Oldham, where the BNP polled almost 8,000 votes, the key factor was residual antagonism towards the local Asian community. Moreover, in certain areas where the asylum issue had taken on particular local resonance, such as Kent and Sussex – the scene of recent demonstrations against the housing of asylum-seekers in local hotels – the BNP did not perform as well as they might have expected.[137] Such counter-examples clearly require further probing but it seems likely that these were areas in which the party's doorstep presence was more subdued.

As was the case with the National Front in the 1970s, the 'race' issue has been the vehicle for the party's electoral emergence. Wherever this politicisation of 'race' occurred, be it through Asian-on-white crime, 'positive discrimination', anti-Islamic sentiment or opposition to asylum-seekers, space has opened up for the British National Party. But most crucial of all, to seize this space, hold on to it and then further widen the party's appeal, legitimacy is essential. As we have seen, extreme-right electoral breakthrough hinges on the construction of legitimacy whether at the broader national level or within the local context. On this point, it is worth recalling that close to 25 per cent of the electorate agreed with the forcible repatriation of immigrants during the 1970s.[138] Yet since the vast majority of voters associated the NF with Nazism, it always struggled to win elections. And if election victories are our measure, the BNP can certainly boast more legitimacy today than the NF had in the 1970s. Even so, nearly half of those questioned in a recent online poll still thought that the BNP was a 'thoroughly unpleasant' party.[139]

At first it was the Tories and then it was Labour. Both have taken on and pandered to the electorate's fears over asylum and immigration. Every inch of the way, the BNP has been able to associate itself with themes that are now considered 'legitimate' and 'normal'. Indirectly, therefore, the political mainstream has given the British National Party's platform respectability and credibility. In the run-up to the 2003 local elections, it was the turn of the Tories yet again. IDS changed tack, blamed Labour for the rise of the BNP and called for an end to the 'shambles' of the asylum system. He even denied that the issue of asylum-seekers was about 'race' – a sop to the collective self-image of British society as intrinsically tolerant.[140] And so the go-ahead was given for Conservatives to exploit the asylum issue at the local level. Notably, in both Dudley and Broxbourne, Tory election literature imitated that of the BNP. But in both cases it was right-wing extremists who emerged victorious. Astonishingly, Broxbourne had no asylum-seekers at all.[141]

Nor should we forget that the British National Party has also taken significant steps towards legitimating itself. It is clearly wrong to argue that the rise of the BNP is exclusively down to external factors. As you might expect, this is the position that John Tyndall has taken.[142] But Tyndall is wrong and Griffin is right – people are not so desperate that 'they'd vote for a pig in a Nazi armband if it stood for the BNP'.[143] Since anti-fascism is so strongly embedded within British popular culture, party image is obviously a key dynamic. And throughout, the 'new' BNP has given out the message that it is a credible, modernised and legitimate constitutional party. Everywhere, it has endeavoured to present itself as a party of respectable 'democratic nationalists' – just ordinary folk who speak up for the 'silent majority'. Aside from the obvious crackdown on asylum-seekers, the BNP pledged low taxes, curbs on bureaucracy, action against corruption, an end to 'political correctness' and 'positive discrimination', restoration of local democracy, a stop on crime, and so on.[144] Every one of its pledges at the May 2003 local elections talked the language of 'common-sense' populism. Significantly such populism (which promises government close to the people) struck a chord with many for whom the mainstream parties offered little more than political spin.

Doubtless, the party has benefited from increasing alienation from the political system and mainstream politicians. The 'crowded centre' where ideological distinctions between the mainstream parties are barely recognisable has certainly been a factor in the localised success of 'outsider' parties and non-traditional candidates (the election of a Monkey mascot in Hartlepool for example).[145] That the BNP has become a receptacle for some 'protest votes' is without doubt, but it is worth bearing in mind that the most disaffected are also those who are the most disengaged and least likely to vote. What the BNP discovered in Halifax, for instance, was that on the 'sink estates' it had difficulty mobilising its natural constituency because they were less likely to be registered to vote and the most disinterested.[146] Moreover, strict protest voters are often 'one-off' voters. But the fact that three BNP councillors in Burnley had made little contribution to council business did not prevent repeat voting for the party in May 2003.

It should be added that levels of canvassing by mainstream parties have also fallen sharply in recent years, which encourages voters to feel neglected. The BNP has capitalised on this by prioritising voter contact, as we have seen canvassing has become a central part of its electioneering method. Furthermore, where BNP activists canvassed, they were more often than not smartly dressed and polite. The fact that the party put up more than 20 women candidates in May 2003 further added to its image of respectability.[147] With that said, however, behaviour was not always impeccable and vestiges of the 'old' BNP remain. During the campaign in Stoke for instance, Steve Batkin accused Jews of profiteering from the Holocaust and fabricating the death toll.[148] And with the BNP facing an anti-fascist campaign described by *Searchlight* as 'the largest and most widespread for at least a generation', British National Party activists also resorted to intimidation of opponents in a number of localities.[149]

As in 2002, anti-fascist groups hammered out the anti-BNP message, and once again they were joined by sections of the national and local press. The *Daily Express* ran a major anti-BNP crusade, and as for local press opposition this was also extensive. Steve Batkin attacked the *Stoke Sentinel* for running a 'vicious, nasty campaign' against the party. Meanwhile, in the north-east, where a quarter of its candidates stood, the regional daily, the *Northern Echo*, came out strongly against the BNP.[150] All the same, and the party's results surely bear this out, its opponents did not necessarily keep the BNP vote down – a further indicator that the party had effected a more credible front of respectability than the National Front in the 1970s.

So what does this all mean? What are we to make of the party's triumphal declaration that 'HISTORY WAS MADE on Thursday 1st May 2003 when the British National Party walked out from the fringe of British politics and stepped into the mainstream'?[151] For sure, in some areas, the party has established itself within mainstream political life. This is especially true in Burnley where it is now part of the fabric of the town. But even here the controlling Labour group has, within the chamber, endeavoured to both isolate and destroy confidence in BNP councillors.[152] As for the wider picture, it is probably more accurate to say that the British National Party stands on the cusp of the political mainstream. In other words, it may have acquired *partial* respectability but it is still some way from the *full* political legitimacy that Griffin so desperately craves. We can evidence this from a number of factors. First, the national and local press run campaigns against it (and will probably do so again in 2004). Secondly, since the local elections of 2002, the BBC has also tried to limit interviews with the BNP.[153] Unlike the UK Independence Party, for instance, it has never featured on BBC's popular *Question Time* even when the show was broadcast from Burnley itself. Indeed, more recently, an eleventh-hour decision was taken by the BBC to cancel the party's involvement in a special day of programming on asylum.[154]

On the other hand, some parts of the broadcast media still continue to give it a platform, such as *Sky News* (6 May 2003; 24 June 2003). Of course, one might argue that this is bound to happen considering the proliferation of satellite and digital radio and TV channels. Moreover, where media boycotts do occur, the BNP can partly circumvent them. In 2003, its website became the most visited political party site in Britain, and, as I write, it receives more visitors than the sites of many provincial daily newspapers.[155] But with all this said, the mainstream parties are the final gatekeepers. Unlike France, for instance, the electoral system gives the BNP little hope of being incorporated into any mainstream electoral pact or coalition. But should the British National Party achieve a national breakthrough, then its demands to be recognised as a legitimate political party may finally become too strong to dismiss outright. And, as we shall see in the chapter that follows, once a far-right party enters the political mainstream, exorcising this particular demon is easier said than done.

7
The British National Party in Comparative Perspective

In the postwar cultural climate, the odious atrocities associated with Nazism starved Western Europe's extreme right of social and political respectability. Not surprisingly, right-extremist parties were pushed to the very margins of mainstream society, and hence for many years, while the extreme right continued to draw breath, it barely existed as a political force. Admittedly, it would emerge from the shadows every once in a while, but these episodes were short-lived and sporadic. The examples of Pierre Poujade in 1950s France[1] or the National Democratic Party in 1960s Germany[2] readily spring to mind. Since the 1980s, however, after Jean-Marie Le Pen's *Front National* had blazed the trail, right-extremists have taken on a more serious and lasting presence in the party systems of several Western European countries. The times change and over the course of last two decades right-wing extremism in continental Europe has been given a new lease of life. In this, our final chapter, we will place our subject within its broader West European context.[3]

This raises a number of important questions. In the first place, how far is the recent electoral emergence of the British National Party a reflection of wider phenomena and trends? Secondly, what does the experience elsewhere tell us about the British National Party and its electoral prospects? Finally, having considered the similarities and differences with its continental counterparts, what challenge to democracy does the British National Party present and can it be met?

Right-wing extremism: a rising tide?

Weaving through Western Europe, France is our first port of call. During the 1980s, the French political landscape underwent a dramatic transformation when, after more than a decade on the margins, the *Front National* rose to prominence. Following a run of local electoral gains over the period 1982–83, the FN first broke through at the national level in 1984 when it captured 11 per cent of the vote in the European elections. From this point on, the *Front National's* electoral success has become an enduring feature of French political life. By the 1990s the FN was collecting around 15–16 per cent of the vote.[4] Towards the end of 1998, however, Bruno Mégret, its deputy-leader, split from the party and established his own breakaway organisation.[5] This schism brought the FN to the brink of disintegration, and sure enough the party's vote slumped. At the 1999 European elections, the FN polled just 5.7 per cent of the vote and commentators predicted a return to obscurity.[6] Yet Le Pen more than weathered the storm. As we mentioned earlier, he spectacularly bounced back. When Le Pen became the first far-right leader to win through to the second round of the French presidential elections in 2002, it was written about in terms of a 'political earthquake' and with some justification – his second-round score of 18 per cent (5.8 million votes) was the highest ever recorded for a far-right candidate in French history.[7]

Looking to emulate the success of its sister party in France, a name-sake to the FN was formed in the French-speaking part of Belgium in 1985. Whilst this incarnation has had some limited success,[8] Belgium's most important far-right party is found in the Dutch-speaking part of the country. Here, the *Vlaams Blok* (Flemish Block – VB) experienced its first significant breakthrough in 1988. Across 10 municipalities it captured 23 local council seats. In Antwerp, which has since become its major bastion, the party won some 17.7 per cent of the vote. By 1991, the year in which the VB captured 10 per cent of the vote in parliamentary elections, it had become the largest party in the city.[9] Over half a million votes were won by the VB at the 1999 European elections, and the May 2003 general election saw the *Vlaams Blok* garner some 11.6 per cent of the national vote (17.9 per cent in Flanders) and thereby consolidate its position as Belgium's fifth largest political party.[10]

Whilst the electoral gains of the far right in France and Belgium are undoubtedly significant, their achievements have been partly eclipsed by developments elsewhere. Winning votes is one thing, but contemporary right-wing extremists have also managed to enter their respective national governments in two countries, namely Italy and Austria. The *Movimento Sociale Italiano* (Italian Social Movement – MSI), Italy's premier neo-fascist party, emerged from the political wilderness in

1993 when its mayoral candidates were elected to four provincial capitals and 19 medium-sized communes; it also narrowly missed out on winning the mayoralties of Rome and Naples. The following year, when rebranded as the *Alleanza Nazionale* (National Alliance – AN) it won 13.5 per cent of the vote and entered national government as part of the right-wing Freedom Pole coalition led by media tycoon, Silvio Berlusconi. For the first time in postwar Europe, a far-right party could boast ministers in government. What's more, this coalition also included the *Lega Nord* (Northern League), a regional populist organisation that took on many of the trappings of right-wing extremism.[11] But in next to no time at all – after only seven months – Italy's right-wing governing coalition had collapsed. Yet this was not the end of the matter. As part of Berlusconi's new coalition, the *Alleanza Nazionale* found itself back in government in 2001. The AN's leader Gianfranco Fini, who once described Mussolini as 'the greatest statesman of the century', was now sworn in as Italy's deputy prime minister.[12]

From its inception in the mid-1950s down to 1990, Austria's Freedom Party (FPÖ) struggled to break through the 10 per cent barrier in parliamentary elections.[13] Its level of support stood at less than 5 per cent when, at its Innsbruck congress in 1986, Jörg Haider took control of the party. But once the youthful and dynamic Haider was at the helm, the party's fortunes were soon transformed. Significantly, the FPÖ turned its back on social liberalism (it had become a member of the Liberal International in 1979) and swung towards the neo-conservative extreme right. The results were dramatic, and by the mid-1990s it was regularly winning more than 20 per cent of the national vote. In October 1999 it captured some 26.9 per cent of the poll, and four months later Haider's party was in government as the junior partner in a right-wing coalition with the *Österreichische Volkspartei* (Austrian People's Party – ÖVP). Though its stay in government lasted longer than its Italian counterpart, this coalition disintegrated in September 2002.[14] By November 2002 support for the Freedom Party had plummeted to 10.2 per cent. All the same, the Freedom Party was once again invited to become a junior coalition partner in Austria's centre-Right government in February 2003.[15]

Since the 1980s, then, as our all-too-brief overview shows, a tide of right-wing extremism has advanced across Western Europe. Yet as the examples above reveal, this rise has not been inexorable – it has ebbed and flowed. Nor should we exaggerate the geographical spread of right-wing extremism either. Even if we put Britain to one side, it still remains true that some countries have been less affected by this trend than others. In Germany, for instance, there was a surge in support for the far-right *Republikaner* (Republicans – REP) in 1989 when the party took 7.1 per cent of the national vote (2 million votes) at the European elections (14.6 per cent in Bavaria). A downward trend followed before the *Republikaner* regained ground in April 1992 when it took 10.9 per cent of the poll in state elections in Baden-Württemberg. But no sooner had it reemerged than it went into a steep decline. In European elections in 1994 the party failed to muster more than 4 per cent of the poll, and in 1999 support fell back under 2 per cent. Throughout the 1990s, notwithstanding the occasional strong showing in regional elections (the *Land* elections in Saxony-Anhalt in 1998, for example, when the rival German People's Union captured 12.9 per cent of the vote), right-wing extremist parties in Germany have generally stagnated. But Germany's experience has been double-edged. As a wave of racist violence spread across the country during the 1990s, militant neo-Nazi activity intensified.[16]

Around the same time as the Republicans enjoyed their fleeting success, over the border in the Netherlands the principal far-right parties, namely the deceptively titled Democratic Centre and Centre Party'86, also started making an impression. At local elections in 1990 they won a total of 15 seats. Four years later, 85 seats were obtained and, across those municipal seats contested, the vote for the extreme right averaged out at 7.4 per cent. Momentarily, a national breakthrough looked possible. But thereafter, at parliamentary elections in 1994, the combined vote for the far right totalled just 2.9 per cent (CD 2.5 per cent; CP'86 0.4 per cent) and support melted away. At the 1999 European elections, CD managed to scrape together just 0.5 per cent of the vote. As for CP'86, an Amsterdam court dissolved the party in November 1998.[17]

More recently, however, the spectacular success of the 'pink populist' Pim Fortuyn aroused concern among media pundits that even Dutch society – supposedly a stronghold of liberal tolerance – was not immune to the onward march of the extreme right. But the flashy Fortuyn, who met his untimely death in May 2002 from an assassin's bullet, was no right-wing extremist.[18] On the contrary, he was an economic and social neo-liberal. His opposition to immigration, and to Islam above all, stemmed from his belief that Dutch liberal society needed protection from the threat of Islam's 'reactionary' views. The idea that Fortuyn can be classified as a 'very Dutch variety of fascist' gets it wrong altogether.[19] To tell the truth, his blend of hostility towards immigrants, support for right-libertarianism and the fact that he absented himself from ultra-nationalism, took him closer to Scandinavia's tradition of populism rather than right-wing extremism.[20]

Moving our compass point north, in Scandinavia right-wing populist parties lay claim to significant levels of electoral support. At the 2001 general election in Norway for instance, the Progress Party won 14 per of the vote. For sure, these populist parties draw sustenance from the same racist and politically alienated soil that nourishes the growth of the far right elsewhere. However, with the probable exception of the Danish People's Party (a breakaway organisation from the Danish Progress Party, which has a strongly nationalist core), we need not include them in our extreme-right political family.[21] Neither should we dwell on the xenophobic Swiss People's Party, a conservative mainstream party that polled 23 per cent of the vote in the country's general election in 1999. As Chris Husbands cleverly remarked, 'to equate it...with, say, the French Front National or the German Deutsche Volksunion would be inaccurate and simplistic. After all, this is Switzerland: land of the cuckoo clock, not the Borgias!'[22]

Once these populist (but not national-populist) parties are removed from our equation, and we take into account the wider reality of the failure of contemporary far-right parties to register on the party systems of Spain, Portugal, Greece or Ireland, the temptation to overstate our phenomenon is markedly reduced. Therefore, even if xenophobic parties are more widespread, the tide of right-wing extremism remains geographically limited. The flow is not relentlessly rising; nor is it monolithic. Within the European parliament, for instance, there is little sense of a highly coordinated trans-European extreme right. Haider has given Le Pen a wide berth. As for Fini, he will have nothing to do with either the FN or the FPÖ. Nonetheless, our basic premise still holds true. Since the 1980s Western Europe has undoubtedly experienced an alarming resurgence of right-wing extremism. Clearly, the extreme right is no longer the pariah it once was.

Explaining the rise of far-right parties in Western Europe

When we come to isolate the conditions behind the rise of the far right, commentators frequently turn to the immigration issue in the first instance. This is undoubtedly of central importance. It is a standard point of reference, in fact so much so that for some scholars, extreme-right parties are by definition 'single-issue' parties. However, some words of caution are called for. In the first place, extreme-right parties ordinarily have broad ideological programmes even if within the extent of their propaganda, immigration emerges as the dominant theme. Moreover, rather than 'single-issue' anti-immigrant electors and no-one else, the electorates of right-extremist parties contain '*both* extreme right/xenophobic supporters *and* diffuse anti-party protesters', as Cas Mudde appreciates.[23] The truth of the matter is that far-right parties cannot be reduced to one 'single-issue'. But be that as it may, immigration has undoubtedly been, as Paul Hainsworth once described it, the extreme right's issue '*par excellence*'.[24]

To illustrate, we need only think in terms of the classic model of supply and demand. On the supply side, almost every one of our extreme-right parties adopted anti-immigrant populism prior to elect-oral take-off. The *Front National* led the way from 1977 onwards (although the FN was aware of the relative success of the British National Front in this period and almost certainly looked to emulate it).[25] The *Vlaams Blok* followed from the early 1980s (but especially so from 1987), the *Republikaner* from the mid-1980s and the FPÖ from 1989. As soon as popular demand for anti-immigrant policies appeared, which in some cases right-extremists had been instrumental in creating, the far right has worked hard to supply this demand. But there were exceptions to the rule and the MSI is a case in point, of which more later. On the demand side, the key dynamic in mobilising voters against immigration has been the politicisation of 'race'. As we have already seen from our study of Britain, the mainstream can prime the far right's agenda by increasing both the saliency and the respectability of the 'race' issue. Moreover, mainstream parties are fre-quently forced to coopt and further legitimise the far-right agenda once right-extremists acquire greater relevance within the party system.

In France, to quote the leading case, the 'race' issue was depoliticised until the late 1970s. This was largely the consequence of a decision-making process in which immigration policy was restricted to the realm of the technocrat, detached from the political arena and thus removed from mainstream political debate.[26] However, towards the end of the 1970s and during the early 1980s, the 'race' issue was politicised at both central and local levels. A range of factors occasioned this but to single out merely one or two, the more interventionist immigration policy of Giscard and (surprisingly) the racism of the French Communist Party were crucial. At first, the FN followed on the back of this emerging political agenda rather than setting it. However, after the FN had broken through at a local level and in the run-up to the 1984 European elections, the media imparted political salience to Le Pen and

his themes. By 1984, the point at which the FN experienced its electoral take-off, the immigration issue had arrived at the very centre of
French political life. Not surprisingly, by this stage voter demand for a
hard-line policy on immigrants had grown significantly.[27]

Likewise, in Belgium, mainstream politicisation of 'race' occurred
prior to the VB's electoral breakthrough. From the late 1970s onwards,
Flemish politicians had raised objections to the influx of North African
immigrants, particularly in Brussels where there were fears that these
new arrivals would favour Francophone candidates. This goes a long
way to explaining why support for political xenophobia in Dutch-
speaking parts of Belgium is greater: the presence of immigrants
aggravates Flemish concerns over the 'Francification' of Belgium, as
Patrick Hossay points out.[28] But this does not mean to say that the
'race' issue was not politicised in Francophone areas as well. Roger
Nols, the mayor of Schaerbeek (a suburb of Brussels) ran a series of
anti-immigrant campaigns in the 1980s.[29] More generally, there were
also partisan debates regarding the introduction of Islam to Belgium's
state schools. In 1987, the Minister of the Interior had referred to
immigrants as 'barbarians', and in that same year the automatic right
to asylum was abolished.[30] In the Netherlands, too, when the Dutch
extreme right experienced its limited surge in support during the early
1990s, 'race' had increasingly established itself within the mainstream
political debate. The Dutch government adopted a new integration
policy and questions of illegal immigration and asylum became more
important.[31] In Austria, when the influx of asylum-seekers sharply
increased after 1989, the press, in particular the tabloid *Kronen Zeitung*,
pushed the panic button. By May 1990, opinion polls were indicating
that two-thirds of the population thought that too many refugees were
entering the country.[32] At the 1990 federal elections, the mainstream
ÖVP adopted the xenophobic slogan 'Vienna for the Viennese' – a
saying more openly racist than 'Vienna must not become Chicago', the
Freedom Party's law and order slogan.[33] Yet during the 1990s it was
Haider who turned the growing climate of resentment towards foreigners to his party's advantage, especially amongst working-class constituencies.[34]

The cross-national perspective offered by Germany seems to fit this
pattern too. For Thomas Faist, in (West) Germany as in the rest of
Western Europe, immigration bècame a 'highly politicised' issue during
the 1980s.[35] In the city-state of West Berlin, where the Republicans first
made notable gains at local elections in January 1989, the influx of
ethnic Germans and foreigners was a key issue.[36] Besides, there was

further surge in popular support for the German extreme right during 1992 at a time when mainstream politics was dominated by the issue of asylum-seekers – the so-called *Asyldebatte* (asylum debate). In 1991 Germany received a quarter of a million asylum-seekers, and by the end of 1992 this figure was close to half a million. These numbers came in addition to the 222,000 and 230,000 ethnic Germans that had resettled in the country in 1991 and 1992 respectively – many for whom German was a foreign language. Not surprisingly, between October 1991 and August 1993, the asylum/foreigners issue dominated the concerns of ordinary Germans. As Marcel Lubbers and Peer Schappers have pointed out, the pattern of extreme-right voting in Germany 'is above all explained by anti-immigrant attitudes and the changes in these'.[37] Hence, when the mainstream parties reached a compromise and made changes to the Basic Law in order to tighten up Germany's liberal asylum system (passed by a majority of two-thirds in the Bundestag in May 1993), both the numbers of asylum-seekers and support for the extreme-right declined significantly.[38]

The real problem of course runs deeper still. At its root, it is the popular racism that remains stubbornly embedded within the fabric of mainstream European society. This means that both mainstream parties and extreme-right parties continue to see a value in prioritising immigration as an electoral issue. Even before the rise in Islamophobia that followed the events of '9/11', a Eurobarometer survey conducted in 2000 found that in terms of the proportion of the European Union's population that favoured the repatriation of all immigrants (whether legal or illegal), the EU average was one in five. In Belgium and Germany it rises to one in four. France follows with 22 per cent, Britain with 18 per cent and Austria with 17 per cent.[39] But because overt forms of political racism, in particular scientific racism, have become largely discredited in the post-Auschwitz era, for racism to be turned into a political force now requires more legitimate forms of ideological expression. As Robert Miles understands, 'what is conjuncturally novel about the past two decades is not an increase in racism *per se* ... but the intensification of ideological and political struggle around the expression of a racism that often claims not to be a racism'.[40] Therefore we now frequently encounter what some observers call the 'new racism' or 'neo-racism' – a type of racist discourse that denies that it is racist. On the sliding scale, it ranges from the stress on cultural differences (popular with the contemporary far right) through to the 'common-sense' or watered-down versions that major mainstream politicians all too often deploy when they raise the spectre of a 'flood of immigrants', or invariably refer to asylum-seekers in terms of negative stereotypes.

When we come to analyse the electorates of the far-right parties themselves, the immigration issue features highly. Supporters of Le Pen have shown a level of hostility towards ethnic minorities that is twice or three times greater than the national average.[41] North Africans in particular attract the lion's share of their vilification – a massive 94 per cent of Le Pen supporters admitted to disliking North Africans in one opinion poll.[42] As for further cross-national comparisons, a Eurobarometer (no. 37) survey of 50 FN, 42 VB, and 50 *Republikaner* sympathisers revealed that some 68.1 per cent of the FN, 68.4 per cent of the VB and 66 per cent of the REP cohorts demonstrated high levels of xenophobia.[43] Moreover, a study of voters for seven anti-immigrant parties at the 1994 European elections has revealed that most votes for these parties were not protest votes but rational choice votes, that is to say, political factors or salient issues shaped electoral decisions in the majority of cases. And the key determinants were ideological proximity and negative attitudes towards immigrants.[44]

However, since Austria did not become part of the EU until 1995, the Freedom Party was not included in this analysis. But the FPÖ is interesting not least because amongst its voters the protest dimension features more highly – its supporters are defined less by their racism. What accounts for this is Austria's specific national context where Haider's vote often represented a protest against a postwar political system dominated by ÖVP-SPÖ Catholic-conservative/Socialist-secular consociationalism and the tradition of *Proporz* (the distribution of state employment according to party affiliation). Nonetheless, in 1992, FPÖ sympathisers were, as Hans-Georg Betz has noted, at least twice as likely as other Austrians in considering it unpleasant to have Turks, Romanians or Jews as their neighbours.[45] Moreover, the immigration issue still accounted for 49 per cent of FPÖ votes in 1994 and 47 per cent in 1999.[46]

This brings us to Italy, our counter-example. Here, the approach to the immigration issue jarred with the norm. In the MSI's neo-fascist world-view, immigrants were largely seen as the victims of capitalist domination over the Third World.[47] On a visit to Le Pen in 1988, for instance, a leading party figure made it clear that the MSI would not be following Le Pen's xenophobic example.[48] In actual fact, given the ideological inheritance of Mussolini's fascist régime, where the racial laws (which many felt had corrupted Italian fascism) remained a divisive issue, adopting anti-immigrant populism threatened intra-party unity. In any case, for Italian society in general, the immigration issue was neither here nor there – a subject that attracted little public hostility or concern during the 1980s. In relative terms, immigration into Italian society remained modest, and despite the fact that there was a national debate triggered by the Albanian refugee crisis in 1991, at the general election in 1992, the year before the MSI made its breakthrough, immigration did not feature as a partisan issue at all.[49]

In truth, the Italian electorate had to think about issues of far more pressing concern. By 1994 Italy's postwar party system, which had been for decades monopolised by the Christian Democrats (DC) and various coalition partners such as the Socialist Party (PSI), disintegrated. The cause was endemic corruption on the part of Italy's political and business elite. A series of investigations led by the judiciary, which had started in Milan in early 1992, soon spread across Italy. At its peak, it encompassed as many as 211 deputies in the 1992 parliament, five former party leaders, four ex-prime ministers and countless other ministers and former ministers.[50] Italian public opinion was stunned. In a country where, even before the investigations had started levels of political dissatisfaction and cynicism were relatively high, the effect was to wipe the Christian Democrats and Socialists from Italy's political map. It had a crushing effect. Membership haemorrhaged, votes were lost and internal divisions ripped the DC and PSI apart. In December 1993, the point at which this corruption scandal reached its zenith, Fini came close to winning the race for mayor in Rome and Alessandra Mussolini (the Duce's granddaughter) narrowly missed out on Naples. Rather than the immigration issue, it was the collapse of the Italy's corrupt party system that brought the MSI its piece of good fortune.

Admittedly, Italy's example is an extreme one. Nonetheless, across all our cases, right-extremist parties have drawn varying degrees of strength from the ongoing crisis of political representation that is currently afflicting Western democracies. Across Western Europe, surveys repeatedly reveal that many voters feel dissatisfied, disconnected and alienated from the political system and establishment politicians. This most obviously manifests itself in rising levels of voter abstention and apathy. But observers have also noticed that amongst far-right electorates voter alienation, disaffection and cynicism are overrepresented. Le Pen's electorate is, for instance, more dissatisfied with democracy than all other partisan groups. The same is true for REP sympathisers who in 1991 had a 'satisfaction with democracy' rating of only 57 per cent compared to the western German average of 81 per cent.[51] In

Austria, as we have mentioned already, Freedom Party voters distinguish themselves by their anti-establishment mood. Yet it would be wrong to dismiss all this simply as a 'protest vote'. This suggests a negative reaction, in other words a form of issueless protest where voting for an extreme-right party is merely an expression of frustration with the political establishment. If this were the case, extreme-right electorates would be highly volatile. But this does not square with the electoral entrenchment of parties like the FN. Evidently, one can protest and yet still have affinity with an extreme-right party. For some, this affinity might stretch across the party's entire programme; for others, anti-immigrant populism clearly serves as the primary pole of attraction.

Over the years, the low standing of traditional parties and institutions has been incorporated by a variety of international scholars into a broader and more sophisticated theoretical framework. This links the rise of right-wing extremism to the onset of post-industrial society and the rejection of the post-material agenda of left-libertarianism. The argument, which became increasingly influential during the 1990s, maintains that Western society has undergone profound structural transformation since the 1970s. A central part of this process has been the fragmentation of society whereby traditional socio-economic cleavages, such as class, that underpinned electoral behaviour in the past, have largely disappeared. The consequence has been partisan de-alignment, increasing voter volatility and the emergence of issue-politics. The agenda that dominated this new era of issue-based politics, so the theory goes, was shaped by left-wing post-material values (environmentalism, feminism, multiculturalism, and so on). But this triggered what Piero Ignazi calls a 'silent counter-revolution',[52] a growth in authoritarian and anti-system attitudes by those, particularly blue-collar workers (traditionally aligned with the left), who felt that their concerns were not being addressed by the established political elites.

In some cases, these concerns were taken up by the mainstream right (Thatcher in Britain, for example), but in many cases, as mainstream right parties converged on the centre, space was abandoned on the right for non-traditional actors to provide a platform for a new, disaffected constituency, pregnant with what Betz calls 'the politics of resentment'.[53] This, then, is the context in which the contemporary extreme right now finds itself – its 'political opportunity structure', to borrow the jargon of new social movement theory. And the extreme right will optimise its chances of being successful by supplying, so

Hebert Kitschelt argues, the 'winning formula' of economic neo-liberalism, ethnocentrism and social authoritarianism.[54]

If this grand theory is accepted, the overarching reason for the emergence of the extreme right is not the immigration issue but macro-structural change. However, notwithstanding its failure to note the importance of local conditions, if we take the FN as our 'test case', we soon see that this theory starts to suffer from serious flaws. In the first place, attitudinal analyses of the FN electorate reveal that its voters are heterogeneous and do not necessarily conform to the standard anti-post-materialist stereotype. For sure, their position on immigration and insecurity is hostile to left-libertarianism, but FN sympathisers are more liberal on other issues and, in this regard, they are sometimes at odds with the party's own programme.[55] Whilst the FN has won over significant blue-collar working-class support, this trend only became apparent in 1988, some four years after the FN experienced its national breakthrough. And as for Kitschelt's winning formula, when the FN moved away from economic neo-liberalism in the early 1990s, Le Pen's support should have fallen back.[56] But in 1995 Le Pen polled over 15 per cent of the vote at the presidential elections – his best score to that point. Moreover, post-materialist values are considered to be stronger in Germany and the Netherlands than in France, yet in Germany and the Netherlands the performance of extreme-right parties has been less robust.

The point that needs to be made is that even if growing numbers of people are evaluating the efficacy of democracy negatively, this has little to do with conflicts arising from the materialism/post-materialism cleavage. It is more a reflection of the decline of the nation-state in an era of ever-increasing globalisation. As the capacity of individual states to control their own national economic and social space reduces, so dissatisfaction with established political elites and their performance is bound to spread, thereby creating the conditions for the emergence of anti-system or anti-establishment parties.[57] And as we have seen, the opportunity for mobilising such disaffection can only be enhanced when governing elites become tarnished with political sleaze and corruption.

Surprisingly, given its critical importance in explaining why some right-extremist parties have been more successful than others, the issue of legitimacy has received far less attention from international scholars. In all probability this stems from a social-science tradition where accounts of far-right electoral success have tended to rely on survey data aggregated after far-right parties have made their electoral breakthroughs (and have already garnered variable degrees of political legitimacy). Thus, more often than not, where legitimacy is considered it is usually related to the aforementioned crisis of *system* legitimacy. But this offers only a partial explanation as to how and why relations between extreme–right parties and their political and social system have changed. Most crucial of all, it ignores the fact that for many years right-wing extremist parties were beyond the pale – political pariahs that were outside the realms of social and political acceptability. And whilst a crisis of confidence in the system might increase the legitimacy of extreme-right parties *qua* anti-establishment parties, it is difficult to see how the far right could offer a socially acceptable alternative without moderating its extremism.

This brings us to the ways in which Western Europe's right-extremists have endeavoured to bring *themselves* in from the cold. In the particularly apt words of Roger Griffin, the extreme right today 'cannot show its true face and hope to gain wide-spread social acceptance without extensive cosmetic surgery'.[58] A glance at the political histories of various extreme-right parties soon reveals periods of relative moderation and system adaptation. During the 1970s, for instance, the FN included amongst its ranks neo-fascists such as François Duprat and his *Groupes nationalistes-révolutionnaires* (Revolutionary Nationalist Groups), hardliners centred on the monthly review *Militant,* and neo-Nazi activists from the FANE (National and European Federation of Action). But in March 1978, chief ideologist Duprat was assassinated and in stepped Jean-Pierre Stirbois and his ally, Michel Collinot. These former militants from the *Groupe action jeunesse* (Youth Action Group), originally part of Duprat's revolutionary nationalist circle, then set about purging the FN of its 'extremist' wing.

By the early 1980s, in a bid to broaden its electorate, the FN was styling Le Pen as the French Ronald Reagan. Increasingly, however, Le Pen put paid to accusations of fascism by appealing less to the Anglo-American New Right and more to a native (non-fascist) tradition of 'national-populism'; that is to say, a vigorous defence of French national identity, authority and direct democracy where 'real' power would be returned to the people.[59] And as for racism, Le Pen embraced the more socially acceptable neo-racist language of cultural difference – the 'right to be different' – pioneered by the French *Nouvelle Droite.* Similarly, in Belgium, as Marc Swyngedouw informs us, despite its platform of Flemish ultra-nationalism and xenophobia, the VB 'rarely allows itself to support a distinction on a purely biological (racial) basis'.[60] It also tries to project a more moderate, respectable and populist image: 'Just look at our meetings', it recently declared, 'women and children have replaced militants with boxing gloves!'[61]

Needless to say, the transition of Italy's neo-fascist MSI into its 'post-fascist' incarnation, the *Alleanza Nazionale* offers a further case in point. Observers at MSI congresses in 1987 and 1990 would have heard Gianfranco Fini, the AN's leader, eulogising Mussolini's fascism. As late as 1992 the MSI celebrated the seventieth anniversary of the March on Rome with a parade of blackshirts and Roman salutes.[62] But the collapse of Christian Democracy gave the MSI its chance. With the DC in disarray, political space opened up for the MSI on the Italian right on condition that Fini distanced the party (at least cosmetically) from neo-fascism. The possibility of a right-wing alliance with Silvio Berlusconi's newly established *Forza Italia* (Go for it, Italy) left no room for doubt. If the MSI were to seize the occasion, it was incumbent on it to moderate and target centre-right ground. The *Alleanza Nazionale* was therefore launched, albeit first as an electoral banner to rally moderate rightists disoriented by the disintegration of Christian Democracy, before finally becoming instituted as a political party in early 1995 (at which point the MSI was dissolved).

Like its counterparts elsewhere, the new face of Italy's extreme right took on 'national-populist' features. While it still veered away from crude immigrant bashing, the *Alleanza Nazionale* committed itself to the renewal rather than the overthrow of the liberal-democratic system. Hence, there were demands for a directly elected presidency and true direct democracy. For many, however, since the internal culture of the AN remained loyal to its original fascist identity this merely represented a change in name only.[63] Others viewed the AN as a curious ideological hybrid where fascist ultra-nationalism stood cheek by jowl with an antithetical commitment to liberal democracy – a form of 'constitutional fascism' where the embrace of the democratic rules of the game was no longer specious but genuine.[64] This might seem an ideological oxymoron; nevertheless the AN has succeeded in further underscoring its commitment to democracy over recent years. Thus, following the party's 1998 Verona Congress, which marked another shift towards moderation, Francesco Cossiga, Italy's former president, saw Fini not as the reincarnation of Mussolini but as the 'Tony Blair of the Italian right'.[65] Nonetheless, the 1998 conference also revealed a darker side. A large majority of middle-ranking party elites still held a positive evaluation of Mussolini's fascist régime. Therefore Piero Ignazi is right: the AN remains on the fringe of the contemporary extreme right albeit on the threshold of its exit.[66]

Compared with the others, the Austrian case is atypical. As we have seen, before Haider became leader of the FPÖ, it had been controlled by the party's liberal wing. Moreover, the FPÖ had been in a government coalition with the Socialists between 1983 and 1986, and accordingly it had already established itself as a fully legitimate actor in the political arena before Haider started moving the party towards the extreme right. His aim was clear: to sharpen a distinction between Austria's tired, 'old' political elite and the FPÖ as the 'new' and dynamic opposition. Rather than moderation, this measure necessarily involved radicalisation, chiefly through verbal provocations. Along the way, so as to draw condemnation from Austria's political establishment, Haider made positive references to Nazism (its employment policy, praise for Second World War Nazi veterans, for example). However, rather than delegitimising the FPÖ, Haider won recognition for being the first major politician in Austria who was prepared to challenge the Second Republic's founding myth that the country had been Hitler's 'first victim'.[67] Even so, his extremism still had its limits. During the 1990s, careful not to overstep the boundaries of social acceptability, neo-Nazi groups and New Right theoreticians were forced out of the FPÖ and pan-German nationalism was exchanged for Austrian nationalism.[68]

But even if right-extremists have worked hard to appear more respectable, none of this would have been sufficient without the political mainstream also delivering respectability and significance to the far right. As we have seen, mainstream parties have not only politicised and thereby legitimated its themes, they have also included extreme-right parties in electoral coalitions. Take the FN for example. In September 1983 when, at a municipal by-election in Dreux, the mainstream right RPR and UDF incorporated the FN in an electoral alliance, it was awarded 'its long awaited badge of respectability', as Geoffrey Harris puts it.[69] In May 1989 in Belgium, the Flemish parties decided not to cooperate with the *Vlaams Blok* and instead resolved to establish a *cordon sanitaire*. Within weeks it had been abrogated.[70] In Italy, the part played by media mogul Berlusconi in smoothing the legitimation of the MSI was crucial. To begin with, in November 1993 he declared that if he were a resident of Rome he would vote for Fini at the Rome mayoral elections. Then, once Berlusconi had decided to enter the political fray, he invited the MSI to join his coalition. Accordingly, the smartly dressed, bespectacled Fini, who looked far removed from an archetypal right-wing extremist, was given access to Berlusconi's private media network. As a result Fini was conferred both legitimacy and credibility. Before long, this one-time neo-fascist had become Italy's most popular and respected politician.[71]

In accounting for the relative success of Western Europe's extreme right, there are, of course, other dynamics that need to be factored in. Without doubt, the personal qualities of the party leader is one. In an age where the media increasingly personalises politics, it is significant that Le Pen, Fini, Haider and the VB's Filip Dewinter are all regarded as charismatic figures. Even the less successful *Republikaner* Party has cashed in on the personality factor in the past; Franz Schönhuber (its leader until 1994) was a popular figure on Bavarian television during the early 1980s. Clearly the personality of the party leader helps to pull in votes but it does not stop there. A strong personality can also provide the party with a sense of identity, purpose and unity. It was said that Le Pen's greatest strength was his ability to keep the FN, which includes numerous ideological tendencies, together. But over the longer term, as the example of the FN shows, the domination of the party by one central, 'charismatic' figure can give rise to internal dissension. The experience of Haider and the Austrian Freedom Party also bears this out. In February 2000, after some 13 years as party leader, Haider stepped down. But he left the FPÖ in an unstable position. Unenthusiastic about ceding control to his successor, Susanne Riess-Passer, the result was a bout of damaging internal conflict and a consequent drop in popular support during 2002.

A final point to consider is the variable effect of different electoral systems. Whilst Britain's far right has faced the major obstacle of a first-past-the-post majority electoral system, its counterparts in Western Europe have been more fortunate. In many cases, elections to respective national parliaments have been carried out on the basis of PR – Austria, Belgium and France (in 1986), for example. Moreover, should the mainstream right succumb to the exigencies of electoral opportunism, other electoral systems carry a greater potential for the integration of right-extremists into electoral coalitions. But too much can be made of the vagaries of electoral systems, and the extent to which they necessarily guide voters is a moot point. In the Netherlands for instance, an extreme system of proportional representation has not stopped its extreme right from being relatively weak. Moreover, in France the reversion to a two-ballot majority system after 1986 did not stop the electoral consolidation of the FN. Nonetheless, as a general rule, an electoral system based on proportionality and a low representation threshold does tend to favour the extreme right.[72]

The British National Party: similarity and difference

The British National Party might claim to be Britain's fastest growing political organisation but it has yet to make any national break-through. To date, the 1 per cent that it obtained at the 1999 European elections is its highest score in a national election. Meanwhile the Freedom Party polled over 23 per cent, the AN over 10 per cent, the VB close to 9.5 per cent, and, when combined, the FN and MNR polled some 9 per cent. By this standard of comparison, the BNP remains small beer. As I write, the British National Party has 17 local council-lors,[73] but by 1989 the *Front National* had over 1,300 councillors and close to 2,000 by the end of the 1990s. And as for party members, the FN could call on 40,000–50,000.[74] The FN's youth organisation alone was over four times larger than the 3,487 members that the British National Party could boast in November 2002. Clearly the proportions of the phenomenon on the continent are of a different scale entirely. But if, at the 2004 European elections, the BNP were to duplicate the regional averages that it secured in 2003, it stands a chance of obtaining a handful of seats. New heights would be scaled by Britain's far right and it would find itself mixing in the company of its more distinguished overseas brethren. Ominously, after the local elections in 2003 Nick Griffin met Jean-Marie Le Pen in London in order to discuss the possibility of mutual cooperation should the BNP enter the European Parliament in 2004.[75]

For the moment, however, we do not need to know how the British National Party's electoral trajectory will develop in the near future to appreciate that its recent local electoral emergence is part of a wider trend. Over the course of the past two decades, right-extremist parties have grown in political significance in various parts of Western Europe, no more so than in France, Belgium, Italy and Austria. The reasons why can be found in a common pool of factors, which includes the socio-political construction of the immigration/asylum 'problem', popular racism, systemic factors such as political alienation and protest, and most significant of all – since right-wing extremists would remain ghet-toised without it – the construction of legitimacy. Furthermore, these are precisely the very same factors that account for the recent rise of the British National Party, as we saw in the previous chapter. For that reason, developments in Britain should not be taken in isolation. They are characteristic of a wider picture which, if necessary, can be extended out of the extreme-right political family to cover the broader canvas of non-extremist anti-immigrant populist parties as well.

Watching the rise of extreme-right parties from a distance, Britain has long comforted itself with the notion that it is an exceptional case. But whilst it may not (as yet) host a far-right party of the size of Le Pen's FN, British society conforms to the wider pattern on 'race'. The level of popular racism in British society broadly corresponds to a median position in European Union rankings. In this respect, it is generally-speaking no more or no less racist than the societies of many other EU countries, including those in which electoral support for right-extremist parties is (or has been) higher, namely France, Austria and Germany.[76] Without doubt, from a significant minority of its population, there are comparable levels of potential 'demand' for anti-immigrant populism. But over the years, the difficulty that right-wing extremists in Britain have encountered has been putting a party together with enough respectability to realise this potential as well as a political mainstream that by sending out reassuring signals to the racist constituency has, until recently that is, managed the race 'issue' effectively and thereby switched off 'demand'.

The experience elsewhere also tells us that it would be wrong to merely equate the extreme-right vote with a 'single-issue' racist vote. Whilst racism is a prime factor (and in most cases, the primary factor), there is also a strong relationship between extreme-right voting and rising levels of voter dissatisfaction with traditional political elites, particularly when conventional parties crowd in on the centre. This relationship is at its strongest, as the examples of Italy and Austria show, when the traditional party system has been built on networks of patronage and, along with it, either actual or perceived corruption. In the British case, there is little danger that the party system will collapse, but there can be no doubt that voters feel increasingly let down both by New Labour (especially in its traditional heartlands) and by an anaemic Conservative opposition. This mood of disaffection is only made worse by a lack of doorstep contact with voters. One study found that at the 2001 general election for instance, just 14 per cent of voters were canvassed compared with 24 per cent in 1997 and 30 per cent in 1992.[77] And if the rise of the BNP were to stretch beyond the current asylum issue–attention cycle, the reduced capacity of the mainstream parties to mobilise voters would be a major reason why. This factor probably accounts more for the electoral entrenchment of far-right parties over the longer term than the issues that right-extremist parties raise. As Martin Schain *et al.* point out, 'If this were not the case, issue co-option should be more effective.'[78]

As far as one can tell, the British National Party has a reservoir of potential support that is comparable to right-extremist parties else-where. That Britain could follow the example of its continental neigh-bours and host an extreme-right party of some significance is a real possibility, and the prospects of it achieving a national breakthrough[79] cannot be lightly dismissed – it has already acquired partial legitimacy and the asylum issue may yet continue to dominate the concerns of ordinary voters. The *Front National* broke through at the European elections in 1984 following a sequence of local electoral gains so the precedent has already been set elsewhere. But for the BNP, there is obviously an element of wishful thinking in all these projections.

For a start the issue–attention cycle could become less propitious. During the first quarter of 2003 for instance, the inflow of asylum-seekers dropped by almost a third.[80] Furthermore, in those local areas where the party represents the greatest threat, all-postal voting could be extended. This factor, which tends to increase turnout, largely accounts for the failure of the BNP to win any seats in Sunderland despite its full slate of candidates capturing almost 14,000 votes across the city.[81] Besides, the mainstream parties could present multiple candidates across those wards where three ward councillors are up for election in 2004. This might reduce the possibility that BNP candidates will be elected by virtue of coming either second or third-placed. With regard to the European elections, these are run on the basis of PR and hence more favourable to minor parties. Yet Griffin's offer of a pact with the UKIP made on 3 May 2003 was rejected. It therefore seems likely that the 'patriotic vote' will split in 2004. And if the UKIP vote is 'talked up' by the media, the party's only realistic chance of winning any seats may well be restricted to the North-West Euro-constituency, the party's strongest region. Then there are leadership and organisa-tional questions to consider. Following the expulsion of John Tyndall in the summer of 2003, there was talk of the former BNP leader plan-ning to fight Griffin through the courts.[82] Since this might have desta-bilised the party, Griffin was forced into a humiliating climbdown – Tyndall was back in the BNP by the end of the year. But be that as it may, Griffin's opportunistic style still carries the risk of alienating those hardliners who remain within the party's rank-and-file.

In March 2003, for instance, Griffin found it necessary to rush to the defence of Martin Wingfield, who in the 1980s had once been derided by Griffin as a moderate.[83] The election agent to a BNP candidate in Cumbria with two 'mixed-race' grandchildren, Wingfield had drawn attention to this fact in order to validate the claim that the BNP was not a 'racist' party.[84] However, this had touched a raw nerve inside the BNP and the prospect of further bouts of internal strife cannot be discounted. For the moment the BNP is in the ascendant. Nonetheless, in building itself up for a major electoral breakthrough in 2004, as the NF did in 1979, it does leave itself open to frustrated expectations. If Griffin does not make the grade, and fails to deliver on his promises, the BNP might well disintegrate before or soon after the next general election. Yet all this notwithstanding, there is still little scope for complacency. An online poll quoted in the *Mail* on 4 May 2003 offered some serious food for thought: of 1,689 adults questioned, one in seven (or 14 per cent) would consider voting for the British National Party.

All the same, even if the BNP should engineer a national electoral breakthrough, there is not much chance that BNP candidates will be elected to Westminster let alone form a government. When faced with a majority electoral system, the experience of the UK Independence Party shows that European election success does not necessarily translate into representation at Westminster. As we have seen, the vast majority of voters would not (and probably would never) consider voting for the BNP. With the electoral system weighted against it, the bridge to Westminster would prove especially gruelling to cross. This is certainly a reassuring thought particularly as the leadership of the BNP remains wedded to a core ideology of revolutionary nationalism.

As we saw in our earlier chapter, Griffin's 'modernisation' programme is all about repackaging itself in terms with which ordinary people find non-threatening and comfortable. The trained eye does not have to look too far, even within the sanitised and glossy pages of *Identity*, to find evidence that Griffin's 'new' BNP is not that different to the BNP of 'old'. In August 2003, for example, Griffin made it clear that if Britain were to be saved from the end-game of multi-cultural destruction, it does not need a 'protest party' but a 'political, cultural and economic revolution'.[85] Moreover, why, if the BNP claims that it is no longer a 'race supremacist' party, did a recent article praise the work of Professor Glayde Whitney, a 'race' scientist?[86] Anti-Semitism and Holocaust denial may have disappeared from view, but despite its preoccupation with the 'Islamification' of the West, the party has not refrained from expressing anti-Zionism. For Jewish conspiracy – still at the core of Griffin's world-view – the fashionable term 'globalisation' is used instead.[87] Admittedly, Griffin does occasionally depart from Tyndall's ideological beliefs but his revisions merely take us back to NF radicalism in the 1980s. Hence, in recent issues of *Identity*, we find articles supporting decentralisation[88] and Distributism.[89] Thankfully, then, the BNP remains a long way from being propelled to Westminster. Yet it is worth bearing in mind that the FN has not held more than one seat in the French parliament since the reversion to a two-ballot majority system in 1988, and thus far the FN has not disappeared from French politics.

As events have proved elsewhere in Western Europe (and there are too many examples to cite here), racism is not only a cause but also a consequence of the electoral success of the far right. It is in this sense that the real threat of the BNP emerges. On the one hand, especially in communities where the BNP is active, its presence can aggravate racial tensions and lead to a growth in racial attacks. To take one example: it seems likely that the local implantation of the BNP gave confidence to those who directed racial abuse towards touring dancers and musicians from South Africa in Sunderland in the summer of 2003.[90] On the other hand, as it gathers more support, the BNP can pressure other parties into taking a more illiberal stand on asylum and immigration issues. Across Western Europe, mainstream parties have taken on the agenda of the far right and Britain seems no different. The Labour government's Nationality, Immigration and Asylum Act passed in November 2002 is a case in point. By withdrawing all support for single people who do not claim asylum as soon as is 'practicable' it was judged to have contravened Article Three of the Human Rights Act (which protects individuals from 'inhuman or degrading treatment'). In the event, however, the Court of Appeal overturned this ruling and backed Blunkett's policy.[91] Moreover, with Labour reportedly determined to 'kill off' the asylum issue before the next general election, the prospect of further illiberal legislation looks likely.[92]

How then are we to meet the challenge presented by the British National Party? With the construction of legitimacy such a central ingredient in extreme-right electoral success, should we, as democrats, seek to divest the BNP of social and political respectability? The BNP is clearly abiding by the democratic rules of the game, but it remains a party that is led by a leadership coterie that seeks a revolutionary transformation of the system. Unlike the *Alleanza Nazionale* (or arguably the FN, even), its essence is not reformist. On these grounds, democrats would certainly be justified in trying to exclude its representatives from the mainstream social and political arena.[93] But given the rapid expansion of electronic media, this is not as easy as it once was. Moreover, as anti-fascist groups have increasingly found out, 'exposing' what the BNP really stands for has become far more difficult, especially since the party has undergone cosmetic surgery, has dispensed with Tyndall, and when a new, more respectable and non-fascist membership rallies to its cause. Over the long run, this will give rise to its own internal contradictions, but for now Griffin is keeping it together by adopting a slick image and a minimalist approach to ideology. Nevertheless, there is still a place for anti-fascist activity – maximising turnout tends to work against the extremists.

Finally, as for the mainstream parties, strategies are urgently required to address the crisis of representative democracy and to reconnect with voters. Most of all, however, a sense of self-control and moderation must return to the asylum debate not only on the part of mainstream politicians but also amongst tabloid journalists. The growth of the far right is not caused by conspiracies of silence, as some right-wing pundits (such as the *Mail*'s Peter Hitchens) seem to think. As we have seen in Britain and now from our wider West European perspective, the correlation between extreme-right electoral gains and the politicisation of 'race' is direct. And so, on this last point, I need only return to the warning that I first gave in 1996. As long as popular racism remains rooted within the bedrock of British society, playing with the 'race' issue is playing with fire.[94]

Conclusion

Over the course of the past two decades, as far-right parties rose to prominence on the continent we could congratulate ourselves on having no domestic equivalent to the French National Front, Belgium's Flemish Block, Austria's Freedom Party or Italy's National Alliance. It seemed that Britain was immune to the scourge of contemporary right-wing extremism. Since the turn of the new millennium, however, while our condition is still far from critical, British society has started to present some worrying symptoms of this 'continental' illness. Although it is clearly less afflicted by it than many of its West European neighbours, it is nevertheless true that at no period throughout the entire history of right-wing extremism in Britain, has a far-right party registered as much success at the ballot box as today's British National Party.

Significantly, Nick Griffin's BNP has now become, in electoral terms, Britain's most successful right-extremist political party ever. With research carried out by the Commission for Racial Equality (CRE) in 2003 suggesting that between 20 to 30 per cent of voters, particularly males between the ages of 18 and 35, were becoming 'susceptible' to the appeal of the British National Party,[1] there is certainly a possibility that it could follow the wider trend and make a national electoral breakthrough. On the other hand, if this breakthrough does not take place in the near future, the British National Party could all too quickly fade from view. And when historians return to the subject in years to come, this episode may well be written about in terms of yet another false dawn in the continuing cycle of failure that has characterised the ill-fated history of British fascism. But whatever the case may be, it is surely time to abandon the myth that Britain is some special case. As this book has shown, the factors that have occasioned the recent growth of the British National Party have generally been responsible for the electoral emergence of right-extremist parties elsewhere.

Clearly the British National Party has undergone a transformation in both image and tactics. Its activists, as the CRE's Trevor Phillips described them, now 'dress like New Labour and ape the community campaigning of the Liberal Democrats'.[2] But more than that, they have also appropriated the quasi-respectable language of Western Europe's 'national-populist' right. Nonetheless, it would be wrong to see the 'new' BNP as anything other than fascist. When it started out, as the first chapter shows, it was a vehicle for the political aspirations of John Tyndall. A veteran of a host of right-extremist organisations, Tyndall marked the British National Party out as a revolutionary force, a party that if elected would bring about the ultra-nationalist rebirth of Britain. Throughout the 'lean years' of the 1980s, however, he found the electoral road blocked. Margaret Thatcher's brand of Conservatism as well as the party's pariah status presented major obstacles to realising his electoral ambitions. As a result, Tyndall's immediate objectives were more modest in scale: to establish the party's name, to have it taken seriously amongst the right-extremist constituency and to displace the National Front as Britain's leading far-right party.

As we saw in Chapter 2, these objectives were met. Yet the contemporaneous achievements of Le Pen's National Front threw the dismal performance of Britain's far right into sharp relief. To the keen observer, what Le Pen had demonstrated was that if right-extremists could dissociate themselves from fascism and nurture respectability, a way out of the electoral ghetto could be found. But Tyndall refused to take this lesson on board. For Tyndall, determined to keep the party's revolutionary mission nestled under his wing, it was the British National Party's lack of credibility with voters sooner than its dearth of social and political respectability that was the problem. Sure enough, as the third chapter showed, rather than Tyndall it was grassroots activists in East London who thought that the party's strategy needed to alter course. As they looked to normalise the party within local communities, in place of 'red-blooded' activism they substituted 'legitimate' forms of political behaviour. This certainly helped to bring about its fleeting success in Tower Hamlets in the early 1990s where this strategy originated, but the organisational disarray wrought by Combat 18 and a lack of enthusiasm on Tyndall's part meant that this strategy stalled – at least until the end of the 1990s when an influx of new activists from the West Midlands brought fresh momentum.

As we have seen, from the mid-1990s onwards, demoralised by the failure of the party to build on its Tower Hamlets breakthrough, a challenge to the tired and ageing leadership of John Tyndall began to take shape. For the most part, this crystallised around those who wanted to see the party push for greater public acceptability. Eddy Butler, Michael Newland, Tony Lecomber – so-called 'modernisers' – took the FN and the FPÖ as their source of inspiration. Since the term 'populism' was a word associated on Britain's far right with breaking faith and selling out on the core principles of revolutionary nationalism, they described their thinking not so much as 'national populism' or 'neo-populism' but as 'new', 'modern' or 'Euro-nationalism'. With *Patriot* magazine playing the supporting role, the 'modernisers' had emerged as the party's dominant faction by the end of the 1990s. Having sensed which way the wind was blowing, Nick Griffin, who originally had been brought into the BNP to take up the cudgels for Tyndall, made an about-turn. At first Griffin saw the party's hardliners as his natural constituency, but he later switched allegiance. With the sole intention of challenging Tyndall for leadership of the BNP, Griffin started speaking for those who favoured modernising the party. And in 1999, as we saw, Griffin finally outmanoeuvred Tyndall and swept the board in the party's first ever leadership contest.

But none of Griffin's 'modernisation' programme envisaged modification to the party's ideological core. All through Tyndall's reign, as Chapter 4 shows, the party was committed to a revolutionary ideology that was intent on creating a new, post-liberal order. And given that the party's modernisation programme was contrived merely for short-term political gain, as Nick Griffin revealed, there is no reason to think that the inner core of today's British National Party has surrendered its radicalism. That many of its new recruits are oblivious to this fact is certain. Under Tyndall, first in the NF and then in the BNP, this radical ideology revealed itself all too easily. The problem the National Front met in the 1970s was that when it started to attract a larger following, its more moderate constituency discovered its radical ideology at the core and soon departed. But under Griffin, exclusive of reference to the 'apple-pie' concepts of freedom, democracy, security and identity, ideology is rarely talked about in any real detail. As a result, there is less hard-line material for new recruits to come across. But this does not mean to say that the British National Party has compromised principles or sold-out. From the start, everything has been about creating an image of the party that ordinary voters would find non-threatening. As Griffin said, 'Nothing is easier for a group of isolated true-believers than to create a fundamentalist programme of ideological perfection which positively petrifies ordinary voters.'[3]

For sure, a change of image and the adoption of more sophisticated tactics (of which local community politics and doorstep contact with voters have taken precedence) could not deliver electoral success without other facilitating factors. On this point, as this book shows, the central and local politicisation of 'race' has played a key role. In the local arena of Tower Hamlets we saw how, by pandering to racism, the Liberal Democrats helped pave the way for the party's local council by-election victory in 1993. In Oldham in 2001, we reflected on sensationalist reporting of Asian-on-white crime; in Burnley, we underscored the part played by the Independents who spread the perception that Asian areas attracted preferential funding. Nor should we forget that superimposed on this has been a national debate on the asylum issue. Of all things, by availing itself of the sort of hysterical language that legitimates the BNP, it is the socio-political construction of the asylum 'problem' that created the opening for the party in the wider context. Where previously its association with fascism hemmed the party in, the shackles are now loosening as legitimacy is brought about both from within and from without. For the first time in its history, the British National Party stands on the brink of entering the political mainstream.

We conclude that wherever 'race' is politicised by the mainstream (and our final comparative chapter provides yet further confirmation that this is true), more often than not it is the far right that benefits. Through this means, the mainstream typically provides the far right with its route into the main run of society. It thus follows that even if in the next year or so the BNP does retreat back into the ghetto from which it has emerged, so long as popular racism continues to flow through the veins of Britain's public, the potential for a rapid growth in support for an extreme-right party will always remain. In this sense, the challenge that the British National Party presents only serves to detract our attention from the real source of the problem.

Without doubt, the 'race' issue has been key to Griffin's initial success and in time, as the asylum debate quietens down, we would expect that support for the BNP would fade away. But it is not as simple as that. The extent to which the party will be able to 'harden-up' its 'softer' support and build a stable electorate will depend on (a) the degree of voter disaffection from the mainstream parties, and (b) its ability to broaden its appeal beyond its support base in popular racism. In the first place, this brings us to the importance of systemic factors.

As our examples from abroad suggest, the extreme-right's electorate typically contains diffuse anti-party voters who show little confidence in established political elites. And there can be little doubt that there is widespread disillusionment with mainstream politics in Britain today. Indeed, if Martin Wingfield's analysis of the state of play in the party's north-west strongholds is accurate, then the BNP is currently taking seven out of ten of its voters from New Labour.[4] It need hardly be added that the Labour Party desperately needs to reconnect with voters and rebuild confidence. However, the other mainstream parties must also start offering a credible alternative too. Secondly, if the party is to continue on its cycle of growth then it will have to widen its appeal in order to catch the diffuse sentiments of anti-establishment voters. Worryingly, it has already started to do this with the introduction of common-sense 'populist' themes such as promising to crackdown on crime, by pledging to restore local democracy, and through its opposition to corruption. But, and this is where we close, so long as the inner core remains committed to revolutionary nationalism, contradictions in this strategy should emerge in time. In the final analysis, when this happens, either the BNP will genuinely turn itself into a reformist 'national-populist' party (and thereby cease to be fascist), or it will surely return to the murky political backwaters from whence it came.

Notes

Introduction

1 See N. Copsey, *Anti-Fascism in Britain* (Basingstoke: Macmillan – now Palgrave, 2000), p. 76.
2 See J. Bean, *Many Shades of Black* (London: New Millennium, 1999).
3 See *Searchlight*, no. 128, Feb. 1986, p. 15.
4 See for example, C.T. Husbands, 'Following the "Continental Model"?: Implications of the Recent Electoral Performance of the British National Party', *New Community*, vol. 20, no. 4 (1994), pp. 563–79.
5 For discussion of legitimacy as a social-scientific concept, see D. Beetham, *The Legitimation of Power* (Basingstoke: Macmillan – now Palgrave, 1991).
6 For more recent work on various aspects of the British fascist tradition, see for instance, R. Thurlow, *Fascism in Britain: From Oswald Mosley's Blackshirts to the National Front* (London: I.B. Tauris, 1998); R. Thurlow, *Fascism in Modern Britain* (Stroud: Sutton, 2000); T. Linehan, *British Fascism 1918–39: Parties, Ideology and Culture* (Manchester: Manchester University Press, 2000); T. Kushner and N. Valman (eds), *Remembering Cable Street: Fascism and Anti-Fascism in British Society* (London: Vallentine Mitchell, 2000) and J.V. Gottlieb, *Feminine Fascism: Women in Britain's Fascist Movement* (London: I.B. Tauris, 2000).
7 For earlier work on the BNP by this author, see N. Copsey, 'Fascism: The Ideology of the British National Party', *Politics*, vol. 14, no. 3 (1994), pp. 101–8 and 'Contemporary Fascism in the Local Arena: The British National Party and "Rights for Whites"', in M. Cronin (ed.), *The Failure of British Fascism: The Far Right and the Fight for Political Recognition* (Basingstoke: Macmillan – now Palgrave, 1996), pp. 118–40. For work by others, see for example C.T. Husbands, 'Following the "Continental Model"? Implications of the Recent Electoral Performance of the British National Party'; R. Eatwell, 'Britain: The BNP and the Problem of Legitimacy', in H.-G. Betz and S. Immerfall (eds), *The New Politics of the Right: Neo-Populist Parties and Movements in Established Democracies* (Basingstoke: Macmillan – now Palgrave, 1998), pp. 143–55; and D. Renton, 'Examining the Success of the British National Party, 1999–2003', *Race and Class*, vol. 45, no. 2 (2003), pp. 75–85.

1   'Back to Front'

1 J. Tyndall, *The Eleventh Hour: A Call for British Rebirth*, 3rd edn (Welling: Albion Press, 1998), p. 42.
2 *Ibid.*, p. 47.
3 G. Thayer, *The British Political Fringe* (London: Anthony Blond, 1965), p. 56.
4 On Chesterton's conspiracy theory see A.K. Chesterton, *The New Unhappy Lords* (London: Candour Publishing Co., 1965).

5 R. Thurlow, *Fascism in Modern Britain* (Stroud: Sutton, 2000), p. 136.
6 It should be pointed out that *Searchlight* has previously maintained that Tyndall was involved with the pre-1960 British Nazi 'underground' at the age of 19, see *Searchlight*, no. 35, 1978, p. 8. According to *Searchlight*'s sources, this was revealed in a cassette tape that was used in the covert recruitment of new members to Column 88 – a shadowy Nazi paramilitary group formed in Britain in 1970. But if Tyndall was an undercover Nazi at the age of 19, why did it take him several years before he 'infiltrated' the League of Empire Loyalists?
7 See Tyndall, *The Eleventh Hour*, p. 11 and p. 24.
8 *Ibid.*, p. 26.
9 Transcript of Tyndall speech (June 1979) in possession of the Board of Deputies of British Jews.
10 Tyndall, *The Eleventh Hour*, p. 51.
11 *Ibid.*, p. 53.
12 *Ibid.*, p. 63.
13 J. Bean, *Many Shades of Black: Inside Britain's Far Right* (London: New Millennium, 1999), p. 116.
14 See Tyndall, *The Eleventh Hour*, p. 176 and Bean, *Many Shades of Black*, p. 119.
15 See M. Walker, *The National Front*, 2nd edn (London: Fontana/Collins, 1978), p. 33. Bean has subsequently denied that the NLP held any meetings in the area prior to the riots. See Bean, *Many Shades of Black*, p. 121.
16 Bean, *Many Shades of Black*, p. 141.
17 M. Webster, 'Why I am a Nazi', *The National Socialist*, no. 7, 1962.
18 Rosine de Bounevialle as quoted in Walker, *The National Front*, p. 45.
19 R. Hill with A. Bell, *The Other Face of Terror: Inside Europe's Neo-Nazi Network* (London: Grafton, 1988), p. 81.
20 Walker, *The National Front*, p. 105.
21 Alistair Harper, a Scottish schoolteacher, and Roger Pearson, a racist anthropologist, established the Northern League in 1957. It was an international society for the preservation and survival of the 'Nordic race'. Little has been written about this organisation, but a useful summary of its activities can be found in *Searchlight*, no. 108, June 1984, p. 9.
22 See Tyndall, *The Eleventh Hour*, p. 96.
23 J. Tyndall, 'The Jew in Art', copy in possession of the Board of Deputies of British Jews.
24 On A.K. Chesterton and his disillusionment with fascism, see D. Baker, *Ideology of Obsession: A.K. Chesterton and British Fascism* (London: I.B. Tauris, 1996), pp. 184–9.
25 See G. Gable, 'Britain's Nazi Underground', in L. Cheles, R. Ferguson and M. Vaughan (eds), *The Far Right in Western and Eastern Europe*, 2nd edn (London: Longman, 1995), pp. 258–9.
26 See Tyndall, *The Eleventh Hour*, pp. 177–9.
27 See Walker, *The National Front*, pp. 39–40.
28 Tyndall, *The Eleventh Hour*, p. 179.
29 J. Tyndall, *The Authoritarian State* (London: National Socialist Movement, 1962), p. 14 and p. 15.
30 D. Edgar, 'Racism, Fascism and the Politics of the National Front', *Race and Class*, vol. 19, no. 2 (1977), p. 116.

31　Tyndall, *The Authoritarian State*, p. 16.

32　*Ibid.*, pp. 18–20.

33　*Ibid.*, p. 7.

34　See 'Post-Fascists and Neo-Nazis in Britain Today', Part 2, Supplement to the *Institute of Race Relations Newsletter*, Nov. 1962.

35　Estimated by the *Daily Mail*, 10 Aug. 1962.

36　Press Association Special Reporting Service: Report of the proceedings at Bow Street Magistrates Court, 20 Aug. 1962.

37　The former name of Egypt. See *The Times*, 3 Oct. 1962 and the *Sunday Telegraph*, 10 March 1963. In July 1962 Tyndall had requested the sum of £15,000 to cover production of leaflets, pamphlets, the NSM's newspaper, stocking its bookshop, appointment of full-time workers and even the purchase of a pirate broadcasting system.

38　See N. Copsey, *Anti-Fascism in Britain* (Basingstoke: Palgrave Macmillan, 2000).

39　Tyndall, *The Eleventh Hour*, p. 180.

40　*Ibid.*, p. 181.

41　At their 'National Socialist' wedding ceremony, a drop of mixed blood from the happy couple was allowed to drop onto a virgin copy of *Mein Kampf*.

42　Tyndall, *The Eleventh Hour*, p. 191.

43　Walker, *The National Front*, p. 134.

44　See Tyndall, *The Eleventh Hour*, pp. 190–1.

45　National Socialist Movement: 'Statement on Colin Jordan', 13 May 1964.

46　National Socialist Movement, Internal Bulletin, July 1964.

47　*Official Programme of the Greater Britain Movement* (n.d.), p. 3.

48　Tyndall, *The Eleventh Hour*, p. 192.

49　See Walker, *The National Front*, p. 71; and Students Against Fascism, *Briefing Paper on the National Front*, in possession of the Board of Deputies of British Jews.

50　Thayer, *The British Political Fringe*, p. 61.

51　Board of Deputies of British Jews, *Defence with Responsibility* (n.d.), p. 22.

52　*Spearhead*, no. 12, July 1966, p. 9.

53　See M. Billig, *Fascists: A Social Psychological View of the National Front* (London: Harcourt Brace Jovanovich, 1978), pp. 126–38.

54　See Walker, *The National Front*, p. 78.

55　*Candour*, no. 469, Oct. 1967, p. 1.

56　Hill with Bell, *The Other Face of Terror*, p. 83.

57　Chesterton's speech to the NF's first AGM is reprinted in *Candour*, no. 469, Oct. 1967, p. 74.

58　Tyndall, *The Eleventh Hour*, p. 198.

59　Bean, *Many Shades of Black*, p. 184.

60　Billig, *Fascists*, p. 116.

61　*Ibid.*, p. 350.

62　Thurlow, *Fascism in Modern Britain*, p. 150.

63　See A.K. Chesterton. 'Farewell to the National Front', *Candour*, Dec. 1970, pp. 199–200.

64　According to *Searchlight*'s figures in *From Ballots to Bombs: The Inside Story of the National Front's Political Soldiers* (London: Searchlight Publishing Ltd,

1989), p. 4. However, this figure may be somewhat inflated – Tyndall has spoken of a 'quadrupling' of members in the 1972–74 period, although he argues that when he was elected NF Chairman in 1972, membership was below 2,000, see *Spearhead*, no. 183, Jan. 1984, p. 6.

65 Gregor Strasser (1892–1934) and his brother Otto (1897–1974) advocated a form of 'racial bolshevism'. Gregor Strasser was killed at Hitler's 'Night of the Long Knives' in 1934.

66 See C.T. Husbands, *Racial Exclusionism and the City: The Urban Support of the National Front* (London: Allen & Unwin, 1983), p. 11.

67 It later emerged that Verrall was author of the notorious Holocaust denial pamphlet *Did Six Million Really Die?* At the time, he was seen as the NF's leading intellectual after having recently graduated from the University of London with a first-class honours degree in History.

68 *Spearhead*, March 1976, p. 7.

69 *Spearhead*, April 1976, pp. 10–12.

70 On anti-fascist opposition to the National Front, see Copsey, *Anti-Fascism in Britain*, pp. 115–52.

71 *Spearhead*, Oct. 1978, p. 6.

72 S. Taylor, *The National Front in English Politics* (London: Macmillan – now Palgrave, 1982), p. 103.

73 Roger Eatwell for instance; see R. Eatwell, 'The Esoteric Ideology of the National Front in the 1980s', in M. Cronin (ed.), *The Failure of British Fascism: The Far Right and the Fight for Political Recognition* (Basingstoke: Macmillan – now Palgrave, 1996), p. 102.

74 University of Warwick: [M]odern [R]ecords [C]entre, MSS.321 Box 4: British Democratic Party circular.

75 On the Front's rise and demise in a comparative context, see N. Copsey, 'The Extreme Right in Contemporary France and Britain', *Contemporary European History*, vol. 6, no. 1 (1997), pp. 101–16.

76 *Spearhead*, June 1980, p. 17.

77 Transcript of Tyndall speech, June 1979, p. 15.

78 MRC MSS.321 Box 5: *National Front Constitutional Movement Bulletin*, Nov. 1979, p. 15.

79 Hill with Bell, *The Other Side of Terror*, p. 175.

80 See Tyndall, *The Eleventh Hour*, p. 202.

81 Bean, *Many Shades of Black*, p. 201.

82 Hill with Bell, *The Other Face of Terror*, p. 160.

83 *Spearhead*, June 1980, p. 17.

84 See MRC MSS.321 Box 4: New National Front File: J. Tyndall, 'Help us Save the National Front! An Appeal by John Tyndall', June 1980.

85 See MRC MSS.321 Box 5.

86 See J. Tyndall, 'New National Front: The Background and the Facts' (Circular from the Albion Press, Move, 1980?), p. 3.

87 See MRC MSS.321 Box 4: New National Front File: J. Green, 'Help us to Save the National Front', June 1980.

88 See MRC MSS.321/1 Box 1: National Front Directorate Minutes, 5 Oct. 1979.

89 School teacher by profession, Edmonds was organiser of the NF's Lewisham branch.

90 See MRC MSS.321/1 Box 1: National Front Directorate Minutes, 19 Jan. 1980.

91 Tyndall, 'Help us Save the National Front!'.
92 The National Front Constitutional Movement sought support from the far-right fringes of the Conservative Party. It took some 750 followers from the Front but was extremely transient.
93 The British Democratic Party offshoot was formed from the NF's Leicester branch. A respectable solicitor and former Tory, Anthony Reed-Herbert led it. Nonetheless, it quickly sank into oblivion.
94 See 'A New Year's Message from the New National Front', 1981.
95 A former National Front official, Charles Parker became the NNF's National Organiser. Tyndall had married Valerie Parker in November 1977.
96 Dave Bruce became the Director of NNF Activities.
97 Richard Edmonds, always steadfast in his support for Tyndall, was made Head of the Young Nationalist section of the NNF and editor of *Young Nationalist*.
98 *New National Front Members' Bulletin,* March 1981.
99 Hill with Bell, *The Other Face of Terror,* p. 161.
100 *Searchlight*, no. 79, Jan. 1982, p. 2.
101 See *New National Front Members' Bulletin*, March 1981, and *National Front Organisers' Bulletin*, Nov. 1981.
102 *New National Front Members' Bulletin*, Aug. 1981.
103 *New Frontier*, July 1981.
104 Hill with Bell, *The Other Face of Terror*, p. 161.
105 A further-education lecturer by profession, Brons was a former member of both Jordan's National Socialist Movement and Tyndall's Greater Britain Movement.
106 MRC MSS.321/1 Box 1: Minutes of the National Front Directorate Conference, 2–3 Feb. 1980.
107 *Spearhead*, no. 163, May 1982, p. 6.
108 Hill with Bell, *The Other Face of Terror*, p. 165.
109 *Ibid.*, p. 162.
110 *Ibid.*, p. 164.
111 See *Spearhead*, no. 162, April 1982, pp. 18–19.
112 For a report of this press conference, see *Searchlight*, no. 83, May 1982, pp. 3–4.
113 See *Principles and Policies of the British National Party* (1982).
114 J. Tyndall, *The Eleventh Hour: A Call for British Rebirth* (London: Albion Press, 1988), p. 248.
115 *Spearhead*, no. 163, May 1982, p. 6.
116 See *Constitution of the British National Party* (Nov. 1982).
117 Tyndall, *The Eleventh Hour*, 3rd edn, p. 482.
118 *Spearhead*, no. 39, Jan. 1971, p. 6.
119 Tyndall, *The Eleventh Hour*, 3rd edn, p. 482.
120 *Ibid.*, pp. 208–9.
121 Article from *Spearhead*, as quoted in Hill with Bell, *The Other Face of Terror*, p. 288.

2 The Struggle for the Soul of British Nationalism

1 *Searchlight*, no. 197, July 1983, p. 6.

2 See C.T. Husbands, 'Extreme Right-Wing Politics in Great Britain: The Recent Marginalisation of the National Front', *West European Politics*, vol. 11, no. 2 (1988), p. 71.

3 *Spearhead*, no. 179, Sept. 1983, p. 4.

4 R. Hill with A. Bell, *The Other Face of Terror: Inside Europe's Neo-Nazi Network* (London: Grafton, 1988), p. 173.

5 *Spearhead*, no. 162, April 1982, p. 19.

6 See *British National Party Members' Bulletin*, February 1983.

7 *Ibid.*

8 Joe Pearce was also editor of the NF's street-oriented youth magazine *Bulldog*, a magazine that Pearce had established in 1977 at the age of 16. On Joe Pearce, see *Searchlight*, no. 332, Feb. 2003, pp. 12–14.

9 See Hill with Bell, *The Other Face of Terror*, pp. 173–4.

10 See *Constitution of the British National Party* (Nov. 1982) and *British National Party Members' Bulletin*, Feb. 1983.

11 J. Tyndall, *The Eleventh Hour: A Call for British Rebirth*, 3rd edn (Welling: Albion Press, 1998), p. 490.

12 *Searchlight*, no. 84, June 1982, p. 8.

13 Gateshead BNP: *North-East News and Regional Bulletin*, March 1983.

14 Merely two were outside England – once more reflecting the Anglo-centric character of extreme right-wing nationalism in Britain, 'crowded out' by domestic nationalisms in Scotland and Wales.

15 BNP circular: 'Preparation for General Election-First Stage', Dec. 1982.

16 Hill with Bell, *The Other Face of Terror*, p. 178.

17 A figure claimed by Bromley branch of the British National Party in *Counter-Attack*, no. 3, July–Aug. 1983.

18 *Searchlight*, no. 97, July 1983, p. 7.

19 *Vote for Britain*, Manifesto of the British National Party (1983), p. 15.

20 *British National Party Members' Bulletin*, Feb. 1984.

21 See MRC MSS 321/4/1: *NF Organisers' Bulletin*, 8 Oct. 1980.

22 MRC MSS 321/4/1: *NF Organisers' Bulletin*, 13 June 1983 and MRC MSS 321/1/1/: NF Directorate Minutes, 31 July 1983.

23 *British National Party Members' Bulletin*, Feb. 1984.

24 MRC MSS 412/BNP/4/14: *New Frontier*, Feb. 1983. Webster's 'Gay faction' seems to only include Webster's alleged lover, Michael Salt, a member of the NF Directorate.

25 See MRC MSS 321/7: National Front AGM Agenda, 1 Oct. 1983, pp. 22–3.

26 Nick Griffin first attended a National Front meeting as a 15-year-old in Norwich.

27 Derek Holland was a former student at Leicester Polytechnic where the Young National Front Student Organisation enjoyed 'considerable success' in 1979; see *Bulldog*, issue 12, April 1979. Of Irish Catholic descent, Holland was noted for being a Catholic fundamentalist.

28 Graham Williamson first joined the National Front in 1975.

29 Patrick Harrington was soon to achieve notoriety as a student at the Polytechnic of North London, see N. Copsey, *Anti-Fascism in Britain* (Basingstoke: Macmillan – Palgrave, 2000), pp. 154–7. Harrington first joined the National Front in 1979 and was a YNF Organiser.

30 See MRC MSS 321/1/1: Minutes of NF Directorate Conference, 2–3 Feb. 1980.

31 *Ibid.* and NF Directorate Minutes, 29 March 1980.
32 Distributism refers to a political and economic theory that offers a 'third way' between capitalism and socialism. Supported by Hilaire Belloc and G.K. Chesterton in the inter-war period, it promised an end to financial slavery by ensuring the widest distribution of productive property. In the Distributist economy, the restoration of productive property would be based on small-scale craftsmanship and guilds, see H. Belloc, *An Essay on the Restoration of Property* (London: The Distributist League, 1936).
33 MRC MSS 321/5: *National Front Support Group Newsletter*: 'Response to Griffin's *Attempted Murder*', p. 6.
34 See MRC MSS 321/8: National Front, *Introduction to the Movement* (n.d.), p. 3.
35 *Rising*, Summer 1985, p. 11.
36 MRC MSS 321/1/1: NF Directorate Minutes, 5 Nov. 1983.
37 Refers to a type of neo-fascism that seeks a 'third way' between capitalism and communism.
38 Julius Evola (1898–1974), an Italian fascist philosopher who became a cult figure on the contemporary far right. On Evola's political thought, see N. Goodrick-Clarke, *Black Sun. Aryan Cults, Esoteric Nazism and the Politics of Identity* (New York: New York University Press, 2002), pp. 52–71.
39 Corneliu Codreanu (1899–1938), Romanian fascist and leader of the Legion of the Archangel Michael. The Legion proclaimed the need for a cultural-spiritual revolution and the creation of the *omul nou* – the 'new man', see S.G. Payne, *A History of Fascism* (London: UCL Press, 1995), pp. 279–89.
40 In 1985 Fiore was convicted by an Italian court *in absentia* for 'political conspiracy' and for being a member of 'an armed gang', see *Nationalism Today*, issue 40, 1987.
41 See *From Ballots to Bombs: The Inside Story of the National Front's Political Soldiers* (London: Searchlight Publishing, 1989).
42 See, MRC MSS 321/1/1: NF Directorate Minutes, 5 Nov. 1983.
43 See *Searchlight*, no. 103, Jan. 1984, pp. 2–3.
44 *Spearhead*, no. 183, Jan. 1984, p. 8.
45 *Spearhead*, no. 184, Feb. 1984, p. 10.
46 MRC MSS 321/8: National Front, *Introduction to the Movement*, p. 3
47 See, 'Nationalist Unity?' editorial, *New Nation*, no. 6. Winter 1984.
48 *Spearhead*, no. 223, Sept. 1987, p. 4.
49 See for instance, Roger Eatwell's thoughts on the 'political soldiers', MRC MSS 321/2: Transcript of *Disciples of Chaos*, Channel 4, Oct. 1988, p. 30.
50 Clayton-Garnett was a former head-teacher by profession.
51 *Spearhead*, no. 201, July 1985, p. 7.
52 *Ibid.*
53 A secretive national-socialist umbrella organisation that was formed by former Mosleyites in 1973–74.
54 See *Searchlight*, no. 146, Aug. 1987, pp. 3–4. This theory was reiterated by G. Gable, in 'The Far Right in Contemporary Britain', L. Cheles, R. Ferguson and M. Vaughan (eds), *Neo-fascism in Europe* (Harlow: Longman, 1991), pp. 245–63.
55 For a highly entertaining and semi-comical account of the NF's 1986 split from both sides, see MRC MSS 321/2: N. Griffin, *Attempted Murder: The*

State/Reactionary Plot against the National Front (Norfolk: NT Press, 1986), and MSSS 321/5: National Front Support Group Newsletter: 'Response to Griffin's *Attempted Murder*'.

56 MRC MSS 321/2: Unedited interview transcript from Channel 4's 1988 *Dispatches* TV documentary.
57 See MRC MSS 321/5: Circular: 'Will the Real National Front Stand Up?' and *Vanguard*, no. 1, Aug. 1986 and no. 4, Dec. 1986.
58 See *Spearhead*, no. 223, Sept. 1987, p. 4.
59 Leicester BNP: *Just Truth, A Nationalist Review of Policy Affecting British People*, no. 6, Winter 1987.
60 *Spearhead*, no. 223, Sep. 1987, p. 7.
61 *Spearhead*, no. 234, Aug. 1988, p. 7.
62 *Ibid.*, pp. 7–8
63 G. Gable and T. Hepple, *At War with Society* (London: Searchlight, 1993), p. 14.
64 See MRC MSS 321/1/1: NF Directorate Minutes, 8 March 1980.
65 See *Spearhead*, no. 223, Sept. 1987, p. 5. Wingfield is not personally named in this article but his identity is obvious.
66 See *Spearhead*, no. 224, Oct. 1987, p. 12.
67 *British National Party Members' Bulletin*, Jan. 1985.
68 See *Searchlight*, no. 106, April 1984, p. 7.
69 Tyndall, *The Eleventh Hour*, p. 491.
70 A. Roxburgh, *Preachers of Hate. The Rise of the Far Right* (London: Gibson Square Books, 2002), p. 223.
71 *British National Party Organisers' and Activists' Bulletin*, May 1985.
72 *British National Party Members' Bulletin*, Oct. 1985.
73 For offences committed between March and Aug. 1984.
74 See *Spearhead*, no. 221, July 1987, pp. 13–14.
75 BNP circular: 'Important Notice to West London Supporters and Members', 14 May 1987.
76 This branch had been praised as a 'model' BNP branch, having often made the local headlines, see for instance, *The Bromley Leader*, 11 July 1986.
77 Letter from Tyndall to BNP members Bromley area, dated 2 June 1987. Alf Waite later returned to the BNP fold.
78 See 'Fascist power struggle', *City Limits*, 8 Jan.–12 Jan. 1989.
79 'Important Notice to West London Supporters and Members', 14 May 1987.
80 *Searchlight*, no. 151, Jan. 1988, p. 11; and *Spearhead*, no. 227, Jan. 1988, p. 7.
81 See *Spearhead*, no. 227, Jan. 1988, pp. 4–8.
82 *Ibid.*, p. 8.
83 *Ibid.*, p. 7.
84 *Ibid.*, pp. 7–8.
85 See *Searchlight*, no. 155, May 1988, p. 4.
86 *Spearhead*, no. 232, June 1988, p. 5.
87 *Ibid.*, p. 6.
88 The revolutionary-nationalist factions in the *Front National* were cast out by 1981. On Le Pen and the extremist tradition in France, see Peter Fysh and Jim Wolfreys, *The Politics of Racism in France* (Basingstoke: Macmillan – now Palgrave, 1998), pp. 75–106.

89 See R. Eatwell, 'Continuity and Metamorphosis: Fascism in Britain since 1945', in S.U. Larsen (ed.), *Modern Europe After Fascism* (Boulder: Social Science Monographs, 1998), p. 1207.

90 Comments made on BBC Panorama TV interview, 8 April 1991.

91 D. Lipstadt, *Denying the Holocaust* (London: Penguin, 1994), p. 8.

92 First joined the NF in 1978 at the age of 16. Tony Lecomber, from Redbridge, had previously changed his name to Tony Wells or Tony East because he felt that Lecomber was too foreign-sounding.

93 See *Searchlight*, no. 170, Aug. 1989, p. 9.

94 See *Spearhead*, no. 241, March 1989, pp. 13–14.

95 *Spearhead*, no. 232, June 1988, p. 6.

96 See *Spearhead*, no. 227, Jan. 1988, pp. 4–5.

97 See Gable and Hepple, *At War with Society* (London: Searchlight, 1993), pp. 11–12.

98 This Leeds-based incarnation of the British National Party published *BNP Bulletin* and *British News*. On Eddy Morrison's political career, see *Searchlight*, no. 128, Feb. 1986, p. 15.

99 See *Searchlight*, no. 157, July 1988, p. 16.

100 According to *Searchlight*'s figures, see *Searchlight*, no. 170, Aug. 1989, p. 9.

101 See *National Front News*, no. 109, 1988, p. 4.

102 *Bulldog*, no. 36, 1983, p. 1.

103 See *National Front News*, no. 125, Dec. 1989, p. 5.

104 See *Searchlight*, no. 147, Sept. 1987.

105 See *Searchlight*, no. 161, Nov. 1988, pp. 4–5.

106 *Searchlight*, no. 163, Jan. 1989, p. 11.

107 See *Searchlight*, no. 168, June 1989, pp. 10–11.

108 *The Lost Race*, BBC2, 24 March 1999.

109 *Searchlight*, no. 163, Jan. 1989, p. 10.

110 See MRC MSS 321/4/1: 'British National Party Call for Unity' (1989).

111 'Fascist power struggle', in *City Limits*, 8–12 Jan. 1989.

112 See 'British National Party Call for Unity' and *Birmingham Daily News*, 7 June 1989, as reported in *Searchlight*, no. 169, July 1989, p. 7.

113 See 'British National Party Call for Unity'.

114 *Spearhead*, no. 261, Nov. 1990, p. 13.

115 See Gable and Hepple, *At War with Society*, p. 12.

116 *Ibid.*

117 See *Searchlight*, no. 149, Nov. 1987, p. 17.

118 See *Searchlight*, no. 170, Aug. 1989, pp. 4–5 and Gable and Hepple, *At War with Society*, pp. 16–17.

119 Gable and Hepple, *At War with Society*, p. 17.

120 *British Nationalist*, Aug./Sept. 1989, p. 2.

121 Gable and Hepple, *At War with Society*, p. 13.

122 *Searchlight*, no. 175, Jan. 1990, p. 11.

123 A. Heath, 'What has Happened to the Extreme Right in Britain?', *Res Publica*, vol. 37, no. 2 (1995), p. 205.

124 *Spearhead*, no. 259, Sept. 1990, p. 11.

125 *Ibid.*

126 *Ibid.*

3 A False Dawn in Tower Hamlets

1 *Spearhead*, no. 296, Oct. 1993, p. 2.
2 *Ibid.*, p. 3.
3 Board of Deputies of British Jews: CST Elections Department, Local Elections 1998 Briefing Pack, p. 5.
4 A. Roxburgh, *Preachers of Hate: The Rise of the Far Right* (London: Gibson Square Books, 2002), p. 231.
5 See N. Copsey, 'Contemporary Fascism in the Local Arena: The British National Party and 'Rights for Whites'', in M. Cronin (ed.), *The Failure of British Fascism: The Far Right and the Fight for Political Recognition* (Basingstoke: Macmillan – now Palgrave, 1996), pp. 118–40; R. Eatwell, 'The Dynamics of Right-wing Electoral Breakthrough', *Patterns of Prejudice*, vol. 32, no. 3 (1998), pp. 3–31; and C.T. Husbands, 'Following the "Continental Model"?: Implications of the Recent Electoral Performance of the British National Party', *New Community*, vol. 20, no. 4 (1994), pp. 563–79.
6 See R. Eatwell, 'The Dynamics of Right-wing Electoral Breakthrough', pp. 3–31.
7 See *Identity*, issue 28, Jan. 2003, p. 21.
8 The British Brothers' League was struck up as an alliance of Tory back-bench MPs and East End workers, see C. Holmes, *John Bull's Island* (Basingstoke: Macmillan – Palgrave, 1988), p. 70.
9 See T. Linehan, *East London for Mosley* (London: Frank Cass, 1996).
10 On the immediate postwar revival of fascist activity, see D. Renton, *Fascism, Anti-Fascism and Britain in the 1940s* (Basingstoke: Macmillan – now Palgrave, 2000).
11 N. Holtam and S. Mayo, *Learning from the Conflict: Reflections on the Struggle Against the British National Party on the Isle of Dogs, 1993–94* (London: Jubilee Group, 1998), p. 22.
12 *Neither Unique nor Typical: The Context of Race Relations in the London Borough of Tower Hamlets*, An interim report by the Runnymede Trust in the wake of the by-election in Millwall, Isle of Dogs, Dec. 1993, p. 21.
13 *CARF* (Campaign Against Racism and Fascism Magazine), no. 1, Feb./March 1991, p. 4.
14 C.T. Husbands, 'Following the "Continental Model"?: Implications of the Recent Electoral Performance of the British National Party', p. 570.
15 *The British Eastender*, Newsletter for members and supporters of Tower Hamlets British National Party, no. 2, Sept. 1990.
16 *Spearhead*, no. 259, Sept. 1990, p. 12.
17 Holtam and Mayo, *Learning from the Conflict*, p. 24.
18 *The British Eastender*, no. 1, May 1990.
19 See *The British Eastender*, no. 2. Sept. 1990.
20 *Neither Unique nor Typical*, p. 50, and *Spearhead*, no. 281, July 1992, p. 9.
21 *Patriot*, Spring 1997, p. 9.
22 Beackon had first joined the BNP as an associate member in 1986. He became a full member in 1987.
23 *Spearhead*, no. 296, Oct. 1993, p. 2.
24 *Spearhead*, no. 323, Jan. 1996, p. 9. However, this figure was probably an exaggeration. *Searchlight*'s Nick Lowles claims that the BNP received over

500 enquiries after Millwall and 'few actually joined'; see N. Lowles, *White Riot* (Bury: Milo Books, 2001), p. 36.

25 *Spearhead*, no. 312, Feb. 1995, p. 6.

26 See *Neither Unique nor Typical*, pp. 54–5.

27 *Daily Telegraph*, 18 Sept. 1993.

28 *Daily Mail*, 18 Sept. 1993.

29 *Daily Mirror*, 18 Sept. 1993.

30 The *Guardian*, 14 Oct. 1993.

31 See *New Statesman and Society*, 24 Sept. 1993, p. 33.

32 See *Time Out*, 29 Sept. 1993.

33 See the *Guardian*, 21 Sept. 1993.

34 *The Times*, 18 Sept. 1993.

35 The *Sunday Times*, 19 Sept. 1993.

36 An independent charity that was originally founded in 1968. It concerns itself with matters relating to racial equality and justice.

37 See The *Independent*, 21 Sept. 1993.

38 See The *Guardian*, 23 Sept. 1993.

39 See Copsey, 'Contemporary Fascism in the Local Arena', pp. 118–40.

40 G. Gable and T. Hepple, *At War with Society* (London: Searchlight Magazine Ltd, 1993), p. 22.

41 *Patriot*, Spring 1997, p. 5.

42 *Patriot*, Winter 1997, p. 16.

43 *Ibid.*

44 L. Fekete, 'Europe for the Europeans: East End for the East Enders', p. 74.

45 *Patriot*, Spring 1997, p. 6.

46 *Ibid.*, pp. 6–7.

47 *British Nationalist*, April 1990, p. 8.

48 *Patriot*, Winter 1997, p. 16.

49 *Spearhead*, no. 281, July 1992, p. 9.

50 See *British Nationalist*, Aug./Sept. 1990, p. 7.

51 See *CARF*, no. 6., Jan./Feb. 1992, p. 13.

52 *British Eastender*, no. 1, May 1990.

53 *Fighting Talk*, Journal of Anti-Fascist Action, Sept. 1991, p. 3.

54 *Searchlight*, no. 192, June 1991, p. 3 and *Searchlight*, no. 195, Sept. 1991, p. 6.

55 BNP *Organisers' and Activists' Bulletin*: 'Party Image and Discipline', 1 May 1991.

56 See *Searchlight*, no. 196, Oct. 1991, pp. 10–11.

57 *Patriot*, Winter 1997, p. 16.

58 See Gable and Hepple (1993), p. 36.

59 *Patriot*, Winter 1997, p. 17.

60 See S. Smith, *A Storm Rising*, 2nd edn (Imraldis eBooks, 2003), p. 68 and p. 135.

61 *Patriot*, Spring 1997, p. 9.

62 *East London Advertiser*, 9 Sept. 1993.

63 *Patriot*, Spring 1997, p. 3.

64 *Ibid.*

65 See *Sunday Express*, 12 Sept. 1993.

66 Beackon's campaign leaflet as quoted in *Neither Unique nor Typical*, p. 51.

67 *East London Advertiser*, 23 Sept. 1993.

68 See *Docklands Recorder*, 15 Sept. 1993.

69 ANL leaflet, distributed September 1993. On 11 September 1993, an ANL rally was held at Millwall Park. The main speaker was Leon Greenman, a survivor of Auschwitz and Buchenwald.

70 *Daily Telegraph*, 16 Sept. 1993.

71 *Political Speech and Race Relations in a Liberal Democracy*, Report of an Inquiry into the conduct of the Tower Hamlets Liberal Democrats in publishing allegedly racist election literature between 1990 and 1993, Dec. 1993, p. 3.

72 *The British Eastender*, no. 1. May 1990.

73 *Neither Unique nor Typical*, p. 29.

74 See *Searchlight*, no. 110, Aug. 1984, p. 17.

75 See *Neither Unique nor Typical*, p. 34 and p. 44.

76 *Political Speech and Race Relations in a Liberal Democracy*, p. 30.

77 *East London Advertiser*, 8 Nov. 1991.

78 *Political Speech and Race Relations in a Liberal Democracy*, p. 36.

79 *East London Advertiser*, 10 April 1992.

80 See *Political Speech and Race Relations in a Liberal Democracy*, pp. 36–40.

81 R. Eatwell, 'Britain: The BNP and the Problem of Legitimacy', in H.-G. Betz and S. Immerfall (eds), *The New Politics of the Right: Neo-Populist Parties and Movements in Established Democracies* (Basingstoke: Macmillan – now Palgrave, 1998), p. 152.

82 One leaflet – the so-called 'Toilet' leaflet – was distributed by Liberal Focus describing how Labour councillors had tried to donate £30,000 to Bangladeshi flood relief and had given the Bangladeshi Youth Movement £175,000.

83 Holtam and Mayo, *Learning from the Conflict*, p. 3.

84 C. Mudde, 'England Belongs to Me': The Extreme Right in the UK Parliamentary Election of 2001', *Representation*, vol. 39, no. 1 (2002), p. 41.

85 See *Island Patriot*, BNP leaflet (1992).

86 See *Spearhead*, no. 303, May 1994, p. 14.

87 See Holtam and Mayo, *Learning from the Conflict*, p. 2.

88 *British Nationalist*, Oct. 1993, p. 1.

89 See Eatwell, 'The Dynamics of Right-wing Electoral Breakthrough', pp. 3–31.

90 R. Eatwell, 'Ethnocentric Party Mobilization in Europe: The Importance of the Three-Dimensional Approach', in R. Koopmans and P. Statham (eds), *Challenging Immigration and Ethnic Relations Politics* (Oxford: Oxford University Press, 2000), p. 350.

91 See Tower Hamlets Independent News Service, Press Release, 31 March 1994, p. 3.

92 See *Docklands Recorder*, 3 May 1990.

93 *Ibid.*

94 *Neither Unique nor Typical*, p. 52.

95 See Tower Hamlets Independent News Service, Press Release, 31 March 1994, p. 4.

96 See *Spearhead*, no. 303, May 1994, p. 4.

97 On the mobilisation of this vote, see Holtam and Mayo, *Learning from the Conflict*.

98 See *Spearhead*, no. 305, July 1994, p. 10.

99 See Board of Deputies of British Jews: CST Elections Department, Local Elections 1998 Briefing Pack, p. 11.

100 *Spearhead*, no. 305, July 1994, p. 10.

101 Lowles, *White Riot*, pp. 25–6.

102 Amongst far-right circles, Covington is best-known for his role in the Greensboro massacre in North Carolina in 1979 when he helped organise a counter-demonstration to an anti-KKK rally that led to the deaths of five anti-Klan demonstrators. The author of *The March up Country*, a critique of the failure of white resistance, Covington spent some time in Britain in the early 1990s and may have helped launch Combat 18, see Lowles, *White Riot*, pp. 27–35.

103 A physicist by profession, Dr William Pearce was the most influential neo-Nazi in the United States of America. He was leader of the National Alliance and author of *The Turner Diaries* (1978). This book, which has sold around half a million copies, sets out a blueprint for violent white revolution based on a fictional account of a white supremacist terror group in the USA. Pearce died in July 2002. On Pearce, see *Searchlight*, no. 328, Oct. 2002, pp. 16–19.

104 See Lowles, *White Riot*, pp. 41–2.

105 *Patriot*, Winter 1997, p. 17.

106 *Searchlight*, no. 226, April 1994, p. 5.

107 J. Tyndall, *The Eleventh Hour: A Call for British Rebirth*, 3rd edn (Welling: Albion Press, 1998), p. 501.

108 See Lowles, *White Riot*, p. 58.

109 See *Spearhead*, no. 319, Sept. 1995, pp. 7–8.

110 *Searchlight*, no. 237, March 1995, p. 3.

111 *CARF*, no. 29, Dec. 1995–Jan. 1996, p. 12.

112 See *Spearhead*, no. 311, Jan. 1995, p. 5.

113 See *Searchlight*, no. 241, July 1995, p. 2.

114 *Ibid.*, p. 9.

115 See *Spearhead*, no. 319, Sept. 1995, pp. 6–10.

116 See *Searchlight*, no. 244, Oct, 1995, p. 5.

117 Tyndall, *The Eleventh Hour*, p. 502.

118 'The aims of C18', reproduced in *Searchlight*, no. 225, March 1994, p. 6.

119 See Lowles, *White Riot*, pp. 257–66.

120 On the beginnings of the internal feud in Combat 18, see *Searchlight*, no. 259, Jan. 1997, p. 3. Charlie Sargent was imprisoned for murder in 1997.

121 See *Searchlight*, no. 243, Sept. 1995, pp. 7–8.

122 See MRC MSS 412/BNP/3/1: *British National Party Members' Bulletin*, Nov. 1995.

123 *Patriot*, Summer 2000, p. 9.

124 See *Spearhead*, no. 323, Jan. 1996, p. 9.

125 *Ibid.*, p. 10.

126 See *Spearhead*, no. 325, March 1996, pp. 11–13.

127 See *Searchlight*, no. 290, Aug. 1999, pp. 8–11.

128 Michael Newland to author, 19 May 2003.

129 *Spearhead*, no. 366, Aug. 1999, p. 4.

130 *Ibid.*
131 See *The Rune*, Issue 11, p. 4.
132 *Spearhead*, no. 324, Feb. 1996, p. 11.
133 *Ibid.*, 11–13.
134 *The Rune*, issue 8, p. 9.
135 *Spearhead*, no. 336, Feb. 1997, p. 5.
136 See *Who are the Mind-Benders?* p. 8.
137 *Spearhead*, no. 335, Jan. 1997, p. 8.
138 *Searchlight* claimed that the BNP could only field over 50 candidates as a consequence of a £70,000 donation from William Pearce; the BNP maintained that it was financed from ordinary members.
139 See *Spearhead*, no. 339, May 1997, pp. 4–5 and *Searchlight*, no. 264, June 1997, p. 4.
140 MRC MSS 412/BNP/3/1: *British National Party Members' Bulletin*, July 1997.
141 *Ibid.*
142 See *Searchlight*, no. 264, June 1997, pp. 6–11 and *Searchlight*, no. 265, July 1997, pp. 3–6.
143 See *Spearhead*, no. 339, May 1997, pp. 14–15.
144 *Spearhead*, no. 366, Aug. 1999, p. 6.
145 Tyndall, *The Eleventh Hour*, p. 514.
146 See Board of Deputies of British Jews: Local Elections 1998 Briefing Pack, pp. 3–5 and p. 11.
147 Board of Deputies of British Jews: Local Elections 1998 Briefing Pack, p. 3.
148 See *Identity*, issue 28, Jan. 2003, p. 20.
149 See *Searchlight*, no. 276, June 1998, pp. 6–8.
150 See *Spearhead*, no. 351, May 1998, pp. 14–17.
151 Michael Newland to author, 19 May 2003.
152 On this merger, see *Spearhead*, no. 351, May 1998, pp. 4–7 and *British National Party Members' Bulletin*, May/June 1998.
153 See *British Countryman*, Spring issue, 1998, p. 2. At the London Countryside Rally in March 1998, 30,000 copies of the *British Countryman* were handed out to marchers.
154 See *Spearhead*, no. 357, Nov. 1998, pp. 14–19.
155 *Spearhead*, no. 366, Aug. 1999, p. 6.
156 J. Bean, *Many Shades of Black: Inside Britain's Far Right* (London: New Millennium, 1999), p. 238.

4 Fascism on the Fringe

1 *Fight Back! The Election Manifesto of the British National Party* (1992), p. 23.
2 See MRC MSS 412/4/14: *Spreading the Word: British National Party Handbook on Propaganda*, p. 16.
3 See *Patriot*, Summer 1998, pp. 34–5.
4 See for instance, L. Cheles, R. Ferguson and M. Vaughan (eds), *Neo-fascism in Europe* (Harlow: Longman, 1991); P. Merkl and L. Weinberg (eds), *Encounters with the Contemporary Radical Right* (Boulder, San Francisco and Oxford: Westview Press, 1993); H.-G. Betz, *Radical Right-Wing Parties in Western*

Europe (Basingstoke: Macmillan – now Palgrave, 1994) and P. Taggart, 'New Populist Parties in Western Europe', *West European Politics*, vol. 18, no. 1 (1995), pp. 34–51.

5   See for instance, P. Merkl and L. Weinberg (eds), *The Revival of Right-Wing Extremism in the Nineties* (London: Frank Cass, 1997), and H. Kitschelt, *The Radical Right in Western Europe* (Ann Arbor, University of Michigan Press, 1997).

6   See H.-G. Betz and S. Immerfall, *The New Politics of the Right: Neo-Populist Parties and Movements in Established Democracies* (Basingstoke: Macmillan – now Palgrave, 1998), p. 3.

7   See C. Mudde, *The Ideology of the Extreme Right* (Manchester: University of Manchester Press, 2000), p. 12.

8   See F. Ferraresi, *Threats to Democracy. The Radical Right in Italy after the War* (Princeton, NJ: Princeton University Press, 1996), pp. 3–14.

9   C. Mudde, 'The War of Words: Defining the Extreme-Right Party Family', *West European Politics*, vol. 19, no. 2 (1996), pp. 225–48.

10   See P. Hainsworth (ed.), *The Politics of the Extreme Right* (London: Pinter, 2000), pp. 4–5.

11   See Mudde, 'The War of Words: Defining the Extreme-Right Party Family', p. 229.

12   R. Griffin, 'Nationalism', in R. Eatwell and A. Wright (eds), *Contemporary Political Ideologies* (London: Pinter, 1993), p. 150.

13   By 'ideal type' we call upon Max Weber's concept. Therefore, the type is 'ideal' in so far as it only exists in its purest form at the level of abstraction.

14   R. Griffin, *The Nature of Fascism* (London: Routledge, 1994), p. 166.

15   For the classic statement of this position, see G. Allardyce, 'What Fascism is Not: Thoughts on the Deflation of a Concept', *American Historical Review*, vol. 84, no. 2 (1979), pp. 367–88.

16   See for instance, D. Prowe, '"Classic Fascism" and the New Radical Right in Western Europe: Comparisons and Contrasts', *Contemporary European History*, vol. 3, no. 3 (1994), pp. 289–313.

17   For a recent Marxist riposte, see D. Renton, *Fascism: Theory and Practice* (London: Pluto, 1999).

18   G. Mosse, *The Fascist Revolution* (New York: Howard Fertig, 1999), pp. xi–xii.

19   See Z. Sternhell, *Neither Right Nor Left: Fascist Ideology in France* (Princeton, NJ: Princeton University Press, 1996); S.M. Lipset, *Political Man* (London: Heinemann, 1960); and D.S. Lewis, *Mosley, Fascism and British Society 1931–1981* (Manchester: Manchester University Press, 1987).

20   See N. Copsey, 'Fascism: The Ideology of the British National Party', *Politics*, vol. 14, no. 3 (1994), pp. 102–8.

21   Taggart, 'New Populist Parties in Western Europe', p. 36.

22   See R. Griffin, 'The Primacy of Culture: The Current Growth (or Manufacture) of Consensus within Fascist studies', *Journal of Contemporary History*, vol. 37, no. 1 (2003), pp. 21–43.

23   Renton, *Fascism: Theory and Practice*, p. 18.

24   *Ibid.*, p. 28.

25   R. Paxton, 'The Five Stages of Fascism', *Journal of Modern History*, vol. 70, no. 1 (1998), p. 7.

26 *Ibid.*, p. 11.
27 *Ibid.*, p, 9.
28 See comments by Alexander De Grand, in *Journal of Contemporary History*, vol. 37, no. 2 (2002), p. 266.
29 See R. Eatwell, 'On Defining the "Fascist Minimum": The Centrality of Ideology', *Journal of Political Ideologies*, vol. 1, no. 3 (1996), pp. 303–19.
30 G. Mosse, 'Introduction: The Genesis of Fascism', *Journal of Contemporary History*, vol. 1 (1966), p. 22.
31 See S. Payne, *A History of Fascism 1914–45* (London: UCL Press, 1995), p. 14.
32 Griffin, *The Nature of Fascism*, pp. 32–6.
33 *Ibid.*, p. 26.
34 Mosse, 'Introduction: The Genesis of Fascism', p. 21.
35 The classic model is of course provided by C. Friedrich and Z. Brzezinski in *Totalitarian Dictatorship and Autocracy* (Cambridge, Mass.: Harvard University Press, 1956).
36 For a cogent set of criticisms of Griffin, see Eatwell, 'On Defining the "Fascist Minimum": The Centrality of Ideology', pp. 310–12 and Renton, *Fascism: Theory and Practice*, p. 26.
37 MRC MSS.412/BNP/4/13: *BNP Activists' Handbook*, p. 9.
38 *Ibid.*, p. 7.
39 *Ibid.*, p. 9.
40 J. Tyndall, *The Eleventh Hour*, 3rd edn (Welling: Albion Press, 1998), p. 518.
41 *A New Way Forward: The Political Objectives of the British National Party* (1991), p. 2. This was reprinted in 1992 as *Fight Back! The Election Manifesto of the British National Party*.
42 Tyndall, *The Eleventh Hour*, p. 135.
43 T. Linehan, *British Fascism 1918–39* (Manchester: Manchester University Press, 2000), p. 223.
44 MRC MSS 412/BNP/4/14: *New Frontier*, Sept. 1981.
45 *Vote for Britain. The Manifesto of the British National Party* (1983), p. 3.
46 Tyndall, *The Eleventh Hour*, p. 589.
47 BNP: *NO to Maastricht and NO to Europe! Exploded: The Myth that Britain has No Future Outside the EC*, p. 4.
48 Tyndall, *The Eleventh Hour*, 3rd edn, p. 520.
49 *Ibid.*
50 *Ibid.*
51 BNP *Activists' Handbook*, p. 63.
52 *Ibid.*, p. 62.
53 *Spearhead*, no. 248, Oct. 1989, p. 7.
54 Tyndall, *The Eleventh Hour*, 3rd edn, p. 228.
55 See for instance, *Fight Back!* pp. 4–6.
56 *Ibid.*, p. 23.
57 *Ibid.*, p. 3.
58 R. Muldrew, 'Changes on the Extreme Right in Post-War Britain: A Comparison of the Ideologies of Oswald Mosley and John Tyndall' (University of Liverpool, M. Phil, 1995), p. 115.
59 On Mosley's corporatism, see Lewis, *Illusions of Grandeur*, pp. 33–60.
60 Manifesto for the Revival of Britain, *British Nationalist*, July 1987, p. 3.

61 *Fight Back!* p. 3.
62 On Giovanni Gentile, see A. James Gregor, *Giovanni Gentile: Philosopher of Fascism* (New Brunswick, NJ: Transaction Publishers, 2001).
63 *Fight Back!* pp. 20–1.
64 *Ibid.*, p. 14.
65 *Britain Reborn : A Programme for a New Century*, BNP Election Manifesto 1997, Section 6: 'The Mass Media: Time for a Clean Up', British National Party website, <http://www.ngwwmall.com/frontier/bnp/manint.html> accessed 5 Jan. 1997.
66 *Fight Back!* p. 12.
67 See The *Guardian*, 20 Feb. 1993, p. 3.
68 See MRC MSS 321/1451/54: *Combat*, no. 13, Aug.–Oct. 1961, p. 4.
69 See MRC MSS 21/1551/81.
70 *Fight Back!* p. 26.
71 On Leese's 'race theory', see Linehan, *British Fascism*, pp. 180–6.
72 *Britain Reborn: A Programme for a New Century*, Section 11: 'Race and Immigration'.
73 Tyndall, *The Eleventh Hour*, 3rd edn, p. 244.
74 *Ibid.*, p. 403.
75 *Ibid.*, p. 354.
76 J. Tyndall, *The Authoritarian State* (London: National Socialist Movement, 1962), p. 14 and p. 15.
77 Tyndall, *The Eleventh Hour*, 3rd edn, pp. 88–112.
78 Tyndall, *The Authoritarian State*, p. 15.
79 *Official Programme of the Greater Britain Movement*, p. 3.
80 *Spearhead*, no. 191, Sept. 1984, p. 20.
81 *Britain Reborn: A Programme for a New Century*, Section 11: 'Race and Immigration'.
82 Tyndall, *The Eleventh Hour*, 3rd edn, p. 358.
83 *Official Programme of the Greater Britain Movement*, p. 3.
84 Tyndall, *The Eleventh Hour*, 3rd edn, p. 333.
85 *Ibid.*
86 See *Fight Back!* p. 21.
87 M. Durham, *Women and Fascism* (London: Routledge, 1998), p. 144.
88 Tyndall, *The Eleventh Hour*, 3rd edn, p. 368.
89 See *Spearhead*, no. 284, Oct. 1992, pp. 9–12.
90 Tyndall, *The Eleventh Hour*, 3rd edn, p. 109.
91 A.K. Chesterton, *The New Unhappy Lords* (London: Candour Publishing Co., 1965), pp. 203–4.
92 *Ibid.*, p. 19.
93 *Ibid.*, p. 210.
94 *Ibid.*, p. 204.
95 Tyndall, *The Eleventh Hour*, 3rd edn, pp. 102–3.
96 *Who are the Mind-Benders?* p. 4.
97 MRC MSS 412/BNP/4/10: BNP: *The Enemy Within: How TV Brainwashes a Nation* (1993), p. 2.
98 See *Searchlight*, no. 150, Dec. 1987, p. 4.
99 Tyndall, *The Eleventh Hour*, 3rd edn, p. 104.
100 *Ibid.*, pp. 364–5.

101 See The *Guardian*, 19 June 1962.

102 *Spreading the Word: British National Party Handbook on Propaganda*, p. 18.

103 See for instance, *Spearhead*, no. 303, May 1994, pp. 16–17.

104 See *Searchlight*, no. 206, Aug. 1992, pp. 3–5.

105 R.J. Evans, *Telling Lies About Hitler* (London: Verso, 2002), p. 204.

106 Tyndall, *The Eleventh Hour*, 3rd edn, p. 328.

107 See *Britain Reborn: A Programme for a New Century*, Section 3: 'The regeneration of British Industry'.

108 *Principles and Policies of the British National Party* (1982).

109 *Constitution of the British National Party* (Nov. 1982), p. 2.

110 *Vote for Britain*, Manifesto of the British National Party (1983), p. 11.

111 *Fight Back!* p. 7.

112 See *Fight Back!* p. 9.

113 Tyndall, *The Eleventh Hour*, 3rd edn, p. 296.

114 *Ibid.*, p. 414.

115 *NO to Maastricht and NO to Europe!* pp. 3–4.

116 Tyndall, *The Eleventh Hour*, 3rd edn, p. 423.

117 *Ibid.*, p. 424.

118 See *Official Programme of the Greater Britain Movement*, p. 5.

119 See *Fight Back!* pp. 9–10.

120 See *Principles and Policies of the British National Party* (1982).

121 Tyndall, *The Eleventh Hour*, 3rd edn, p. 521.

122 *Fight Back!* p. 21.

123 Tyndall, *The Eleventh Hour*, 3rd edn, p. 522.

124 See Griffin, *The Nature of Fascism*, p. 164.

125 J. Tyndall, 'There's No Image to Beat the Image of Success!', *Spearhead* website, <http:www.spearhead-uk.com/0103-jt2.html> accessed 16 Jan. 2003.

126 Tyndall, 'There's No Image to Beat the Image of Success!'

127 See *Patriot*, Summer 1998, p. 35.

128 R. Griffin, 'British Fascism: The Ugly Duckling', in M. Cronin (ed.), *The Failure of British Fascism: The Far Right and the Fight for Political Recognition* (Basingstoke: Macmillan – now Palgrave, 1996), p. 162.

5 New Millennium New Leader

1 *Identity*, issue 28, Jan. 2003, p. 21.

2 *British National Party Members' Bulletin*, Oct. 1999.

3 See *Spearhead*, no. 367, Sept. 1999, p. 13.

4 See *Patriot*, Spring 1999, p. 3.

5 See *Spearhead*, no. 334, Dec. 1996, p. 13.

6 *Patriot*, Spring 1999, p. 4.

7 *Ibid.*, p. 5.

8 *Ibid.*, p. 7.

9 *Ibid.*, p. 5.

10 *Spearhead*, no. 351, May 1998, p. 15.

11 On the French New Right, see R. Griffin, 'Plus ça change! The Fascist Pedigree of the Nouvelle Droite', in E.J. Arnold (ed.), *The Development of the Radical Right in France* (Basingstoke: Macmillan – now Palgrave, 2000), pp. 217–52.

12 On the FN's strategy of 'dual discourse', see P. Fysh and J. Wolfeys, *The Politics of Racism in France* (Basingstoke: Macmillan – now Palgrave, 1998), pp. 129–32.

13 *Spearhead*, no. 351, May 1998, p. 17.

14 *Patriot*, Spring 1999, p. 7.

15 See H.-G. Betz, 'Introduction' in H.-G. Betz and S. Immerfall (eds), *The New Politics of the Right: Neo-Populist Parties and Movements in Established Democracies* (Basingstoke: Macmillan – now Palgrave, 1998), esp. pp. 3–6.

16 *Patriot*, Spring 1999, p. 8.

17 See *Spearhead*, no. 363, May 1999, p. 28.

18 *Patriot*, Spring 1998, p. 8.

19 *Ibid.*

20 *Searchlight*, no. 288, July 1999, p. 20.

21 *Freedom for Britain and the British*, BNP website <http://www.vote.bnp.net/euroman.html> accessed 17 June 1999.

22 For a summary of BNP activity during 1998 by area, see *Searchlight*, no. 285, March 1999, p. 18.

23 British National Party Election Communication: North East Region, 10 June 1999.

24 Griffin had consulted some 75 party activists on the design of the election leaflet.

25 See *Spearhead*, no. 362, April 1999, p. 4.

26 This had resulted in three deaths. All together, over 100 people had been injured as a result of these nail-bomb attacks. On Copeland, see special issue of *Searchlight*, no. 301, July 2000.

27 *White Nationalist Report* (published in Support of the NF), issue no. 5, Oct. 1999.

28 As quoted in *Searchlight*, no. 289, July 1999, p. 17.

29 See *For a Britain Strong and Free: An Introduction to the British National Party* (1999), p. 3.

30 *Identity*, issue 28, Jan. 2003, p. 21.

31 *Searchlight*, no. 288, June 1999, p. 12.

32 *Spearhead*, no. 351, May 1998, p. 5.

33 *Patriot*, Summer 2000, p. 13.

34 *Patriot*, Spring 1999, p. 5.

35 Dr Phil Edwards, a former academic (real name – Dr Stuart Russell) ran this operation from the East Midlands.

36 See N. Copsey, 'Extremism on the Net: The Extreme Right and the Value of the Internet', in R. Gibson, P. Nixon and S. Ward (eds), *Political Parties and the Internet: Net Gain?* (London: Routledge, 2003), esp. pp. 226–9.

37 *Patriot*, Spring 1999, p. 6.

38 *Identity*, issue 28, Jan. 2003, p. 20.

39 *Patriot*, Spring 1999, p. 6.

40 See N. Griffin, *Attempted Murder: The State/Reactionary Plot against the National Front* (Norfolk: NT Press, 1986), p. 13.

41 *Patriot*, Spring 1999, p. 7.

42 For a quick guide to these 'circles', see for instance, E.G. Declair, *Politics on the Fringe. The People, Policies and Organization of the French National Front* (Durham and London: Duke University Press, 1999), pp. 167–9.

43 *Spearhead*, no. 358, Dec. 1998, p. 12.

44 *Searchlight*, no. 298, April 2000, p. 11.

45 On the American Friends of the BNP, see *Searchlight*, no. 292, October 1999, pp. 18–19. In November 2000, the Political Parties Elections and Referendums Act became law. This imposed restrictions on foreign and anonymous donations to political parties.

46 Nick Griffin's official leadership election address: 'The Future, not the Past', posted out with *British National Party Members' Bulletin*, Aug.–Sept. 1999.

47 'The Future, not the Past'.

48 Michael Newland to author, 19 May 2003.

49 John Tyndall's official election address: 'We've Come a Long Way – Don't Let's Ruin It!', posted out with *British National Party Members' Bulletin*, Aug.–Sept. 1999.

50 See *Spearhead*, no. 367, Sept. 1999, p. 5.

51 See 'The Leadership Election' column in *Moving On, Moving Up: Why People Are Voting for Nick Griffin*.

52 *Spearhead*, no. 367, Sept. 1999, p. 7.

53 See 'Image Does Matter', by Bruce Crowd in *Moving On, Moving Up*.

54 See 'The Challenge of the New Millennium', by Nick Griffin in *Moving On, Moving Up*.

55 *Spearhead*, no. 367, Sept. 1999, p. 9.

56 See *Spearhead*, no. 367, Sept. 1999.

57 See *Searchlight*, no. 292, Oct. 1999, pp. 8–11.

58 See *Patriot*, Summer 2000, p. 15.

59 *Searchlight*, no. 292, Oct. 1999, p. 6.

60 'We've Come a Long Way – Don't Let's Ruin It!'

61 *Searchlight*, no. 292, Oct. 1999, p. 4.

62 See *British National Party Members' Bulletin*, Oct. 1999.

63 Quoted in *British National Party Members' Bulletin*, Oct. 1999.

64 See *Spearhead*, no. 370, Dec. 1999, p. 14.

65 At a special BNP tribunal held in Chigwell in Essex in August 2003, Tyndall was briefly expelled from the BNP having been found guilty of under-mining the party through a series of attacks made on the leadership in *Spearhead*. See *Searchlight*, no. 339, Sept. 2003, p. 7.

66 See *Identity*, issue no. 1, Jan./Feb. 2000, p. 2.

67 *Patriot*, Summer 2000, p. 15.

68 Michael Newland to author, 19 May 2003.

69 *Identity*, issue 3, May/June 2000, p. 12.

70 Born in Potters Bar in 1944, Newland was educated at South Bank University and then Guildhall University. He joined the BNP in the 1990s after the election victory in Millwall.

71 *Patriot*, Summer 2000, p. 3.

72 Michael Newland to author, 19 May 2003.

73 *Searchlight*, no. 300, June 2000, p. 6.

74 Newland's election address is reprinted in *Patriot*, Summer 2000, p. 10.

75 See Board of Deputies of British Jews, CST Elections Research Unit, *Local Elections 2000 Including London and London Mayoral*, Thursday 4 May 2000 and *Patriot*, Summer 2000, pp. 3–6.

76   Interview with branch organiser Steve Smith, in *The Voice of Freedom*, BNP website <http://www.bnp.org.uk/freedom/burnley.html> accessed 11 Sept. 2002.

77   See Patriot, Summer 2000, p. 4, and Board of Deputies of British Jews: *Local Elections 2000 Including London and London Mayoral*, Thursday 4 May 2000, p. 3.

78   See *Searchlight*, no. 308, Feb. 2001, p. 15.

79   For a report on this campaign and a photograph of Smith, wearing a swastika armband and clothed in British Movement regalia, see *Searchlight*, no. 302, Aug. 2000, p. 7. On how the local community in Bexley then fought back against the BNP, see the *Guardian*, 27 May 2003.

80   See *CARF*, no. 15, July/Aug. 1993, p. 3.

81   See *CARF*, no. 5, Nov./Dec. 1991, p. 3 and no. 6, Jan./Feb. 1992, p. 10.

82   See P. Statham, 'United Kingdom' in J. ter Wal (ed.), *Racism and Cultural Diversity in the Mass Media* (European Monitoring Centre on Racism and Xenopobia, 2002), pp. 395–419.

83   The *Guardian Magazine*, 20 May 2000.

84   See Home Office: Asylum Statistics: United Kingdom 1999, HOSB 17/00.

85   See *CARF*, no. 58, Oct./Nov. 2000, p. 12.

86   See *CARF*, no. 56, June/July 2000, pp. 5–7. The Macpherson Report argued that institutionalised racism in the police force was endemic.

87   See *Searchlight*, no. 299, May 2000, p. 9.

88   See 'Race to the Right' in The *Guardian Magazine*, 20 May 2000.

89   Michael Newland to author, 19 May 2003.

90   See *Identity*, issue 5, Jan. 2001, pp. 4–5.

91   With 40.54 per cent of the vote, Sharron Edwards of the Freedom Party won her first council seat in May 2003 at Wombourne in south Staffordshire.

92   See *Searchlight*, no. 322, April 2002, p. 7.

93   See *British Nationalist*, Members' Bulletin of the BNP, Nov./Dec. 2000.

94   Michael Newland to author, 19 May 2003.

95   At the start of 2001, Tyndall had announced that it was his intention to challenge for the leadership of the party, see *British Nationalist*, Members' Bulletin of the BNP, Feb. 2001.

96   See *British Nationalist*, Members' Bulletin of the BNP, Jan. 2001. *Searchlight* had previously noted that the original design of *Identity* owed much to a prewar Communist format.

97   *British Nationalist*, Members' Bulletin of the BNP, March 2001.

98   *Identity*, Jan. 2001, p. 5.

99   *Identity*, July 2001, p. 13.

100   See *Spearhead*, no. 366, Aug. 1999, p. 5.

101   *Patriot*, Spring 1999, p. 7.

102   *Ibid.*, p. 5.

6   Into the Political Mainstream?

1   A BUF councillor was elected at Eye in Suffolk in 1938.

2   See *Lancashire Evening Telegraph*, 2 May 2003.

3 A consequence of revised and updated warding for all metropolitan authorities.
4 *Oldham Chronicle*, 8 June 2001. This figure also includes the 1,617 votes that the BNP candidate polled in the adjacent constituency of Ashton-under-Lyne, which includes the Oldham wards of Hollinwood and Failsworth.
5 *Identity*, June 2001, p. 11. This is a different Steve Smith to the local BNP organiser in Tower Hamlets.
6 *Oldham Independent Review* (2001), p. 43.
7 See *Oldham Chronicle*, 31 Jan. 2001.
8 See *CARF*, no. 63, Aug./Sept. 2001, p. 4.
9 See letter by Jawaid Iqbal to *Oldham Chronicle*, 15 Feb. 2001.
10 See Hewitt's response in the *Oldham Chronicle*, 19 Feb. 2001.
11 See for instance, 'Chronicle Comment', in *Oldham Chronicle*, 1 Feb. 2001.
12 See *Oldham Independent Review*.
13 Oldham is listed by *Spearhead* as having had a BNP unit in the mid-1990s. Eighteen months before the riots in Oldham, the BNP had no membership in Oldham, see the *Guardian*, 30 May 2001.
14 *Searchlight*, no. 300, June 2000, p. 7.
15 See *Oldham Chronicle*, 8 Feb. 2001. Mick Treacy joined the party in 2000 and works as a local taxi-driver.
16 *British Nationalist*, Members' Bulletin of the BNP, Feb. 2001.
17 For a brief report, see *Oldham Chronicle*, 5 March 2001. For a video stream of this demonstration, see BNP website <http://www.bnp.org.uk/audio2.html> accessed 24 June 2003.
18 *Identity*, June 2001, p. 4.
19 See *Oldham Chronicle*, 6 April 2001.
20 See S. Smith, *A Storm Rising*, 2nd edn (Imladris eBooks, 2003), p. 113.
21 See for instance *Oldham Chronicle*, 25 and 27 April 2001.
22 *Ibid.*, 24 April 2001.
23 For BNP involvement, see *Searchlight*, no. 337, July 2003, pp. 4–7.
24 See *Oldham Chronicle*, 28 May 2001.
25 For a chronology of events, see *Oldham Independent Review*, pp. 69–71.
26 The coverage of the other main local newspapers, the *Manchester Evening News* and the *Oldham Advertiser* attracted less criticism from the Asian community, see *Oldham Independent Review*, pp. 64–6.
27 See *Oldham Chronicle*, 28 May 2001.
28 *Ibid.*, 27 April 2001.
29 See *Oldham Independent Review*, p. 64.
30 On 'race' and readers' letters, see J.E. Richardson and B. Franklin, 'Dear Editor: Race, Readers' Letters and the Local Press', *Political Quarterly*, vol. 74, no. 2 (2003), pp. 185–92.
31 *Oldham Independent Review*, p. 65.
32 *Searchlight*, no. 314, Aug. 2001, p. 12.
33 See N. Lowles, *White Riot* (Bury: Milo Books, 2001), pp. 322–3.
34 Nick Griffin, on *Today* programme, BBC Radio 4, 28 May 2001. See BNP website <http://www.bnp.org.uk/audio2.html> accessed 25 June 2003.
35 *Oldham Chronicle*, 29 May 2001.
36 See *Voice of Freedom*, June 2001, p. 11.

37 See *Oldham Chronicle*, 6 June 2001.

38 *Runnymede Quarterly Bulletin*, June 2001, p. 19.

39 See *Oldham Chronicle*, 28 May 2001.

40 As quoted in *CARF*, 62, June/July 2000, p. 7.

41 See *Runnymede Quarterly Bulletin*, June 2001, p. 13.

42 Nick Griffin, on *Today* programme, BBC Radio 4, 28 May 2001.

43 C. Mudde, 'England Belongs to Me: The Extreme Right in the UK Parliamentary Election of 2001', *Representation*, vol. 39, no. 1 (2002), p. 39.

44 In Barking, Mark Tolman had polled 6.4 per cent of the vote; in Poplar and Canning Town, Paul Borg had captured 5.2 per cent.

45 *Identity*, June 2001, p. 5.

46 See *Oldham Chronicle*, 8 June 2001.

47 See *Burnley Express*, 10 July 2001.

48 See *Burnley Task Force Report* (2001), p. 7.

49 See *Burnley Express*, 12 May 2000.

50 See *Burnley Express*, 21 April 2000. The upshot of both BNP candidates having failed to reveal their political affiliation on their nomination papers.

51 *Burnley Task Force Report*, p. 66.

52 See *Burnley Express*, 9 May 2000.

53 See *Burnley Task Force Report*, Appendix 2c: Labour Group submission. Also see letter by Councillor Kenyon to *Burnley Express*, 27 July 2001.

54 See *Burnley Express*, 26 June 2001.

55 A shop-cum-museum in Burnley's town centre.

56 See *Burnley Express*, 1 June 2001.

57 *Voice of Freedom*, June 2001, p. 11.

58 For opposition to the BNP, see *Burnley Express*, 25 May 2001 and 1 June 2001.

59 *Identity*, June 2001, p. 11.

60 *Runnymede Quarterly Bulletin*, June 2001, p. 19.

61 On these disturbances, see *Burnley Task Force Report*, Section 2.

62 See *Burnley Task Force Report*, Appendix 2a: submission by the Burnley and Pendle Branch of the British National Party.

63 *Newsnight*, BBC2, 26 June 2001. See BNP website <http:www.bnp.org.uk/audio2.html> accessed 1 July 2003.

64 See N. Copsey, *Anti-Fascism in Britain* (Basingstoke: Macmillan – now Palgrave, 2000), p. 142.

65 See the *Observer*, 9 Sept. 2001.

66 *Today* programme, BBC Radio 4, 30 June 2001. See BNP website <http:www.bnp.org.uk/audio2.html> accessed 2 July 2003.

67 *Tonight with Trevor McDonald*, ITV1, 5 July 2001. See BNP website <http:www.bnp.org.uk/audio2.html> accessed 2 July 2003.

68 *Hardtalk*, BBC News 24, 3 Aug. 2001. See BNP website <http:www.bnp.org.uk/audio2.html> accessed 2 July 2003.

69 As quoted in the *Observer*, 9 Sept. 2001.

70 See the *Mirror*, 24 Aug. 2001.

71 See Smith, *A Storm Rising*, pp. 136–7.

72 See C. Allen and J.S. Nielsen, *Summary Report on Islamophobia in the EU after 11 September 2001* (Vienna: European Monitoring Centre on Racism and Xenophobia, 2002), pp. 29–30.

73 *Ibid.*, p. 39.

74 See *Identity*, Oct. 2001, p. 5.

75 See *Searchlight*, no. 316, Oct. 2001, p. 6, and *Identity*, July 2001, p. 9. Lawrence Rustem briefly fronted the party's Ethnic Liaison Committee. Although he was half-Turkish by descent, he was allowed to join the party as a lone exception to its 'British descent only' rule in 1991 in recognition of his services to the party.

76 See *Identity*, Dec. 2001, p. 14.

77 See *Burnley Express*, 20 Nov. 2001.

78 See *Voice of Freedom*, Dec. 2001, p. 11.

79 'Under the Skin', *Panorama*, BBC1, 25 Nov. 2001. This is transcribed by 1-Stop Express Services, London.

80 *Searchlight*, no. 319, Jan. 2002, p. 12.

81 See *Identity*, Dec. 2001, pp. 8–9.

82 See *Burnley Express*, 27 Nov. 2001, and *Lancashire Evening Telegraph*, 27 Nov. 2001.

83 See BNP *Organisers' Bulletin*, Nov. 2001.

84 See *Identity*, Nov. 2001, pp. 6–7.

85 *Searchlight*, no. 321, March 2002, p. 5.

86 See *Identity*, Aug. 2001, pp. 8–9.

87 BNP *Organisers' Bulletin*, Nov. 2001.

88 See *Identity*, Jan. 2003, pp. 20–1.

89 See *Identity*, Nov. 2001, p. 10.

90 Simon Bennett election leaflet. Bennett was the BNP candidate for Burnley Wood in 2002.

91 See Burnley BNP election leaflet: 'The BNP will Put Burnley People First', and *The Times*, 23 April 2002.

92 See Bradford BNP leaflet: 'People Power: You can't beat it'.

93 See Sunderland BNP leaflets: 'Charity Begins at Home'; and 'Labour Takes you for Granted!'

94 See *Voice of Freedom*, Feb. 2002, pp. 1–2 and p. 11.

95 *Searchlight*, no. 324, June 2002, p. 10.

96 <http://www.burnley.bravepages.com> accessed 17 April 2002.

97 *Ibid.*

98 See *British Worker*, Voice of the North East, Election Special – Thursday, 2 May 2002.

99 See *Searchlight*, no. 324, June 2002, p. 16.

100 The BNP distributed hundreds of 'Helping Hands' flyers on Ravenscliffe and claimed to have pressed Bradford Council into a £1 million housing repair plan.

101 Bradford BNP leaflet: City of Bradford Metropolitan District Local Council Elections, 2 May 2002, Eccleshill Ward.

102 Paul Meszaros, anti-fascist coordinator for Bradford Trades Council, as quoted in *Searchlight*, no. 324, June 2002, p. 17.

103 *Searchlight*, Press Release, 3 May 2002.

104 See for instance, *Daily Mirror*, 24 April 2002; *Daily Express*, 25 April 2002 and 2 May 2002.

105 See *Oldham Chronicle*, 1 May 2002.

106 See *Burnley Express*, 20 April 2002.

107 It finished either second or third in three multiple member wards.

108 For a thorough breakdown of BNP results, see *Searchlight*, no. 234, June 2002, pp. 8–9.

109 One of eight female candidates, Carol Hughes first stood in the Lowerhouse ward in November 2001. She was a recent recruit to the BNP and hardly fitted the 'thuggish' BNP stereotype. The Labour Party in its *Lowerhouse Rose* newssheet had attacked the BNP as a gang of football hooligans but this only allowed Hughes to portray herself as the real 'Lowerhouse Rose'.

110 <http://www.electoralcommission.org.uk/elections/faqselections.cfm/faqs/59> accessed 10 July 2003.

111 See *Searchlight*, no. 324, June 2002, p. 8.

112 See <http: www.mori.com/digest/2002/pd020621.shtml> accessed 18 July 2003.

113 See the *Guardian*, 11 April 2002.

114 In a television interview on 30 January 1978, Margaret Thatcher had said that new measures were needed to tighten-up on immigration because of the widespread feeling among whites that they were being 'swamped' by immigrants.

115 See *Searchlight*, no. 326, Aug. 2002, p. 10.

116 <http:www.icmresearch.co.uk/reviews/2002/bbc%2Drace%2Dpoll.may%2D2002.htm> accessed 16 July 2003.

117 See Smith, *A Storm Rising*, p. 112.

118 *Searchlight*, no. 313, July 2001, pp. 4–5.

119 *Searchlight*, no. 324, June 2002, pp. 8–9.

120 See *Making your Mark in History. Voting for Stoke-on-Trent's first Elected Mayor Including Election Addresses by Candidates for Mayor* (Stoke-on-Trent City Council, 2002), pp. 24–5.

121 See *Asylum Seeking in Stoke-on-Trent: The Facts. Report of the Elected Mayor's Enquiry into Asylum Seekers in the City of Stoke-on-Trent* (Stoke-on-Trent City Council, Feb. 2003).

122 According to a Mori poll that was carried out between 23–28 May 2002. See <http:www.mori.com/digest/2002/pd020621.shtml> accessed 18 July 2003.

123 Interview with Steve Batkin, BBC Radio Stoke, <http:www.bbc.co.uk/stoke/news/2002/10/mayor_result.shtml> accessed 15 July 2003.

124 *Identity*, issue 26, Nov. 2002, p. 3.

125 See *Identity*, issue 27, Dec. 2002, pp. 14–15.

126 British National Party: Statement of Accounts for Year ending 31 December 2002. See <http: www.electoral commission.gov.uk> accessed 10 July 2003.

127 See *Identity*, issue 27, Dec. 2002, pp. 4–5.

128 See *Identity*, issue 29, Feb. 2003, pp. 4–7.

129 See *Mixenden Matters. Calderdale By-Election Special* (2003).

130 See the *Guardian*, 24 Jan. 2003.

131 *Identity*, issue 32, May 2003, p. 7.

132 *Ibid.*, p. 5.

133 *Ibid.*, p. 7.

134 See <htttp: //www. mori.com/digest/2002/c020621.shtml> accessed 20 July 2003.

135 As quoted in the *Guardian*, 30 April 2003.

136 See for instance, Burnley BNP: Gannow ward election leaflet.
137 See *Searchlight*, no. 336, June 2003, p. 7.
138 See B. Särlvik and I. Crewe, *Decade of Dealignment* (Cambridge: Cambridge University Press, 1983), p. 243.
139 See *Identity*, issue 32, May 2003, p. 4.
140 See the *Guardian*, 29 April 2003.
141 See the *Guardian*, 26 April 2003, and the *Observer*, 11 May 2003.
142 See *Identity*, issue 34, July 2003, pp. 4–7.
143 *Ibid.*, p. 5.
144 See *BNP Council Manifesto* May 2003. This is reprinted in *Identity*, issue 31, April 2003, pp. 16–19.
145 See the *Guardian*, 4 May 2002.
146 See *Identity*, issue 29, Feb. 2003, p. 9.
147 See *Daily Express*, 29 April 2003.
148 Griffin was forced into a damage limitation exercise and publicly censored him. Batkin went on to win his seat.
149 On the anti-fascist campaign, see *Searchlight*, no. 336, June 2003.
150 See *Northern Echo*, 1 May 2003.
151 See *Voice of Freedom*, BNP website <http://www.bnp.org.uk/freedom/history.html> accessed 16 June 2003.
152 See *Financial Times*, 30 May 2003.
153 See the *Guardian*, 4 May 2003.
154 See BNP website <http:www.bnp.org.uk/news/2003_July21.htm.> accessed 22 July 2003.
155 See BNP website <http:www.bnp.org.uk/articles/internet_tables.htm> accessed 3 July 2003.

7 The British National Party in Comparative Perspective

1 On Poujadism, see R. Eatwell, 'Poujadism and Neo-Poujadism: from Revolt to Reconciliation', in P. Cerny (ed.), *Social Movements and Protest in Modern France* (London: Pinter, 1982), pp. 70–93.
2 For a study of the NPD, see J.D. Nagle, *The National Democratic Party: Right Radicalism in the Federal Republic of Germany* (Berkeley: University of California Press, 1970).
3 Space precludes a study of Eastern Europe. On the far right after the collapse of communism in Eastern Europe, see S.P. Ramet (ed.), *The Radical Right in Central and Eastern Europe since 1989* (Penn State University: The Pennsylvania State University Press, 1999).
4 P. Perrineau, 'The Conditions for the Re-emergence of an Extreme Right Wing in France: The National Front, 1984–98', in E.J. Arnold (ed.), *The Development of the Radical Right in France* (Basingstoke: Macmillan – Palgrave, 2000), p. 255.
5 *Mouvement National*, later *Mouvement National Republicain* (National Republican Movement).
6 See P. Hainsworth, 'The Front National: From Ascendancy to Fragmentation on the French Extreme Right', in P. Hainsworth (ed.), *The Politics of the Extreme Right* (London: Pinter, 2000), pp. 18–32.

7 See Institute of Race Relations: *European Race Bulletin*, no. 41, Aug. 2002, p. 11.

8 The Belgian FN polled 5.6 per cent of the vote in Wallonia at the May 2003 general election.

9 On the success of the *Vlaams Blok* in Antwerp, see M. Swyngedouw, 'Belgium: Explaining the Relationship between Vlaams Blok and the city of Antwerp', in Hainsworth (ed.), *The Politics of the Extreme Right*, pp. 121–43.

10 Institute of Race Relations: *European Race Bulletin*, no. 44, July 2003, p. 13.

11 On the populist politics of the Northern League, see A.C. Bull and M. Gilbert, *The Lega Nord and the Northern Question in Italian Politics* (Basingstoke: Palgrave Macmillan, 2001).

12 On the Italian far right, see for instance, T. Gallagher, 'Exit from the Ghetto: The Italian Far Right in the 1990s', in Hainsworth (ed.), *The Politics of the Extreme Right*, pp. 64–86; P. Ignazi, *Extreme Right Parties in Western Europe*, pp. 35–61, and A. Roxburgh, *Preachers of Hate: The Rise of the Far Right* (London: Gibson Square Books, 2002), pp. 131–53.

13 For a useful table of Freedom Party results, see Ignazi, *Extreme Right Parties in Western Europe*, p. 113.

14 On the performance of the Freedom Party in government, see R. Heinisch, 'Success in Opposition – Failure in Government: Explaining the Performance of Right-Wing Populist Parties in Office', *West European Politics*, vol. 26, no. 3 (2003), pp. 91–130.

15 Institute of Race Relations: *European Race Bulletin*, no. 44, July 2003, p. 13.

16 See for instance, L. McGowan, *The Radical Right in Germany*. 1870 to the Present (Harlow: Longman, 2002), pp. 147–206.

17 See C. Mudde and J. Van Holsteyn, 'The Netherlands: Explaining the Limited Success of the Extreme Right', in Hainsworth (ed.), *The Politics of the Extreme Right*, pp. 144–71.

18 Volkert van der Graaf, an animal rights activist, was convicted of his murder. Van der Graaf likened the rise of Fortuyn to Adolf Hitler and claimed that he was acting in defence of the country's Muslim community.

19 The journalist Angus Roxburgh refers to him as such; see Roxburgh, *Preachers of Hate*, pp. 157–77.

20 On Scandinavia, see for instance J.G. Andersen and T. Bjørklund, 'Radical Right-Wing Populism in Scandinavia: From Tax Revolt to Neo-Liberalism and Xenophobia', in Hainsworth (ed.), *Politics of the Extreme Right*, pp. 193–223; Ignazi, *Extreme Right Parties in Western Europe*, pp. 140–61.

21 As Bjørklund and Andersen point out, nationalism rather than individual freedom was the core idea in the Danish People's Party's 1998 manifesto. At the 2001 general election, it won 12 per cent of the vote, see T. Bjørklund and J.G. Andersen, 'Anti-Immigrant Parties in Denmark and Norway: The Progress Parties and the Danish People's Party', in M. Schain, A. Zolberg and P. Hossay (eds), *Shadows over Europe: The Development and Impact of the Extreme Right in Western Europe* (New York: Palgrave Macmillan, 2002), pp. 107–36.

22 C.T. Husbands, 'Switzerland: Right-Wing and Xenophobic Parties, from the Margin to Mainstream?', *Parliamentary Affairs*, vol. 53, no. 3 (2000), p. 515.

23 See C. Mudde, 'The Single-Issue Party Thesis: Extreme Right Parties and the Immigration Issue', *West European Politics*, vol. 22, no. 3 (1999), pp. 182–97.

24 P. Hainsworth, 'The Cutting Edge: The Extreme Right in Post-War Western Europe and the USA', in P. Hainsworth (ed.), *The Extreme Right in Europe and the USA* (London: Pinter, 1992), p. 7.

25 Links with the British NF had been established in 1977 when two FN members had attended a rally in Birmingham. The far-right press in France had also taken note of the NF's relative success. See for instance, *Patterns of Prejudice*, vol. 12, no. 2 (1978), p. 13, and *Militant*, no. 84, Dec. 1976–Jan. 1977, pp. 14–15.

26 On immigration and the decision-making process in France (and Britain) in the postwar period, see G.P. Freeman, *Immigrant Labor and Racial Conflict in Industrial Societies* (Princeton, NJ: Princeton University Press, 1979).

27 See for instance, J. Marcus, *The National Front and French Politics* (Basingstoke: Macmillan – now Palgrave, 1995), pp. 73–99.

28 See P. Hossay, 'Why Flanders?', in Schain, Zolberg and Hossay (eds), *Shadows over Europe*, pp. 159–85.

29 C.T. Husbands, 'Belgium: Flemish Legions on the March', in Hainsworth (ed.), *Extreme Right in Europe and USA*, p. 133.

30 See H. Cools, 'Belgium: Fragile National Identity(s) and the Elusive Multicultural Society', in B. Baumgartl and A. Favell (eds), *New Xenophobia in Europe* (London: Kluwer Law International, 1995), p. 40.

31 See J. Ter Wal, A. Verdun and K. Westerbeek, 'The Netherlands: "Full or at the Limit of Tolerance"', in Baumgartl and Favell (eds), *New Xenophobia in Europe*, pp. 238–9.

32 R. Knight, 'Haider, the Freedom Party and the Extreme Right in Austria', *Parliamentary Affairs*, vol. 45, no. 3 (1992), p. 297.

33 See M. Riedlsperger, 'The Freedom Party of Austria: From Protest to Radical Right Populism', in H.-G. Betz and S. Immerfall (eds), *The New Politics of the Right: Neo-Populist Parties in Established Democracies* (Basingstoke: Macmillan – now Palgrave, 1998), p. 34.

34 See D. Morrow, 'Jörg Haider and the New FPÖ: Beyond the Democratic Pale?', in Hainsworth (ed.), *The Politics of the Extreme Right*, p. 51.

35 T. Faist, 'How to Define a Foreigner? The Symbolic Politics of Immigration in German Partisan Discourse, 1978–1992', in M. Baldwin-Edwards and M. Schain (eds), *The Politics of Immigration in Western Europe* (Ilford: Frank Cass, 1994), p. 51.

36 D. Childs, 'The Far Right in Germany since 1945', in L. Cheles, R. Ferguson and M. Vaughan (eds), *Neo-fascism in Europe* (Harlow: Longman, 1991), p. 79.

37 See M. Lubbers and P. Scheepers, 'Explaining the Trend in Extreme-Right Voting: Germany 1989–1998', *European Sociological Review*, vol. 17, no. 4 (2001), p. 444.

38 On the German extreme right and the immigration thesis, see R. Karapin, 'Far-Right Parties and the Construction of Immigration Issues in Germany', in Schain, Zolberg and Hossay (eds), *Shadows over Europe*, pp. 186–219.

39 See E. Thalhammer *et al.*, *Attitudes Towards Minority Groups in the European Union: A Special Analysis of the Eurobarometer 2000 Survey* (Vienna: European Monitoring Centre on Racism and Xenophobia, 2001), p. 47.

40 R. Miles, 'Explaining Racism in Contemporary Europe', in A. Rattansi and S. Westwood (eds), *Racism, Modernity, and Identity on the Western Front* (Oxford: Polity Press, 1994), p. 214.

41 See N. Mayer, 'Is France Racist?', *Contemporary European History*, vol. 5, no. 1 (1996), p. 122.

42 See P. Perrineau, 'The Conditions for the Re-emergence of an Extreme Right Wing in France: The National Front, 1984–98', in Arnold (ed.), *The Development of the Radical Right in France*, p. 266.

43 G. Ivaldi, 'Cognitive Structures of Xenophobic Attitudes among Supporters of Extreme Right-Wing Parties in Europe', Paper presented to the Workshop on Racist Parties in Europe, 23rd ECPR Joint Sessions – Bordeaux, 27 April–2 May 1995, p. 7.

44 See W. Van Der Brug, M. Fennema and J. Tillie, 'Anti-Immigrant Parties in Europe: Ideological or Protest Vote?', *European Journal of Political Research*, vol. 37 (2000), pp. 77–102.

45 Betz, *Radical Right-Wing Populism in Western Europe*, p. 105.

46 See P. Ignazi, *Extreme Right Parties in Western Europe*, p. 119.

47 *Ibid.*, p. 47.

48 H. Kitschelt, *The Radical Right in Western Europe*, p. 173.

49 J. Veugelers, 'Recent Immigration Politics in Italy: A Short Story', in Baldwin-Edwards and Schain (eds), *The Politics of Immigration in Western Europe*, p. 39.

50 M.J. Bull and J.L. Newell, 'Italy Changes Course? The 1994 Elections and the Victory of the Right', *Parliamentary Affairs*, vol. 48, no. 1 (1995), p. 74.

51 H.-J. Veen, N. Lepszy and P. Mnich, *The Republikaner Party in Germany* (Westport, Connecticut: Praeger, 1993), p. 43.

52 See P. Ignazi, 'The Silent Counter-revolution. Hypotheses on the Emergence of Extreme Right Parties in Europe', *European Journal of Political Research*, vol. 22 (1992), pp. 3–34.

53 H.-G. Betz, 'The New Politics of Resentment. Radical Right Wing Parties in Western Europe', *Comparative Politics*, vol. 16 (1993), pp. 413–27.

54 See H. Kitschelt, *The Radical Right in Western Europe* (Ann Arbor: University of Michigan Press, 1997).

55 See J.W.P. Veugelers, 'Right-Wing Extremism in Contemporary France: A "Silent Counterrevolution"?', *The Sociological Quarterly*, vol. 41, no. 1 (2000), pp. 19–40.

56 See S. Bastow, 'The Radicalization of Front national Discourse: A Politics of the "Third Way"?', *Patterns of Prejudice*, vol. 32, no. 3 (1998), pp. 55–68.

57 This argument is explored in the case of France, in B. Jenkins and N. Copsey, 'Nation, Nationalism and National Identity in France', in B. Jenkins and S. Sofos (eds), *Nation and Identity in Contemporary Europe* (London: Routledge, 1996), pp. 101–24.

58 R. Griffin, 'Afterword: Lost Rights?', in Ramet, *The Radical Right in Central and Eastern Europe since 1989*, p. 317.

59 For an excellent analysis of FN doctrine, see P.-A. Taguieff, 'The Doctrine of the National Front in France (1972–1989): A "Revolutionary Programme"? Ideological Aspects of a National-Populist Mobilization', *New Political Science*, vol. 16–17 (1989), pp. 29–70.

60 Swyngedouw, 'Belgium: Explaining the Relationship between Vlaams Blok and the city of Antwerp', in Hainsworth (ed.), *The Politics of the Extreme Right*, p. 136.

61 See A. Dézé, 'An Alternative to the System or an Alternative within the System?' An Analysis of the Relationship of Extreme Right Parties with the

Political Systems of Western Democracies', Paper presented to the 92th ECPR Joint Sessions of Workshops, 'Democracy and the New Extremist Challenge in Europe', Grenoble, 6–11 April 2001, p. 25.

62 P. Ignazi, 'From Neo-Fascists to Post-Fascists? The Transformation of the MSI into the AN', *West European Politics*, vol. 14, no. 4 (1996), p. 704.

63 See Ignazi, *Extreme Right Parties in Western Europe*, esp. pp. 45–53.

64 Roger Griffin for instance, see R. Griffin, 'The "Post-Fascism" of the Alleanza Nazionale: A Case-Study in Ideological Morphology', *Journal of Political Ideologies*, vol. 1, no. 2 (1996), pp. 123–45.

65 See P. Tripodi, 'The National Alliance and the Evolution of the Italian Right', *Contemporary Review*, vol. 272 (1998), pp. 295–300.

66 Ignazi, *Extreme Right Parties in Western Europe*, p. 52.

67 See L. Höbelt, *Defiant Populist: Jörg Haider and the Politics of Austria* (Indiana: Purdue University Press, 2003), pp. 117–42.

68 Ignazi, *Extreme Right Parties in Western Europe*, p. 115.

69 G. Harris, *The Dark Side of Europe. The Extreme Right Today* (Edinburgh: Edinburgh University Press, 1990), p. 73.

70 See M. Swyngedouw, 'The Extreme Right in Belgium: Of a Non-existent Front National and an Omnipresent Vlaams Blok', in Betz and Immerfall (eds), *The New Politics of the Right* (Basingstoke: Macmillan – now Palgrave, 1998), p. 72.

71 See T. Gallagher, 'Exit from the Ghetto: The Italian Far Right in the 1990s', in Hainsworth (ed.), *The Politics of the Extreme Right*, esp. pp. 70–80.

72 See R.W. Jackman and L. Volpert, 'Conditions Favouring Parties of the Extreme Right in Western Europe', *British Journal of Political Science*, vol. 26, no. 4 (1996), pp. 515–16.

73 In August 2003, the BNP won a local council seat in Kirklees, West Yorkshire, but since one of its councillors in Burnley resigned its total number fell back to 16. In September 2003, the BNP won a further seat – this time at the Grays Riverside by-election at Thurrock in Essex. Robin Evans, BNP councillor in Blackburn, resigned from the party due to 'organisational differences' in October 2003. In early December, a Tory councillor defected to the BNP on Calderdale Council, West Yorkshire.

74 N. Mayer, 'The French National Front' in Betz and Immerfall (eds), *The New Politics of the Right*, p. 15.

75 *Identity*, issue 32, May 2003, p. 4.

76 See *Attitudes Towards Minority Groups in the European Union*, p. 25. By country, the percentage of respondents who were classed as intolerant towards minority groups: France (19 per cent), Germany (18 per cent), UK (15 per cent), Austria (12 per cent).

77 See R. Worcester and R. Mortimore, *Explaining Labour's Landslide* (London: Politico's Publishing, 2001), p. 166.

78 M. Schain, A. Zolberg and P. Hossay, 'The Development of Radical Right Parties in Western Europe', in Schain, Zolberg and Hossay (eds), *Shadows over Europe*, p. 14.

79 What constitutes a national electoral breakthrough for an extreme-right party is typically defined after the event and in context.

80 Home Office Asylum Statistics: First Quarter 2003. See <http://www.homeoffice.gov.uk/rds/pdss2/asylumq103.pdf> accessed 25 July 2003.

81   See *Sunderland Echo*, 2 May 2003.
82   See *Identity*, issue 30, March 2003, pp. 6–7.
83   In the 1980s Griffin said of Wingfield: he 'may have impeccable credentials as a racialist, but so has the extreme right-wing of the Tory party, which is where Wingfield belongs', see *Attempted Murder: The State/Reactionary Plot against the National Front* (Norfolk: NT Press, 1986), p. 31.
84   See *Identity*, issue 30, March 2003, p. 6.
85   *Identity*, issue 35, p. 5.
86   See *Identity*, issue 33, June 2003, pp. 10–11.
87   See K. Taylor, 'Hatred Repackaged: The Rise of the British National Party and Antisemitism', in P. Iganski and B. Kosmin (eds), *A New Antisemitism? Debating Judeophobia in 21st Century Britain* (London: Profile Books, 2003), pp. 231–48.
88   See *Identity*, issue 34, July 2003, p. 6.
89   See *Identity*, issue 28, Jan. 2003, pp. 18–19, and issue 29, Feb. 2003, pp. 12–14.
90   See the *Northern Echo*, 6 Aug. 2003.
91   The *Independent*, 24 Sept. 2003.
92   See the *Observer*, 21 Sept. 2003.
93   For a philosophical discussion of this issue with regard to the French National Front, see M. Fennema and M. Maussen, 'Dealing with Extremists in Public Discussion: Front National and "Republican Front" in France', *Journal of Political Philosophy*, vol. 8, no. 3 (2000), pp. 379–400.
94   N. Copsey, 'Contemporary Fascism in the Local Arena: The British National Party and Rights for Whites', in M. Cronin (ed.), *The Failure of British Fascism: The Far Right and the Fight for Political Recognition* (Basingstoke: Macmillan – now Palgrave, 1996), p. 139.

Conclusion

1   See the *Guardian*, 16 Sept. 2003.
2   *Ibid.*
3   *Patriot*, Spring 1999, p. 5.
4   See *Identity*, issue 36, Sept. 2003, pp. 8–9.

Select Bibliography

Baker, D. (1996) *Ideology of Obsession: A.K. Chesterton and British Fascism* (London: I.B. Tauris).

Baumgartl, B. and Favell, A. (eds) (1995) *New Xenophobia in Europe* (London: Kluwer Law International).

Bean, J. (1999) *Many Shades of Black: Inside Britain's Far Right* (London: New Millennium).

Betz, H.-G. (1994) *Radical Right-Wing Parties in Western Europe* (Basingstoke: Macmillan – now Palgrave).

Betz, H.-G. and Immerfall, S. (eds) (1998) *The New Politics of the Right: Neo-Populist Parties and Movements in Established Democracies* (Basingstoke: Macmillan – now Palgrave).

Billig, M. (1978) *Fascists: A Social Psychological View of the National Front* (London: Harcourt, Brace Jovanovich).

Cheles, L., Ferguson, R. and Vaughan, M. (eds) (1995) *The Far Right in Western and Eastern Europe*, 2nd edn (London: Longman).

Chesterton, A.K. (1965) *The New Unhappy Lords* (London: Candour Publishing Co.).

Copsey, N. (1994) 'Fascism: The Ideology of the British National Party', *Politics*, vol. 14, no. 3, pp. 101–8.

—— (1997) 'A Comparison between the Extreme Right in Contemporary France and Britain', *Contemporary European History*, vol. 6, no. 1, pp. 101–16.

—— (2000) *Anti-Fascism in Britain* (Basingstoke: Macmillan – now Palgrave).

—— (2003) 'Extremism on the Net: The Extreme Right and the Value of the Internet', in R. Gibson, P. Nixon and S. Ward (eds), *Political Parties and the Internet: Net gain?* (London: Routledge), pp. 218–33. ← on my

Cronin, M. (ed.) (1996) *The Failure of British Fascism: The Far Right and the Fight for Political Recognition* (Basingstoke: Macmillan – now Palgrave).

Declair, E.G. (1999) *Politics on the Fringe: The People, Policies and Organization of the French National Front* (Durham and London: Duke University Press).

Durham, M. (1998) *Women and Fascism* (London: Routledge).

Eatwell, R. (1995) *Fascism: A History* (London: Chatto & Windus).

—— (1996) 'On Defining the "Fascist Minimum": The Centrality of Ideology', *Journal of Political Ideologies*, vol. 1, no. 3, pp. 303–19.

—— (1998) 'The Dynamics of Right-Wing Electoral Breakthrough', *Patterns of Prejudice*, vol. 32, no. 1, pp. 3–31.

—— (2000) 'The Rebirth of the "Extreme Right" in Western Europe?', *Parliamentary Affairs*, vol. 53, no. 3, pp. 407–25.

—— (2000) 'Ethnocentric Party Mobilization in Europe: The Importance of the Three-Dimensional Approach', in R. Koopmans and P. Statham (eds), *Challenging Immigration and Ethnic Relations Politics* (Oxford: Oxford University Press), pp. 348–67.

Fysh, P. and Wolfreys, J. (1998) *The Politics of Racism in France* (Basingstoke: Macmillan – now Palgrave).

Griffin, R. (1994) *The Nature of Fascism* (London: Routledge).

—— (1996) 'The "Post-Fascism" of the Alleanza Nazionale: A Case-Study in Ideological Morphology', *Journal of Political Ideologies*, vol. 1, no. 2, pp. 123–45.

Gable, G. and Hepple, T. (1993) *At War with Society* (London: Searchlight).

Goodrick-Clarke, N. (2002) *Black Sun: Aryan Cults, Esoteric Nazism and the Politics of Identity* (New York: New York University Press).

Hainsworth, P. (ed.) (1992) *The Extreme Right in Europe and the USA* (London: Pinter).

—— (ed.) (2000) *The Politics of the Extreme Right: From the Margins to the Mainstream* (London: Pinter).

Harris, G. (1994) *The Dark Side of Europe: The Extreme Right Today* (Edinburgh: Edinburgh University Press).

Heath, A. (1995) 'What has Happened to the Extreme Right in Britain?', *Res Publica*, vol. 37, no. 2, pp. 197–206.

Hill, R. with Bell, A. (1988) *The Other Face of Terror: Inside Europe's Neo-Nazi Network* (London: Grafton).

Höbelt, L. (2003) *Defiant Populist: Jörg Haider and the Politics of Austria* (Indiana: Purdue University Press).

Husbands, C.T. (1983) *Racial Exclusionism and the City: The Urban Support of the National Front* (London: Allen & Unwin).

—— (1988) 'Extreme Right-Wing Politics in Great Britain: The Recent Marginalisation of the National Front', *West European Politics*, vol. 11, no. 2, pp. 65–79.

—— (1994) 'Following the "Continental Model"?: Implications of the Recent Electoral Performance of the British National Party', *New Community*, vol. 20, no. 4, pp. 563–79.

Ignazi, P. (2003) *Extreme Right Parties in Western Europe* (Oxford: Oxford University Press).

Kitschelt, H. (1997) *The Radical Right in Western Europe* (Ann Arbor: University of Michigan Press).

Larsen, S.U. (ed.) (1998) *Modern Europe After Fascism* (Boulder: Social Science Monographs).

Lowles, N. (2001) *White Riot* (Bury: Milo Books).

Marcus, J. (1995) *The National and French Politics: The Resistible Rise of Jean-Marie Le Pen* (Basingstoke: Macmillan – now Palgrave).

Mudde, C. (1999) 'The Single-Issue Party Thesis: Extreme Right Parties and the Immigration Issue', *West European Politics*, vol. 22, no. 3, pp. 182–97.

—— (2000) *The Ideology of the Extreme Right* (Manchester: Manchester University Press).

—— (2002) '"England Belongs to Me": The Extreme Right in the UK Parliamentary Election of 2001', *Representation*, vol. 39, no.1, pp. 37–43.

Merkl, P. and Weinberg, L. (eds) (1997) *The Revival of Right-Wing Extremism in the Nineties* (London: Frank Cass).

Paxton, R. (1998) 'The Five Stages of Fascism', *Journal of Modern History*, vol. 70, no. 1, pp. 1–23.

Renton, D. (1999) *Fascism: Theory and Practice* (London: Pluto Press).

—— (2003) 'Examining the Success of the British National Party, 1999–2003', *Race and Class*, vol. 45, no. 2, pp. 75–85.

Roxburgh, A. (2002) *Preachers of Hate: The Rise of the Far Right* (London: Gibson Square Books).

Ryan, N. (2003) *Homeland: Into a World of Hate* (Edinburgh: Mainstream Publishing).

Schain, M., Zolberg, A. and Hossay, P. (eds) (2002) *Shadows over Europe: The Development of the Extreme Right in Western Europe* (New York: Palgrave Macmillan).

Simmons, H. (1996) *The French National Front: The Extremist Challenge to Democracy* (Boulder: Westview Press).

Smith, S. (2003) *A Storm Rising*, 2nd edn (Imraldis eBooks).

Taggart, P. (1995) 'New Populist Parties in Western Europe', *West European Politics*, vol. 18, no. 1, pp. 34–51.

Taylor, K. (2003) 'Hatred Repackaged: The Rise of the British National Party and Antisemitism', in P. Iganski and B. Kosmin (eds), *A New Antisemitism? Debating Judeophobia in 21st Century Britain* (London: Profile Books), pp. 231–48.

Taylor, S. (1982) *The National Front in English Politics* (London: Macmillan – now Palgrave).

Thayer, G. (1965) The British Political Fringe (London: Anthony Blond).

Thurlow, R. (1998) *Fascism in Britain: From Oswald Mosley's Blackshirts to the National Front* (London: I.B. Tauris).

—— (2000) *Fascism in Modern Britain* (Stroud: Suttton).

Tyndall, J. (1998) *The Eleventh Hour: A Call for British Rebirth*, 3rd edn (Welling: Albion Press).

Veen, H.-J., Lepszy, N. and Mnich, P. (1993) *The Republikaner Party in Germany* (Westport, Connecticut: Praeger).

Walker, M. (1978) *The National Front*, 2nd edn (London: Fontana/Collins).

Index